SOFTWARE RELIABILITY
Measurement, Prediction, Application

Professional Edition

Other McGraw-Hill Books in Software Engineering

ISBN	AUTHOR	TITLE
0-07-040235-3	Marca, McGowan	*SADT: Structured Analysis and Design Technique*
0-07-036948-8	Lecarme, Pellissier, Gart	*Software Portability*
0-07-057299-2	Shumate	*Understanding Concurrency in ADA®*
0-07-046536-3	Nielsen, Shumate	*Designing Large Real-Time Systems with ADA®*
0-07-042632-5	Modell	*A Professional's Guide to Systems Analysis*
0-07-016803-2	Dickinson	*Developing Quality Systems*
0-07-023165-6	General Electric Company Staff	*Software Engineering Handbook*
0-07-010646-0	Wallace et al.	*A Unified Methodology for Developing Systems*
0-07-010645-2	Charette	*An Introduction to Software Engineering Environments*
0-07-067922-3	Wallace	*Practitioner's Guide to ADA®*
0-07-044119-7	Musa, Iannino, Okumoto	*Software Reliability*
0-07-010661-4	Charette	*Risk Analysis and Management*
0-07-002394-8	Arnell, Davis	*Handbook of Disaster Recovery Planning*
0-07-065086-1	Towner	*Case Concepts and Implementation*

Ranade IBM Series

ISBN	AUTHOR	TITLE
0-07-065087-X	Towner	*IDMS/R*
0-07-002673-4	Azevedo	*ISPF*
0-07-050686-8	Prasad	*IBM Mainframe*
0-07-046263-1	McGrew, McDaniel	*Online Text Management*
0-07-039822-4	Malamud	*DEC Networks and Architectures*
0-07-071136-4	Wipfler	*CICS Application Development and Programming*
0-07-051144-6	Ranade	*SNA Introduction to VTAM*
0-07-583963-6	Ranade	*VSAM: Concepts, Programming, and Design*
0-07-051198-5	Ranade, Ranade	*VSAM: Performance, Design, and Fine Tuning*

For more information about other McGraw-Hill materials, call 1-800-2-MCGRAW in the United States. In other countries, call your nearest McGraw-Hill office.

SOFTWARE RELIABILITY

Measurement, Prediction, Application

Professional Edition

John D. Musa

Anthony Iannino

Kazuhira Okumoto

AT&T Bell Laboratories
Whippany, NJ

McGraw-Hill Publishing Company

New York   St. Louis   San Francisco   Auckland   Bogotá
Caracas   Hamburg   Lisbon   London   Madrid   Mexico
Milan   Montreal   New Delhi   Oklahoma City
Paris   San Juan   São Paulo   Singapore
Sydney   Tokyo   Toronto

Library of Congress Cataloging-in-Publication Data

Musa, John D.
    Software reliability : measurement, prediction, application / John
D. Musa, Anthony Iannino, Kazuhira Okumoto. — Professional ed.
        p.   cm.
    Includes bibliographical references.
    ISBN 0-07-044119-7
    1. Computer software — Testing.   2. Computer software — Reliability.
I. Iannino, Anthony.   II. Okumoto, Kazuhira.   III. Title.
QA76.76.T48M87   1990
005.1'4 — dc20   89-13005

To MARILYN   J.D.M.
    To JILL   A.I.
  To LILLIE   K.O.

1234567890   DOC/DOC   895432109

0-07-044119-7

Printed and bound by R. R. Donnelley & Sons Company.

For more information about other McGraw-Hill materials,
call 1-800-2-MCGRAW in the United States. In other
countries, call your nearest McGraw-Hill office.

ABOUT THE AUTHORS

John D. Musa is Supervisor of Software Quality at AT&T Bell Laboratories, Whippany, N.J. He has been involved in the field of software reliability since 1973, developing two models (one with Okumoto) and making many theoretical contributions. Musa has published over 40 papers. A manager of a wide variety of software projects, he has been a leader in the practical application of software reliability measurement and prediction to guiding engineering and management decisions. He has created two courses at AT&T to integrate this extensive experience in both theory and practice and impart it to software practitioners. This book has benefited greatly from that effort.

Musa brings a wealth of experience in software engineering to his writing. As chairman of the IEEE Technical Committee on Software Engineering, he won a Meritorious Service Award for innovative leadership. His wide participation and leadership in a range of conferences and publications results in an unusual breàdth of perspective and depth of technical judgment. He has been Chair of the Steering Committee for the International Conferences on Software Engineering. He is currently a member of the editorial boards of *IEEE Software* and *IEEE Proceedings* and has been a member of the editorial board of *IEEE Spectrum*. He has served as Vice President for Publications, Vice President for Technical Activities, and 2nd Vice President of the IEEE Computer Society. He is a fellow of the IEEE, cited for his "contributions to software engineering, in particular, software reliability."

Anthony Iannino is currently a Member of Technical Staff in the Software Quality Group at AT&T Bell Laboratories. He received his Ph.D. in Computer Science from Stevens Institute of Technology, where he was holder of the Robert Crooks Stanley Fellowship. He has been an active researcher in the field of software reliability for over seven years and has published several papers in professional journals and conference proceedings. He has consulted on software reliability with numerous projects, both internal and external to Bell Laboratories. He is a member of Tau Beta Pi.

Kazuhira Okumoto is Supervisor of the User/Performance Tools Development Group at AT&T Bell Laboratories, where he has been involved in various research and development activities such as software reliability, computer performance evaluation and capacity planning. He received his Ph.D. in Industrial Engineering and Operations Research from Syracuse University. He has been an active researcher in the field of software reliability for over ten years, including work toward his Ph.D. dissertation which was partly supported by the Air Force Systems Command's Rome Air Development Center. While he was an Assistant Professor at Rutgers University, he wrote a research proposal on software reliability modeling, which was accepted by NSF. He has published over 25 papers in professional journals and conference proceedings in the field and related topics, and has presented technical papers at numerous national conferences and workshops. He is a member of Alpha Pi Mu and was a committee member of the 5th Minnowbrook workshop on software performance evaluation.

CONTENTS

Part II   Practical Application

4   System Definition   77

5   Parameter Determination   113

6   Project-Specific Techniques   151

PREFACE

HOW TO USE THIS BOOK

Two large general groups of people need practical information on software reliability measurement. These needs have been carefully and systematically analyzed, and this book has been organized to meet them.

The first and largest group consists of those who need to develop a general understanding of software reliability measurement and what it can be used for, even though they may not directly apply it. This category includes high-level managers, engineers who use or whose designs interface with software, and people who purchase, lease, or use software. Part I of the book has been written for them. This part treats the basic concepts and illustrates a number of uses. The treatment is graphically oriented and can be understood in those terms. We have emphasized this approach, finding that about three-fourths of our readers prefer it. You can look at the plots, ignoring the symbols, and clearly understand the relationships. However, symbols are provided for the other one-fourth who understand a mathematical presentation more clearly. We also provide them with formulas illustrated with examples.

The second and also large group of people involves those who will be using and applying software reliability measurement. It also includes practitioners in related disciplines such as risk analysis, management decision sciences, and quality assurance. Part II has been written for this group (of course, they should also read Part I). Members of this group may play different roles, as noted in Chapter 3. The introduction to Part II indicates which topics are important to which roles. We present formulas when needed for calculation, but there are no derivations. Procedures are explained in step-by-step fashion, and examples are liberally provided.

A "road map" for the book is presented in Figure P.1, based on questions on the reader's background and interests. It should be noted that our objective has been that the reader with no background in probability and statistics can read Parts I and II with nearly complete understanding. If a reader lacks technical background in computers, the brief overview of Appendix A should be read. The reader who is unfamiliar with how software is developed should begin with Section 4 of Appendix A. Otherwise, readers should start with the Overview, Part I. The short introductory summaries for Parts I and II are important for placing the individual chapters in perspective.

The reader who wants a comprehensive treatment might consider the foregoing "two pass" approach to the subject illogical or inefficient. However, we believe that he or she will quickly find it is indeed superior for the following reasons. The overview of Part I rapidly creates a structure in which the rest of the material can be understood. The practical application section, Part II, provides the rich fabric of experience.

Professors and instructors will find this structure extremely flexible. The book can be easily adapted to the needs of widely varying courses. Courses that treat the areas of software engineering, computer science, management sciences, and reliability in a survey fashion will find Part I well-suited to their needs. Courses involving more depth in practical application will wish to add Part II as well.

Examples, case studies, and problems have been provided to illustrate the concepts and give the background needed to develop judgment. They were included because identifying problems and determining which are worth solving is usually much more difficult than solving the problems themselves. Immersion in a wide variety of realistic experiences in a field is necessary to develop the former capabilities. Some of the problems are essentially thought questions, designed to deepen and expand one's understanding of the material. You may not always find them directly answered in the preceding text. However, solutions are always discussed in Appendix E. Although much "how to do it" information is provided, the value of practically oriented insight is recognized throughout as well. There has been a conscious effort to avoid theoretical exuberance in conveying this insight. The book has been thoroughly indexed so that it can serve as a reference, and a glossary of terms (Appendix C) and a glossary of notation (Appendix D) have been provided for this same purpose. The glossary of terms includes those few probability terms used in Parts I and II. Terms used in the book reflect present standard usage. In most cases they are in conformance with the *IEEE Standard Glossary of Software Engineering Terminology* [IEEE (1983)], which is also an ANSI (United States) standard. The practitioner will find a summary of all the formulas likely to be needed for hand calculations in one place, Appendix B. In certain cases, detailed discussions of topics that might otherwise interrupt the flow of a chapter are placed at the end just before the summary.

In concentrating on software reliability *measurement*, the authors do not mean to imply that investigation of the *causes* and means of reducing software faults is unimportant. However, it is helpful to know how bad a situation is before one attacks it and just what economic benefits can be obtained from improving things, so that one knows how hard to attack. A discussion of the causes and cures for software faults would be a book (or books) in itself. Fault introduction and removal are related to such topics as cognitive psychology and software engineering technology. Reliability

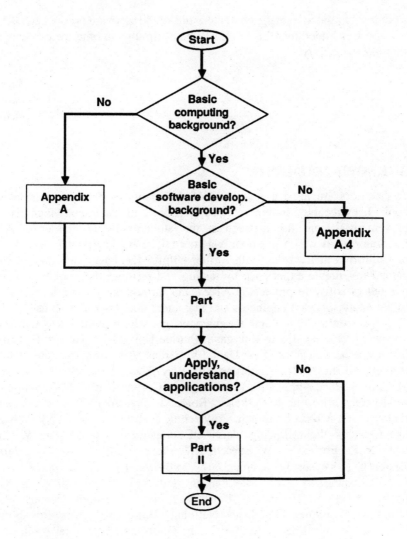

FIGURE P.1
Guide to reading the book.

is obviously related to many characteristics of the software product and development process. It is hoped that this book will be a stimulus to other researchers to explore them *quantitatively*.

John D. Musa
Anthony Iannino
Kazuhira Okumoto

ACKNOWLEDGMENTS

The authors are most appreciative of the many people who contributed to this book. They received innumerable suggestions and reactions (which also led to improvements) from the instructors and students in 11 classes at AT&T Bell Laboratories in which the book was used. The book was also used at University of California at Berkeley with further helpful feedback. In addition, the authors gained invaluable experience by testing and refining the book's ideas on a large number of software projects at AT&T and throughout the world. We are indebted to the many software engineers and managers that worked with us.

We would like to thank the many people who provided thorough and incisive reviews, including Bharat Bhargava, Purdue University; Richard E. Fairley, Wang Institute of Graduate Studies; Daniel V. Ferens, Air Force Institute of Technology; Herbert Hecht, Sohar Incorporated; Way Kuo, Iowa State University; J.A. McCall, Science Applications International Corporation; C.V. Ramamoorthy, University of California at Berkeley; Roger S. Pressman, R.S. Pressman and Associates; and Martin Shooman, Polytechnic Institute of New York. We would also like to thank the following identified colleagues: S.J. Amster, W. Chen, L.H. Crow, W.K. Ehrlich, W.W. Everett, L.T. Frase, M.R. Garzia, D.A. James, N.K. Kester, C.J. Keyser, W. Kremer, C.L. Mallows, J.D. Patterson, N.D. Prabhakar, J. Vizcarrondo, A. von Mayrhauser, and A.S. Wang (all from AT&T Bell Laboratories), C. Brehmer (China Lake Naval Weapons Center), R. Cairone (Grumman Aircraft), C.J. Dale (National Centre of Systems Reliability, United Kingdom Atomic Energy Authority), E. Girard and P. Saunier (both of CIMSA), and S. Sherer (Wharton School, University of Pennsylvania). We are appreciative of the efforts of M.A. Brana, S. Cole, C. Hubner, and D. Nolte, who helped coordinate the orderly revision of the book through its many drafts. Our special thanks go to C.A. Lopata, our indefatigable, efficient, and dedicated word processor, and her several colleagues who have helped at various times.

SOFTWARE RELIABILITY
Measurement, Prediction, Application

Professional Edition

OVERVIEW

This part of the book has three principal objectives:

1. to demonstrate the great potential value of software reliability measurement in engineering and managing software,
2. to convey enough basic concepts such that the reader will be able to communicate intelligently with software reliability measurement practitioners and interpret the results of their studies, and
3. to increase awareness of possible uses for software reliability measurement.

Some material is also presented on how to plan and organize for applying these ideas to a project or a system in operation.

Chapter 1 focuses on general introductory material and basic concepts. Chapter 2 presents two selected software reliability models and discusses how the model parameters are determined. Chapter 3 discusses a range of potential uses and includes a section on overall planning and organization for application.

ONE

INTRODUCTION TO SOFTWARE RELIABILITY

This chapter places software reliability in the context of software engineering and shows its importance. A comparison with hardware reliability will be made. Then we will present basic definitions and concepts. Availability, a measure related to reliability, will be defined. There will be a general discussion of software reliability modeling. Finally, we will discuss some of the uses of software reliability measurement and prediction.

1.1 IMPORTANCE

Information processing is probably the most significant industry in the world economy today and in the foreseeable future. It has expanded and continues to expand at a rapid rate. This expansion is, in part, related to the increase in cost-effectiveness of computer hardware. Cost-effectiveness has increased by a factor of about 1000 every decade [Musa (1985)]. As long as this rate of change continues, the range of tasks that can be handled most economically by computing is likely to grow rapidly. Since software is the major part of most computer systems, the field of software engineering can expect similar rapid growth.

The major forces affecting the software engineering field today include:

1. the increasing level and truly international nature of business competition,
2. the increasing cost of both information system development and information system failure,
3. the increasing pace of change in computing technology, and
4. the increasing complexity of managing information system development.

Most information system customers are, in turn, businesses. The increasing level of business competition that they face makes them acutely aware of their needs in regard to software products. Since there is also more competition among software producers, software customers are more aware of the products and services available to them. These customers, once relatively naive and dependent on their suppliers, have become increasingly sophisticated and demanding. Software producers must understand their needs thoroughly and precisely. Three of the most significant needs are level of quality required, time of delivery, and cost.

At the same time, both the development and operational cost of software have increased substantially. The size, complexity, and degree of distribution of systems are increasing. We have many multicomputer systems linked by networks. They may have many diverse pieces of software that run simultaneously and interact. Consequently, development costs are becoming higher. The proliferation of information system applications has increased the heavy dependence of institutions on such systems. This dependence is extending to smaller organizations and down to lower levels of organizations. A growing proportion of the systems operate in real time. The operational effects of failure are large and often critical. For example, consider the effects of breakdowns of airline reservations, banking, automatic flight control, military defense, and nuclear power plant safety control systems, to name just a few. The economic results can be large and even catastrophic. Costs of failure include not only direct expenses but also product liability risks and damage to a company's reputation. The latter can have a dramatic impact on a company's market share and profitability.

The increasing pace of change in computing technology means that information systems become economically obsolete more rapidly. Software can become obsolete either as the result of new hardware technology or new software technology. The time of delivery of a system has become increasingly crucial. The *market window,* or time period available for the introduction of a new product before that product is surpassed in capability or cost by another, has shortened.

With the cost and schedule pressures we have discussed, it is becoming increasingly impossible to create a software product that is "generous" in the sense of simultaneously providing high quality, rapid delivery, and low cost. The view that such characteristics are simply desired objectives to be achieved is obsolete. For example, it would be nice to have programs that are "correct," but in this real world we must settle for something less. The need for trade-offs is pressing, and the characteristics of the software must be carefully selected to meet customer needs. This means that measurement and prediction of software product characteristics is essential.

The management of information system development has become more complex as the size and complexity of the systems have increased. Many systems are now divided into components that are developed by different companies. A definite need exists for the clear identification of the characteristics of the system and its components and for indicators of progress during development. Such identification is important from managerial, contractual, and legal viewpoints. Again, the result is that measurement and prediction of software product characteristics and the current status of those characteristics during development has become increasingly important.

We have indicated that three of the most important software product characteristics are quality, cost, and schedule. Note that these are primarily user-oriented rather than developer-oriented attributes. Quantitative measures exist for the latter two characteristics, but the quantification of quality has been more difficult. It is most important, however, because the absence of a concrete measure for software quality generally means that quality will suffer when it competes for attention against cost and schedule. In fact, this absence may be the principal reason for the well known existence of quality problems in many software products.

Reliability is probably the most important of the characteristics inherent in the concept "software quality." It is intimately connected with defects, and as Jones (1986) points out, defects represent the largest cost element in programming. Software reliability concerns itself with how well the software *functions* to meet the requirements of the customer. We define software reliability precisely in Section 1.3, but simply, it is the probability that the software will work without failure for a specified period of time. "Failure" means the program in its functioning has not met user requirements in some way. "Not functioning to meet user requirements" is really a very broad definition. Thus reliability subsumes, totally or partially, many properties that are often quoted as aspects of quality. One example is correctness. Another is program *behavior* that is not user-friendly. Some properties like software safety are actually specialized aspects of software reliability. Two of the few aspects of quality that probably cannot be related to reliability are modifiability and understandability of documentation. In addition to its preeminent importance, software reliability has proved to be the most readily quantifiable of the attributes of software quality.

Reliability represents a user-oriented view of software quality. Initial (and many present) approaches to measuring software quality were based on *attempting* to count the faults or defects found in a program. This approach is developer-oriented. Also, what was usually counted were either failures (the occurrences of malfunction) or repairs (for example, maintenance or correction reports), neither of which are equivalent to faults. Even if faults found are correctly counted, they are not a good status indicator (is a large number good or bad?). Faults remaining may be. Faults found can only be used to make rough comparisons with other projects. Such comparisons are commonly made in terms of faults per 1000 developed source lines of code. Reliability is a much richer measure. It is customer- or user-oriented rather than developer-oriented. It relates to operation rather than design of the program, and hence it is dynamic rather than static [Saunier (1983)]. It takes account of the frequency with which problems occur. It relates directly to operational experience and the influence of faults on that experience. Hence, it is easily associated with costs. It is more suitable for examining the significance of trends, for setting objectives, and for predicting when those objectives will be met. It permits one to analyze in common terms the effect on system quality of both software and hardware, both of which are present in any real system. Thus, reliability measures are much more useful than fault measures.

This does not mean that some attention to faults is without value. But the attention should be focused on faults as predictors of reliability and on the nature of faults. A better understanding of faults and the causative human error processes should lead to strategies to avoid, detect and remove, or compensate for them.

Understanding software reliability measurement and prediction has become a vital skill for both the software manager and software engineer. This knowledge is also important to managers and engineers of products that include software, and to users of these products. Fortunately, in the past 15 years a body of knowledge has been developed to help meet this need. Software reliability measures and models have been developed, and much practical knowledge has been gathered by applying them to actual projects. This history is recounted in Musa, Iannino, and Okumoto (1987). Since this area appears ripe for exploitation, it seemed desirable to organize the information and disseminate it. Some problems remain, but further progress in solving them is dependent on confronting them in real project situations and gathering relevant data. The models are sufficiently accurate [see Musa, Iannino, and Okumoto (1987)] and useful (see Chapters 3 and 7) that the benefits in using them exceed their costs.

Experience with the application of software reliability measurement and prediction on projects indicates a cost of implementation of around 0.1 to 0.2 percent of project development costs. This includes the cost of education, the cost of data collection and processing, and the cost of studies. On many projects some of the costs are already being incurred. For example, many projects have formal mechanisms for reporting troubles. Also, many projects already conduct studies of the kind that we will describe, but decisions are arrived at in a less quantitative and a less satisfactory way. These costs, therefore, should represent an upper bound for the incremental costs involved.

A primary objective of this book is to help the engineer, manager, or user of software learn to make more precise decisions. A strong secondary objective is to make everyone more concretely aware of software quality by focusing attention on its most important characteristic, software reliability. Better decisions can save money on a project or during the life cycle of a piece of software in many ways. We will discuss some of these in the next section. In general, the total savings that we expect are more than 10 times greater than the cost of applying these ideas. Consider the following simple example for illustrative purposes. A 2-year software project with a system test period of about 6 months is fairly typical. The amount of testing is usually highly correlated with reliability, although it is not the only factor. Suppose you could establish that only 5 months of test are needed to get the reliability that is required for the particular application. Then you might well be able to save 4 percent of the development cost of the project. Compare this with the cost of application noted above. The cost effectiveness of the methodology is high.

1.2 SOFTWARE RELIABILITY AND HARDWARE RELIABILITY

The field of hardware reliability has been established for some time. Hence, you might ask how software reliability relates to it. In reality, the division between hardware and software reliability is somewhat artificial. Both may be defined in the same way. Therefore, you may combine hardware and software component reliabilities to get system reliability. Both depend on the environment. The source of failures in software is design faults, while the principal source in hardware has generally been physical deterioration. However, the concepts and theories developed for software reliability could really be applied to any design activity, including hardware design. Once a software (design) defect is properly fixed, it is in general fixed for all time. Failure usually occurs only when a program (design) is exposed to an environment that it was not developed or tested for. Although manufacturing can affect the quality of physical components, the replication process for software (design) is trivial and can be performed to very high standards of quality. Since introduction and removal of design faults occur during software development, software reliability may be expected to vary during this period.

The "design reliability" concept has not been applied to hardware to any extent. The probability of failure due to wear and other physical causes has usually been much greater than that due to an unrecognized design problem. It was possible to keep hardware design failures low because hardware was generally less complex logically than software. Hardware design failures had to be kept low because retrofitting of manufactured items in the field was very expensive. The emphasis in hardware reliability may be starting to change now, however. Awareness of the work that is going on in software reliability, plus a growing realization of the importance of design faults, may be having an effect. This growing awareness is strengthened by the parallels that people are starting to draw between software engineering and chip design.

A final characteristic of software reliability is that it tends to change continually during test periods. This happens either as new problems are introduced when new code is written or when repair action removes problems that exist in the code. Hardware reliability may change during certain periods, such as initial burn-in or the end of useful life. However, it has a much greater tendency than software toward a constant value.

Despite the foregoing differences, we can develop software reliability theory in a way that is compatible with hardware reliability theory. Thus system reliability figures may be computed using standard hardware combinatorial techniques [Shooman (1986) and Lloyd and Lipow (1977)]. Hardware and software reliability share many similarities and some differences. One must not err on the side of assuming that software always presents unique problems, but one must also be careful not to carry analogies too far.

1.3 BASIC CONCEPTS

We need to first thoroughly understand the basic terms and concepts of software reliability modeling before specific models or practical applications can be addressed. The reader will then find that the task of mastering software reliability will be much easier. This modeling background is frequently essential to making intelligent decisions in practical applications. For example, how do we model software reliability for a multiprocessor or a distributed system? This background will be deepened in Part II, when it is related to the application of software reliability models and to the analysis of system reliability as well. We will build up to the concept of software reliability in several steps, introducing some other concepts en route.

1.3.1 Failures and Faults

What do we mean by the term *software failure*? It is the departure of the external results of program operation from requirements (requirements are discussed in detail in Chapter 4). So our "failure" is something dynamic. The program has to be executing for a failure to occur. The term failure relates to the behavior of the program. Note that a failure is not the same thing as a "bug" or, more properly, "fault." This very general definition of failure is deliberate. It can include such things as deficiency in performance attributes and excessive response time.

A *fault* is the defect in the program that, when executed under particular conditions, causes a failure. There can be different sets of conditions that cause failures, or the conditions can be repeated. Hence a fault can be the source of more than one failure. A fault is a property of the program rather than a property of its execution or behavior. It is what we are really referring to in general when we use the term "bug." A fault is created when a programmer makes an *error*. It's *very* important to make the failure-fault distinction! This may not be apparent to you now, but hopefully it will be after you have delved more deeply into the field. There has been, and frequently remains, much confusion because these terms were mixed up and erroneously used interchangeably. If you get them clear in your mind, you will avoid much trouble that has bedeviled people trying to learn software reliability measurement.

Consider this simple example. A user requests a display at program start-up. It does not appear. That departure from how the program should behave is a failure. The fault associated with the failure might be that an initialization instruction for a variable was not provided. Note, however, that a fault does not have to be localized in nature. The fault could be an inefficient routine that has to be rewritten.

Reliability quantities have usually been defined with respect to time, although it would be possible to define them with respect to other variables. We are concerned with three kinds of time. The *execution time* for a program is the time that is actually spent by a processor in executing the instructions of that program. The second kind of time is *calendar time*. It is the familiar garden variety of time that we normally experience. Execution time is important, because it is now generally accepted that models based on execution time are superior. However, quantities must ultimately be related back to calendar time to be meaningful to engineers or managers. Sometimes the term *clock time* is used for a program. It represents the elapsed time from start to end of program execution on a running computer. It includes wait time and the execution time of other programs. Periods during which the computer is shut down are not counted. If computer utilization by the program, which is the fraction of time the processor is executing the program, is constant, clock time will be proportional to execution time. As an example of these three types of time, consider a word processing system serving a group of secretaries. In 1 week of calendar time, there may be 50 hr of clock time during which the system is running. There might be 25 hr of execution time for the word processing program itself. Note that when either execution time or clock time is used, any down time of a system is excluded. In this book, general descriptions of models, estimation, and techniques for adapting models to specific projects will be formulated in terms of a generic time t, so that they will have the widest possible applicability. However, when specific execution time models or outputs of programs using these models are described, discussions will be in terms of execution time τ and calendar time t.

There are four general ways of characterizing failure occurrences in time:

1. time of failure,
2. time interval between failures,
3. cumulative failures experienced up to a given time, and
4. failures experienced in a time interval.

These are illustrated in Tables 1.1 and 1.2.

Note that all the foregoing four quantities are random variables. By "random," we mean that the values of the variables are not known with certainty. There are many possible values, each associated with a probability of occurrence. For example, we don't really know when the next failure will occur. If we did, we would try to prevent or avoid it. We only know a set of possible times of failure

TABLE 1.1
Time-based failure specification

Failure number	Failure time (sec)	Failure interval (sec)
1	10	10
2	19	9
3	32	13
4	43	11
5	58	15
6	70	12
7	88	18
8	103	15
9	125	22
10	150	25
11	169	19
12	199	30
13	231	32
14	256	25
15	296	40

TABLE 1.2
Failure-based failure specification

Time (sec)	Cumulative failures	Failures in interval
30	2	2
60	5	3
90	7	2
120	8	1
150	10	2
180	11	1
210	12	1
240	13	1
270	14	1

occurrence and the probability of each. The probability of each time of occurrence is the fraction of cases for which it occurs. Note that "random" does not carry any connotation of true irrationality or unpredictability, as some mistakenly assume. "Random" means "unpredictable" only in the sense that the exact value is not known. However, the average value and some sense of the dispersion *are* known. It does not mean "unaffected by other variables." Although failure occurrence is random, it is decidedly affected by such factors as test strategy and the operational profile. Neither does "random" imply any specific probability distribution, which some mistakenly assume as "uniform."

There are at least two principal reasons for this randomness. First, the commission of errors by programmers, and hence the introduction of faults, is a very complex, unpredictable process. Hence the locations of faults within the program are unknown. Second, the conditions of execution of a program are generally unpredictable. For example, with a telephone switching system, how do you know what type of call will be made next? In addition, the relationship between program function requested and code path executed, although theoretically determinable, may not be so in practice because it is so complex. Since failures are dependent on the presence of a fault in the code *and* its execution in the context of certain machine states, a third complicating element is introduced that argues for the randomness of the failure process.

Table 1.3 illustrates a typical probability distribution of failures that occur within a time period of execution. Each possible value of the random variable of number of failures is given along with its associated probability. The probabilities, of course, add to 1. Note that here the random variable is discrete, as the number of failures must be an integer. We can also have continuous random variables, such as time, which can take on any value. Note that the most probable number of failures is 2 (probability 0.22). The mean or average number of failures can be computed. You multiply each possible value by the probability it can occur and add all the products, as shown. The mean is 3.04 failures.

A random process can be viewed as a set of random variables, each corresponding to a point in time. We can have a discrete or continuous time random

TABLE 1.3
Typical probability distribution of failures

Value of random variable (failures in time period)	Probability	Product of value and probability
0	0.10	0
1	0.18	0.18
2	0.22	0.44
3	0.16	0.48
4	0.11	0.44
5	0.08	0.40
6	0.05	0.30
7	0.04	0.28
8	0.03	0.24
9	0.02	0.18
10	0.01	0.1
Mean failures		3.04

process. One characteristic of a random process is the form of the probability distributions of the random variables. For example, one common form for failure random processes is Poisson. The other principal characteristic is the variation of the process with time.

We will look at the time variation from two different viewpoints, the mean value function and the failure intensity function. The *mean value function* represents the average cumulative failures associated with each time point. The *failure intensity function* is the rate of change of the mean value function or the number of failures per unit time. For example, you might say 0.01 failure/hr or 1 failure/ 100 hr. Strictly speaking, the failure intensity is the derivative of the mean value function with respect to time, and is an instantaneous value.

Table 1.4 illustrates an example of the random process of failures in simplified fashion, showing failure distributions of the cumulative number of failures experienced at two different time points. Note that the random variables are given at elapsed time t_A of 1 hr and elapsed time t_B of 5 hr. A random process whose probability distribution varies with time is called *nonhomogeneous*. Most failure processes during test fit this situation. Figure 1.1 illustrates the mean value and the related failure intensity functions at times t_A and t_B. Note that the mean failures experienced increases from 3.04 to 7.77 between these two points, while the failure intensity decreases.

Failure behavior is affected by two principal factors:

1. the number of faults in the software being executed, and
2. the execution environment or operational profile of execution.

TABLE 1.4
Probability distributions at times t_A and t_B

Value of random variable (failures in time period)	Probability	
	Elapsed time t_A = 1 hr	Elapsed time t_B = 5 hr
0	0.10	0.01
1	0.18	0.02
2	0.22	0.03
3	0.16	0.04
4	0.11	0.05
5	0.08	0.07
6	0.05	0.09
7	0.04	0.12
8	0.03	0.16
9	0.02	0.13
10	0.01	0.10
11	0	0.07
12	0	0.05
13	0	0.03
14	0	0.02
15	0	0.01
Mean failures	3.04	7.77

FIGURE 1.1
Mean value and failure intensity functions.

The number of faults in the software is the difference between the number introduced and the number removed.

Faults are introduced when the code is being developed by programmers. They may introduce the faults during original design or when they are adding new features, making design changes, or repairing faults that have been identified. The term *developed code,* defined as instructions that have been created or modified, is used deliberately. In general, only code that is new or modified results in fault introduction. Code that is *inherited* from another application does not usually introduce any appreciable number of faults, except possibly in the interfaces. It generally has been thoroughly debugged in the previous application. Note that the process of fault removal introduces some new faults because it involves modification or writing of new code. Hopefully (if you have a programming staff of reasonable competence!), the new faults entered are fewer than the faults being removed. Data on the introduction of faults is presented in Tables 5.2 to 5.4.

Fault removal obviously can't occur unless you have some means of detecting the fault in the first place. Thus fault removal resulting from execution depends on the occurrence of the associated failure. Occurrence depends both on the length of time for which the software has been executing and on the execution environment or operational profile. When different functions are executed, different faults are encountered and the failures that are exhibited tend to be different—thus the environmental influence. We can often find faults without execution. They may be found through inspection, compiler diagnostics, design or code reviews, or code reading.

Fault removal is also dependent on the efficiency with which faults are found and removed. For example, a failure correction team may remove 95 faults for every 100 failures reported. The efficiency depends on factors such as how well the circumstances surrounding the failure are documented and the degree of structuring and clarity of the program.

Finally, the failure process and hence software reliability is directly dependent on the environment or the operational profile for the program. For example, you can expect that an electronic switching system that is being used in a business district will have a software reliability different from that in a residential area.

We have seen that the failure process depends on the *system* being built, the nature of the development process for a particular *project,* and the *use* of the system. Since the system and the project are so closely associated, they are often used interchangeably in naming a particular failure process.

1.3.2 Environment

Let us scrutinize the term *environment*. The environment is described by the operational profile. We need to build up to the concept of the operational profile through several steps. It is possible to view the execution of a program as a single entity. The execution can last for months or even years for a real time system. However, it is more convenient to divide the execution into runs. The definition of *run* is somewhat arbitrary, but it is generally associated with some function that the program performs. Thus, it can conveniently describe the functional environment of the program. Runs that are identical repetitions of each other are said to form a *run type*. The proportion of runs of various types may vary, depending on the functional environment. Examples of a run type might be:

1. a particular transaction in an airline reservation system or a business data processing system,
2. a specific cycle in a closed loop control system (for example, in a chemical process industry), or
3. a particular service performed by an operating system for a user.

During test, the term *test case* is sometimes used instead of run type.

We next need to understand the concept of the *input variable*. This is a variable that exists external to the program and is used by the program in executing its function. For an airline reservation system, "destination" might be an input variable. One generally has a large quantity of input variables associated with the program, and each set of values of these variables characterize an *input state*. In effect, the input state identifies the particular run type that you're making. Therefore, runs can always be classified by their input states. Again, taking the case of the airline reservation system, the input state might be characterized by particular values of origin, destination, airline, day, and flight number. The set of all possible input states is known as the *input space*, illustrated in Figure 1.2.

Similarly, an *output variable* is a variable that exists external to a program and is set by it. An *output state* is a set of values of all output variables associated with a run of a program. In the airline reservation system, an output state might be the set of values of variables printed on the ticket and on different reports used in operating the airline. It can now be seen that a failure involves a departure of the output state from what it is expected to be.

The run types required of the program by the environment can be viewed as being selected randomly. Thus, we define the *operational profile* as the set of run types that the program can execute along with the probabilities with which they will occur. In Figure 1.2, we show two of many possible input states, A and B,

FIGURE 1.2
Input space.

with their probabilities of occurrence. The part of the operational profile for just those two states is shown in Figure 1.3. In reality, the number of possible input states is generally quite large. A realistic operational profile is illustrated in Figure 1.4. Note that the input states have been located on the horizontal axis in order of the probabilities of their occurrence. This can be done without loss of generality. They have been placed close together so that the operational profile would appear to be a continuous curve. The operational profile is an extremely useful concept. However, it may not always be practical to determine all the input states and their probabilities in full detail, because of the large number that can be involved. We can reduce the large number by the use of equivalence partitioning, as described in Chapter 4. With a reasonably small number of such classes, an operational profile based on the classes may be established in practice. One possible source of data for such an operational profile is a marketing study of the uses of a system.

1.3.3 Software Reliability

The definition that we will present here for *software reliability* is one that is widely accepted throughout the field. It is the probability of failure-free operation of a computer program for a specified time in a specified environment. For example, a time-sharing system may have a reliability of 0.92 for 8 hr when employed by the "average user." This system, when executed for 8 hr, would operate without failure for 92 of these periods out of 100. As a result of the general way in which we defined failure, note that the concept of software reliability incorporates the notion of performance being satisfactory. For example, excessive response time at a given load level may be considered unsatisfactory, so that a routine must be recoded in more efficient form.

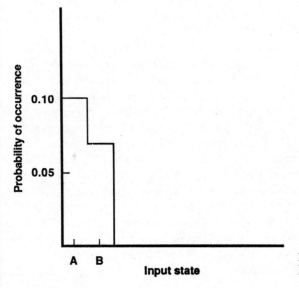

FIGURE 1.3
Portion of operational profile.

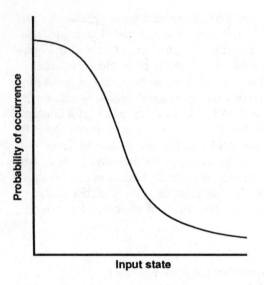

FIGURE 1.4
Operational profile.

This definition implies that you should, for accurate reliability measurement during test, select runs randomly with the same probability expected to occur in operation. Alternatively, if you use different probabilities, compensate for them as discussed in Chapter 6. The effect of selecting runs by plan rather than randomly depends on whether the instructions and machine states exercised are localized or not. If a localized part of the program is exercised, the failures that occur will only be the result of faults in that part. Removal of the faults will be more rapid than usual. Since the failure intensity curve will reflect just the part of the program examined, it will initially drop more rapidly than would be expected. When a transition to a new set of instructions and machine states occurs, the failure intensity curve will probably rise. This reflects the greater number of faults remaining in the new part of the program.

The definition also implies that the input space must be "well covered" for accurate reliability measurement. To measure input space coverage, take the sum of the probabilities in the operational phase associated with the test runs selected. The sum gives the probability that a run occurring during operation will have already been tested. Thus you will know whether it results in failure. The coverage can be small when the input space is very large. The number of tests in any practical test effort is limited. Equivalence partitioning, described in Chapter 4, is a technique for increasing the coverage. Assume equal run lengths. Then any error in reliability measurement due to insufficient coverage can not exceed the difference between 1 and the coverage. Thus we want input space coverage to be substantially closer to 1 than the level of reliability being measured. For example, one might attempt coverage of 0.9999 for a reliability measurement expected to be near 0.99. The probability that a run occurring in operation will not have been tested is 0.0001. If we assume equal run lengths, our reliability measurement will have an error of 0.0001 or less. This is about 1 percent.

Failure intensity is an alternative way of expressing reliability. We just gave the example of the reliability of a particular system being 0.92 for 8 hr of time. An equivalent statement, based on Equation (2.13), is that the failure intensity is 0.01 failure/hr. Each specification has its advantages. The failure intensity statement is more economical, as you only have to give one number. However, the reliability statement is better suited to the combination of reliabilities of components to get system reliability. If the risk of failure at any point in time is of paramount concern, failure intensity may be the more appropriate measure. This would be the case for a nuclear power plant. When proper operation of a system to accomplish some function with a time duration is required, reliability is often best. An example would be a space flight to the moon. Figure 1.5 shows how failure intensity and reliability typically vary during a test period, as faults are removed. Note that we define failure intensity, just like we do reliability, with respect to a specified environment. The relationship between failure intensity and reliability depends on the reliability model employed if these values are changing.

As faults are removed (for example, during a test phase), failure intensity tends to drop and reliability tends to increase. When faults are being introduced, they often accompany new features or design changes that are all made at one time. This situation can occur in test or operation. There tends to be a step increase in failure intensity and a step decrease in reliability in this situation. It is also common, particularly in the field, to introduce repairs in batches. There can be a step increase or decrease in failure intensity, depending on whether new code and its faults or repairs predominate. There will be a corresponding decrease or increase in reliability. If a system is stable (that is, the code is unchanging), both failure intensity and reliability tend to be constant. This might be the situation for a program that has been released to the field, with no changes in code and no repairs being made.

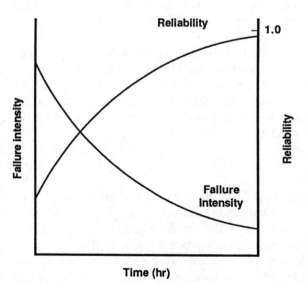

FIGURE 1.5
Reliability and failure intensity.

The term *mean time to failure (MTTF)* is used in the hardware reliability field and to a decreasing extent in software reliability. It is the average value of the next failure interval. The use of MTTF is attractive, in that "larger" indicates "better." However, there are many cases in software reliability in which MTTF is undefined. Failure intensity is preferred because it always exists. Also, failure intensities are simple to work with because they combine additively. In an approximate nonrigorous sense, the two are inverses of each other. The term *mean time between failures (MTBF)* is used in the hardware reliability field when repair or replacement is occurring. It is the sum of MTTF and *mean time to repair (MTTR)*.

1.4 AVAILABILITY

Software availability is usually defined as the expected fraction of time during which a software component or system is functioning acceptably. Assume that the program is operational and is not being modified by new features or repairs. Hence, it has a constant failure intensity. We can compute availability for software as we do for hardware. It is the ratio of up time to the sum of up time plus down time, as the time interval over which the measurement is made approaches infinity. The down time is the product of the failure intensity and the mean time to repair (MTTR). Usually the failure intensity applied here is a figure computed for serious failures and not those that involve only minor degradation of the system. It is generally not practical to hold up operation of the system while performing fault determination and correction in the field. Therefore, we ordinarily determine MTTR as the average time required to restore the data base for a program, reload the program, and resume execution.

A Markov model was developed by Shooman and Trivedi (1976) that depicts the concept of software availability. Okumoto and Goel (1978) extended this model by assuming that a failure may be imperfectly repaired. A more recent paper by Laprie (1984) deals with the evaluation of availability during the operational phase.

Note that the term *maintainability* usually has somewhat different meanings for hardware and software. Hardware is considered "maintainable" if it can be repaired quickly so that its total down time is low. The term "maintainable" for software relates to the speed and ease with which a program can be corrected. However, since these repairs are not generally performed in a way that idles the program, software maintainability does not relate to down time.

1.5 MODELING

To model software reliability one must first consider the principal factors that affect it: fault introduction, fault removal, and the environment. Fault introduction depends primarily on the characteristics of the developed code (code created or modified for the application) and development process characteristics. The most significant code characteristic is size. Development process characteristics include software engineering technologies and tools used and level of experience of personnel. Note that code can be developed to add features or remove faults. Fault removal depends on time, operational profile, and the quality of the repair activity. The environment directly depends on the operational profile. Since some of the foregoing factors are probabilistic in nature and operate over time, software reliability models are generally formulated in terms of random processes. The models are distinguished from each other in general terms by the probability distribution of failure times or number of failures experienced and by the nature of the variation of the random process with time.

A software reliability model specifies the general form of the dependence of the failure process on the factors mentioned. We have assumed that it is, by definition, time-based (this is not to say that non-time-based models may not provide useful insights). The possibilities for different mathematical forms to describe the failure process are almost limitless. We have restricted ourselves to considering well-developed models that have been applied fairly broadly with real data and have given reasonable results. The specific form can be determined from the general form by establishing the values of the parameters of the model through either:

1. estimation—statistical inference procedures are applied to failure data taken for the program, or
2. prediction—determination from properties of the software product and the development process (this can be done before any execution of the program).

There is always some uncertainty in the determination of the specific form. This is generally expressed in terms of *confidence intervals* for the parameters. A confidence interval represents a range of values within which a parameter is expected to lie with a certain confidence. For example, the 0.75 confidence interval of total failures that will be experienced in infinite time may be 150 to 175.

Once the specific form has been established, many different characteristics of the failure process can be determined. For many models there are analytic expressions [see Musa, Iannino, and Okumoto (1987)] for:

1. the average number of failures experienced at any point in time,
2. the average number of failures in a time interval,
3. the failure intensity at any point in time,
4. the probability distribution of failure intervals.

A good software reliability model has several important characteristics. It

1. gives good predictions[1] of future failure behavior,
2. computes useful quantities,
3. is simple,

---

[1] The term *prediction* has two different but commonly used meanings in this book, "prediction of parameter values" and "prediction of failure behavior." One must be careful to distinguish them.

4. is widely applicable, and

5. is based on sound assumptions.

Prediction of future failure behavior assumes that the values of model parameters will not change for the period of prediction. If the net effect of the opposing influences of fault introduction and fault repair should change substantially, we must either compensate for the change or wait until enough new failures have occurred so that we can reestimate the model parameters. Incorporating such changes into the models themselves has generally been impractical due to the added complexity. In any event, the complexity is not worthwhile, considering the accuracy with which parameters are generally known.

In general, software reliability models are based on (although this is often not stated explicitly) a stable program executing in a constant environment. This means that neither the code nor the operational profile are changing. If the program and environment do change, they often do so and are usually handled in a piecewise fashion. Thus, the models focus mainly on fault removal. Most models can account for the effects of slow fault introduction, however. Some assume that the average net long-term effect must be a decrease in failure intensity. If neither fault introduction, fault removal, or operational profile changes are occurring, the failure intensity will be constant and the model should simplify to accommodate this. It is assumed that the behavior of the program is compared with the requirements with enough thoroughness that all failures are detected. It is possible to compensate for programs (Chapter 6) or environments that are changing.

For a program that has been released and is operational, it is common to defer installation of both new features and repairs to the next release. Assuming a constant operational profile, the program will exhibit a constant failure intensity.

In general terms, a good model enhances communication on a project and provides a common framework of understanding for the software development process. It also enhances visibility to management and other interested parties. These advantages are valuable, even if the projections made with the model in a specific case are not particularly accurate.

Developing a practically useful software reliability model involves substantial theoretical work, tool building, and the accumulation of a body of lore from practical experience. This effort generally requires several person years. In contrast, the application of a model that is well established in practice requires a very small fraction of project resources. Consequently, we will consider this factor as one of the criteria for selection in Chapter 2.

It has sometimes been suggested that a range of models be applied to each project. The ones that perform best (or some weighted combination of them) would be used. This approach may be suitable for research investigations. However, the authors consider the use of more than one or two models conceptually and economically impractical for real projects.

1.6 USES

Pressures have been increasing for achieving a more finely tuned balance among product and process characteristics, including reliability. Trade-offs among product components with respect to reliability are also becoming increasingly important. This has made "seat-of-the-pants" engineering increasingly unacceptable. Quantitative approaches are essential. Thus an important use of software reliability measurement is in system engineering. However, there are at least four other ways in which software reliability measures can be of great value to the software engineer, manager, or user.

First, you can use software reliability measures to evaluate software engineering technology quantitatively. New techniques are continually being proposed for improving the process of developing software, but unfortunately they have been exposed to little quantitative evaluation. Software engineers and managers greeted many of these innovations with enthusiasm at first, because of the strong need for them. This attitude often turned to skepticism when their cost seemed to outweigh their effectiveness. The inability to distinguish between good and bad new technology has often led to a general resistance to change that is counterproductive. Software reliability measures offer the promise of establishing at least one criterion for evaluating the new technology. For example, you might run experiments to determine the decrease in failure intensity (failures per unit time) at the start of system test resulting from design reviews. A quantitative evaluation such as this makes the benefits of good software engineering technology highly visible. This is likely to stimulate the investment of more money and effort in this field, in addition to making the investment more informed and efficient.

Second, a software reliability measure offers you the possibility of evaluating development status during the test phases of a project. Methods such as intuition of designers or test team, percent of tests completed, and successful execution of critical functional tests have been used to evaluate testing progress. None of these have been really satisfactory and some have been quite unsatisfactory. An objective reliability measure (such as failure intensity) established from test data provides a sound means of determining status. Reliability generally increases with the amount of testing. Thus, reliability can be closely linked with project schedules. Furthermore, the cost of testing is highly correlated with failure intensity improvement. Since two of the key process attributes that a manager must control are schedule and cost, reliability can be intimately tied in with project management.

Third, you can use a software reliability measure to monitor the operational performance of software and to control new features added and design changes made to the software. The reliability of software usually decreases as a result of such changes. A reliability objective can be used to determine when, and perhaps how large, a change will be allowed. The objective would be based on user and other requirements. For example, a freeze on all changes not related to debugging can be imposed when the failure intensity rises above the performance objective.

Finally, a quantitative understanding of software quality and the various factors influencing it and affected by it enriches your insight into the software product and the software development process. You are then much more capable of making informed decisions.

The following case study shows some of the uses of software reliability measurement.

CASE STUDY 1.1
THE DATCOM PROJECT

A bank desiring to set up the data network shown in Figure 1.6 hires an outside firm to design the hardware for the front end processor and system controller. In addition the firm is also contracted to develop the necessary software that will run on both of these processors. Wishing to monitor their progress toward a failure intensity objective for the system controller software, the firm decides to use a software reliability model. They will collect failure interval data during system test. In practice the firm would also monitor the reliability of the front end processor software. Combining the failure interval data with estimates for the amount of available resources and some project parameters, a report similar to that shown in Figure 1.7 can be generated.[2] The report shows the most likely value of the indicated quantity in the center. The lower and upper confidence bounds (for various confidence limits) are shown sandwiched around it. For example, we are 75 percent confident that the present failure intensity is between 0.079 and 0.125 failure/CPU hr. The "completion date" refers to the date of meeting the failure intensity objective. It is in month-day-year format.

The 75 percent confidence interval has been found from experience to be a good compromise between a higher confidence and the resultant larger interval. Plots of estimated present failure intensity and completion date for this project are shown in Figures 1.8 and 1.9, respectively. The plots show running histories throughout the course of system test for the project, as indicated by the dates on the horizontal axis. They represent the behavior one expects on real projects. In both figures, the solid center curve is the most likely value and the dashed outer curves delineate the bounds of the 75 percent confidence interval. The jaggedness of the curves is a result of statistical fluctuations. Figure 1.8 is a plot of present failure intensity; it is useful for indicating progress toward the failure intensity objective. Note that failure intensity drops steadily throughout system test as the program is debugged. Figure 1.9 is a plot of the current estimate of project completion date. The left hand sides of the curves should be disregarded. Large fluc-

---

[2]The reports and plots for the DATCOM project were generated using Musa's (1975) basic execution time model. Hence we will be dealing with both execution time and calendar time.

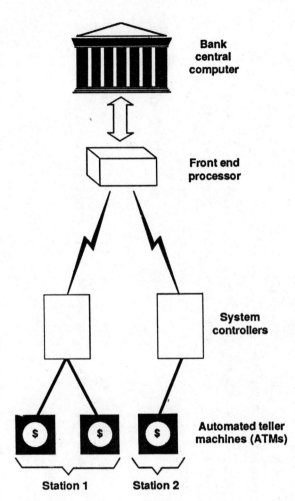

FIGURE 1.6
Hypothetical bank data network.

tuations are occurring because of the small size of the data sample in this time period. Note that they stabilize about halfway through system test.

A software reliability model can be used to help answer managerial questions relating to project status and scheduling. Three such questions are:

1. *Is* this software ready for release?
2. *When* will it be ready for release?
3. Should we regress to a previous version from the present one?

To answer the first question, compare the present failure intensity with the project's failure intensity objective. The report of Figure 1.7 is helpful, but plotting the recent history of the present failure intensity (Figure 1.8) will make additional information available for managerial judgments. The present failure intensity will normally exhibit steady (ignoring statistical fluctuations) improvement with time during testing. A sharp rise in failure intensity usually indicates new

SOFTWARE RELIABILITY PREDICTION
BASIC MODEL
DATCOM EXAMPLE

BASED ON SAMPLE OF 180 TEST FAILURES
EXECUTION TIME IS 450.57 HR
FAILURE INTENSITY OBJECTIVE IS .20e-03 FAILURES/CPU HR
CALENDAR TIME TO DATE IS 180 DAYS
PRESENT DATE 9/1/86

	CONF. LIMITS				MOST	CONF. LIMITS			
	95%	90%	75%	50%	LIKELY	50%	75%	90%	95%
TOTAL FAILURES	190	191	193	196	199	204	208	213	217

FAILURE INTENSITIES (FAILURES/1000 CPU HR)

	95%	90%	75%	50%	MOST LIKELY	50%	75%	90%	95%
INITIAL F.I.	850.1	878.6	924.1	968.8	1033	1099	1147	1197	1230
PRESENT F.I.	66.9	71.5	79.1	87.2	99.8	114.0	125.0	137.4	145.8

*** ADDITIONAL REQUIREMENTS TO MEET FAILURE INTENSITY OBJECTIVE ***

	95%	90%	75%	50%	MOST LIKELY	50%	75%	90%	95%
FAILURES	10	11	13	15	19	24	28	33	37
EXEC. TIME (CPU HR)	899.6	939.5	1007	1080	1197	1336	1450	1586	1684
CAL. TIME (DAYS)	36.0	37.9	41.4	45.3	51.8	59.8	66.7	75.2	81.5
COMPLETION DATE	100786	100986	101386	101786	102386	103186	110786	111686	112286

FIGURE 1.7
Sample project status report.

FIGURE 1.8
Estimates of present failure intensity for bank project.

faults introduced by code change or exposed by extension of testing into new environments. If the system test phase is marked by many unforeseen new environments, test planning may have been inadequate. Unusually slow improvement in failure intensity usually indicates that a substantial number of faults remain. Alternatively, one could be introducing or exposing new faults at roughly the same rate that they are being corrected.

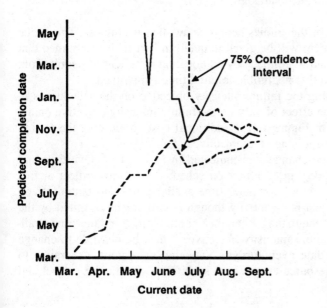

FIGURE 1.9
Predicted completion date for bank project.

The question regarding when the software will be ready for release can be answered by observing the completion date line in Figure 1.7.

We can determine whether we should regress to a previous version by tracking present failure intensity for each version. If the new version is not meeting the failure intensity objective and the old one is, and the difference between the failure intensities is substantial, it will probably be worth the effort to regress.

The model can help the manager, through simulation, reach trade-off decisions among schedules, costs, resources, and reliability and can assist in determining resource allocations. One chooses several values of each parameter that is to be varied, applies the model to compute the effects, examines the results, and iterates this procedure as required. Usually one chooses the parameter values to include the extreme values that are reasonably possible, so that the influence of the parameters can be quickly determined.

To illustrate, consider the DATCOM project system test period report (Figure 1.7) for September 1, 1986. The project had a test team of 3 and a debugging team of 5 people. A failure intensity objective of 0.0002 failure/CPU hr for the system controller software was set originally. The estimated completion date was expected to be October 23, with a 75 percent confidence interval of October 13 to November 7. Assuming this date to be unsatisfactory, the effect of several different managerial actions on the schedule can be studied:

1. increasing the failure intensity objective,
2. working up to 50 percent overtime (as required to expedite the project),
3. increasing the size of the test team,
4. increasing the size of the debugging team, or
5. making more computer time available.

We will present the results of the studies here to show their usefulness. The explanation of how to conduct them will be given in detail in Part II. It is assumed that the increases of actions 3 and 4 are made by reallocating experienced people from other parts of the project so that negligible training time is involved.

The effect of increasing the failure intensity objective on the schedule is illustrated in Figure 1.10. The effect of varying the failure intensity objective on additional cost is illustrated in Figure 1.11. "Additional cost" represents the testing and debugging cost required to reach the objective.

The effects of resource changes are indicated in Figure 1.12. Overtime and additional personnel have negligible effect on schedules for this project at this point in its history. Making more computer time available has substantial effect. This indicates that this project is essentially though not completely limited by the computer time available. If the manager can make both more computer time available *and* back off on the failure intensity objective, it may be possible to change the estimated completion date even further. Note that we cannot generalize to other projects. Effects of resource changes are specific to a particular project and time.

FIGURE 1.10
Effect of failure intensity objective on predicted completion date for bank project.

Options 3 through 5 do not affect costs because the total resources required will be the same. The resources will merely be expended at a more rapid rate (unless free time that occurs is not used on another task). Option 2 can affect costs only through the premium pay rates.

We have the capability to combine component reliabilities to determine system reliability. Consider the event diagram shown in Figure 1.13 for our bank data network system. It presents the view of a user at station 1 of how the functioning

FIGURE 1.11
Effect of failure intensity objective on additional cost for bank project.

FIGURE 1.12
**Effect of resource levels on
predicted completion date
for bank project.**

of components affects the functioning of the system. The view from station 2 is similar except that there is only one ATM. This concept and the methods for combining reliabilities will be presented in Chapter 4. We will simply note that the calculation is easily performed and give the results. The bank's central computer is assumed to have a hardware reliability and software reliability of 1 for simplicity in presenting this example. The ATMs have a reliability of 0.995 for a 24-hr period. The front end processor and system controller hardware have 24-hr reliabilities of 0.99 and 0.995, respectively. The front end processor and system controller software each have a failure intensity in execution time of 0.004 failure/CPU hr. The front end processor utilization is 0.95. The system controller utilization is 0.5. We wish to find the reliability of the system for a 24-hr period as seen from station 1 and from station 2 (see Figure 1.6).

The calendar time failure intensities for the front end processor and system controller software will be 0.0038 failure/hr and 0.002 failure/hr, respectively. The 24-hr reliabilities can be calculated, using a standard formula for relating failure

FIGURE 1.13
Bank data network failure event diagram (as seen from station 1).

intensity and reliability, as 0.913 and 0.953. The overall 24-hr period reliability as seen from station 1 is calculated to be 0.857 and that from station 2 turns out to be 0.853. If the bank considers this unacceptable, improvements should be made first in the front end processor software and then in the system controller software.

1.7 SUMMARY

Measurement is a vital element in the practice of software engineering. Good software engineering is important to the information industry. Reliability is one of the most important measurements. An understanding of the failure process is central to any effort to model and comprehend software reliability. Availability is closely related to and can be calculated from reliability.

PROBLEMS

1.1 The term "software reliability" is disturbing. Software doesn't wear out like hardware, so how can you apply a hardware concept?

1.2 How can you apply probability theory to software reliability? In hardware reliability it makes sense because there are a myriad of possible failure mechanisms operating on a microscopic level, and failures are essentially random. But aren't software failures deterministic, being the result of human error?

1.3 How can you talk of a failure intensity for software? It isn't the same situation as we have for hardware. You let me pick the tests and establish their sequence and I'll give any failure intensity estimate you want. For example, if one takes a run that operates without failure and repeats it endlessly, zero failure intensity will be obtained.

1.4 How can you view the usage of a system as a random process? If people learn the weaknesses of a system, they will avoid them.

1.5 If in testing we continually repeat the same set of test cases, will the accuracy of software reliability predictions be affected?

1.6 Aren't software failures due primarily to changes in the environment?

1.7 Are software reliability figures more usage-dependent than hardware reliability figures?

1.8 What is the meaning of mean time to repair (MTTR) for software?

1.9 What is meant when one says that for accurate reliability determination the entire input space must be covered?

1.10 Software reliability theory assumes that tests are selected randomly from the possible input space. This seems inefficient to us. We select the tests in an order that corresponds to our estimate of the likelihood they will occur during use. This removes faults most rapidly and economically. Can the theory be applied in our case?

TWO

SELECTED MODELS

In Chapter 1 the characteristics of a good software reliability model were summarized. In this chapter we present two models for application in detail throughout this book. The models from which the two were selected are described and compared in Musa, Iannino, and Okumoto (1987). Two models were chosen because each has certain advantages not possessed by the other. However, the effort required to learn the lore associated with the application of a model makes presenting more than two a question of sharply diminishing returns. The models are the basic execution time model and the logarithmic Poisson execution time model. We consider first why we selected them; then they are described. You will see that both models have two components, named the execution time component and the calendar time component. Each component will be described with respect to both models. The determination of parameters will also be discussed.

2.1 MODEL SELECTION

Both models were developed with special regard to the needs of the engineers and managers who would use them. Consequently, both yield particularly useful quantities, such as the date for attaining a failure intensity objective. In addition, there were five primary reasons for selecting the basic execution time model:

1. It generally predicts satisfactorily.
2. It is simple and easy to understand.
3. It is the model that is most thoroughly developed and has been most widely applied to actual projects. Several programs have been developed to aid in implementing it.
4. Its parameters have a clear physical interpretation and can be related to information that exists before the program has been executed. The information in-

cludes characteristics of the software such as size and characteristics of the development environment. The foregoing property is important for system engineering studies.

5. It can handle evolving systems (systems that change in size) by adjusting the failure times to estimates of what they would have been if all the code had been present (see Chapter 6).

The logarithmic Poisson execution time model [Musa and Okumoto (1984b)] has high predictive validity, which it attains early in the system test phase. It is a relatively new model, initially published in March 1984. There is less experience with it than with the basic execution time model. However, it is almost as simple. At present, its parameters have not been related to software and development environment characteristics which exist prior to execution. The failure intensity is generally larger for large values of execution time than that of the basic model. The model may be somewhat pessimistic as compared to the basic model with regard to estimating the time, resources, and cost required to reach small failure intensity objectives. However, the nature of the prediction errors is not currently well known.

Both execution time models use an effective dual approach for characterizing failure behavior. Initial modeling is done in terms of execution time, the processor time used by the program. Then the models convert execution time to the more familiar calendar time. Quantities expressed in calendar time are more meaningful to most engineers and managers. The conversion is done through a second component of the model that characterizes the way in which human and computer resources are applied to the project.

Presently, a lot of evidence has accumulated that demonstrates the superiority of execution time over calendar time for initial modeling [Trachtenberg (1985), Musa and Okumoto (1984a), and Hecht (1981)]. This fact is generally accepted in the field. The reason that execution time is preferable is that it best characterizes the failure-inducing stress placed on software. Consider two different facilities associated with an operating system, an editor and a matrix manipulation package. Each is activated by input states that occur randomly in accordance with their operational profiles. The editor, perhaps executing 2 to 3 CPU hr daily, is certainly more stressed than the matrix package, which might execute for only a few CPU minutes. Both of the two models described previously were developed as execution time models. We currently have an interesting phenomenon. Some models, originally developed as calendar time models or without consideration of the kind of time involved, are being interpreted as execution time models.

In evaluating the basic execution time model, Dale (1982) states, "This is arguably the most practical model of all. It is a statistical model, and has been developed to the extent that it takes into account various personnel and resource constraints." Ramamoorthy and Bastani (1982) note that, "(the Musa model) . . . is better developed and is the first model to insist on execution time."

Managers involved in the projects on which these two models have been applied have observed benefits beyond the quantitative measures. They noted that the models provided an intuitively appealing and well-structured conceptual framework that gave a new perspective on the testing process. Developers and their customers were stimulated to think more carefully about just what should be considered a failure for the system involved. Also, they gave more careful consideration to what their reliability objective should be.

Before we leave the subject of model selection, we need to examine why we did *not* choose a number of other models. First, the other models do not use the execution time component–calendar time component approach that has proved so fruitful. Generally, reliability modeling is performed in calendar time, resulting in severe disadvantages, or the time domain is unspecified. If you interpret one of these models in terms of execution time, you may not have a way of relating execution time to calendar time. The calendar time capability is most important for engineers and managers. Most models do not provide many of the useful quantities that the basic execution time and logarithmic Poisson execution time models do. An example of one of these useful quantities is the calendar time required to reach a failure intensity objective. Concepts from several of the models [Goel and Okumoto (1979), Jelinski and Moranda (1972), and Shooman (1972)] have been incorporated in the basic execution time model. Consequently, you can enjoy most of their advantages and those of the basic model itself when you use it. Some models such as the Littlewood-Verrall general model [Littlewood and Verrall (1973)] are very complex. They are difficult to understand and visualize physically and relatively difficult and costly to implement on a computer for practical and economical use. Finally, none of the other models match the basic execution time model in the extent of the practical experience that has been gained with it.

In general, it appears that these models can be applied to any type or size of software project, with the following exception. Very small projects (less than about 5000 lines of code) may not experience sufficient failures to permit accurate estimation of execution time component parameters and the various derived quantities. Some kind of estimate can usually be made, however, yielding a result of the form "present failure intensity is at least X failures/CPU hr."

We'll now take a look at each component in turn. The component will be described for both models and we will discuss parameter determination. We will provide both graphical and mathematical descriptions. The model descriptions and various useful formulas will be grouped in Appendix B for ready reference.

2.2 EXECUTION TIME COMPONENT

2.2.1 Description

The execution time component for both models assumes that failures occur as a random process, to be specific, a nonhomogeneous Poisson process.[1] Don't be

---

[1] The basic execution time model was not at first described as a nonhomogeneous Poisson process.

frightened by the term "nonhomogeneous Poisson process." "Poisson" simply refers to the probability distribution of the value of the process at each point in time. The term "nonhomogeneous" indicates that the characteristics of the probability distributions that make up the random process vary with time. This is exhibited in a variation of failure intensity with time. You would expect that, since faults are both being introduced and removed as time passes.

The two models have failure intensity functions that differ as functions of execution time. However, the difference between them is best described in terms of slope or decrement per failure experienced (Figure 2.1).[2] The decrement in the failure intensity function remains constant for the basic execution time model whether it is the first failure that is being fixed or the last. By contrast, for the logarithmic Poisson execution time model, the decrement per failure becomes smaller with failures experienced. In fact, it decreases exponentially. The first failure initiates a repair process that yields a substantial decrement in failure intensity, while later failures result in much smaller decrements.

The failure intensity λ for the basic model as a function of failures experienced is

$$\lambda(\mu) = \lambda_0 \left[1 - \frac{\mu}{\nu_0} \right]. \tag{2.1}$$

---

[2]In this discussion, since failures occur randomly, we are referring to "average failures experienced."

FIGURE 2.1
Failure intensity functions.

The quantity λ_0 is the initial failure intensity at the start of execution. Note that μ is the average or expected number of failures experienced at a given point in time. The quantity ν_0 is the total number of failures that would occur in infinite time.

Example 2.1. Assume that a program will experience 100 failures in infinite time. It has now experienced 50. The initial failure intensity was 10 failures/CPU hr. The current failure intensity is:

$$\lambda(\mu) = \lambda_0 \left[1 - \frac{\mu}{\nu_0} \right]$$

$$= 10 \left[1 - \frac{50}{100} \right]$$

$$= 5 \text{ failures/CPU hr .}$$ ■

The failure intensity for the logarithmic Poisson model is

$$\lambda(\mu) = \lambda_0 \exp(- \theta\mu) . \tag{2.2}$$

The quantity θ is called the failure intensity decay parameter. Suppose we plot the natural logarithm of failure intensity against mean failures experienced. Then we can see by transforming (2.2) that the failure intensity decay parameter θ is the magnitude of the slope of the line we have plotted. It represents the relative change of failure intensity per failure experienced.

Example 2.2. Assume that the initial failure intensity is again 10 failures/CPU hr. The failure intensity decay parameter is 0.02/failure. We will assume that 50 failures have been experienced. The current failure intensity is:

$$\lambda(\mu) = \lambda_0 \exp(- \theta\mu)$$

$$= 10 \exp[- (0.02)(50)]$$

$$= 10 \exp(- 1)$$

$$= 3.68 \text{ failures/CPU hr .}$$ ■

The slope of failure intensity, $d\lambda/d\mu$, is given by

$$\frac{d\lambda}{d\mu} = - \frac{\lambda_0}{\nu_0} \tag{2.3}$$

for the basic model.

Example 2.3. In Example 2.1, the decrement of failure intensity per failure is given by:

$$\frac{d\lambda}{d\mu} = - \frac{\lambda_0}{\nu_0}$$

$$= - \frac{10}{100}$$

$$= - 0.1/\text{CPU hr}. \qquad\qquad \blacksquare$$

It is

$$\frac{d\lambda}{d\mu} = - \lambda_0 \, \theta \, \exp(- \theta\mu) = - \theta\lambda \qquad\qquad (2.4)$$

for the logarithmic Poisson model.

Example 2.4. In Example 2.2, the decrement of failure intensity per failure is given by:

$$\frac{d\lambda}{d\mu} = - \lambda_0\theta \, \exp(- \theta\mu)$$

$$= - 10(0.02) \, \exp(- 0.02\mu)$$

$$= - 0.2 \, \exp(- 0.02\mu)/\text{CPU hr}.$$

When no failures have been experienced, we have a decrement of $- 0.2/\text{CPU hr}$, greater than that for the basic model. After 50 failures have been experienced, the decrement is $- 0.0736/\text{CPU hr}$. Note the decrease to an amount smaller than the corresponding amount for the basic model. The *relative* change in failure intensity per failure experienced is constant at 0.02. In other words, the failure intensity at a given number of failures experienced is 0.98 of that at the preceding failure. $\qquad \blacksquare$

The basic model implies a uniform operational profile. Studies by both Downs (1985) and Trachtenberg (1985) demonstrate the association of the basic model with a uniform operational profile. They also show that highly nonuniform operational profiles yield failure intensity curves that are convex (of decreasing slope) with respect to number of failures experienced. The logarithmic Poisson model may be superior for highly nonuniform operational profiles, where some functions are executed much more frequently than others. The first occurrences of the input states will, on the average, be in the same order as the frequency rank. If a particular input state stimulates a fault and thus results in a failure, that failure will occur on the first instance of that input state being executed. Once the failure has been identified, the fault will in general be repaired. Then you won't see the failure recurring on subsequent instances of the particular input state. If the repair happens to be imperfect, the failure could return. In general, however, the failures tend to occur only on the early occurrences of the input states. Thus, the early failures that you tend to experience during a period of execution are associated with the frequently occurring input states. Consequently, when you repair the early failures, you tend to have a greater reduction in failure intensity. With a highly nonuniform operational profile, the early failures result in sharp decreases in failure intensity and the later failures show much smaller ones. Thus a highly nonuniform operational profile yields a failure intensity history that tends to be more suitably modeled by the logarithmic Poisson execution time model. We emphasize the point *highly* nonuniform because the basic execution time model appears to be quite tolerant to a substantial degree of nonuniformity. This fact has been demonstrated by both Downs (1985) and Trachtenberg (1985).

Note that failure intensity eventually decreases very slowly for the logarithmic Poisson model. This results from the very infrequent execution of the input states that still contain faults. This may be unrealistic with respect to system test. Often the operational profile is deliberately transformed by the test planners to reduce the system test execution time required to expose the problems. One could adjust for the transformed operational profile. It may be easier, however, to handle the situation indirectly by employing the less pessimistic basic model.

The curve for the logarithmic Poisson model may or may not cross the straight line characterizing the basic model, depending on its parameter values (see Figure 2.1). Each failure that is experienced will generate some repair activity and the result of this repair activity is a decrement in failure intensity. Neither model makes any assumption about the quality of the repair process (debugging may be imperfect). They both can allow for possible introduction of new faults during repair. Both models assume that the correction of faults following failures is immediate. In actuality, there is always some delay, but the effects of the delay are not serious and can easily be accounted for, as discussed in Chapter 4.

One might be concerned that a potential failure would be masked by a previous failure and that this behavior might affect the validity of the software reliability model. This is not likely. It occurs more frequently in unit test than in subsystem test or later, where software reliability models are commonly applied. The failures that mask other failures tend to have been eliminated by this point.

We can obtain some interesting relationships with some straightforward derivation [see Musa, Iannino, and Okumoto (1987)]. The expected number of failures experienced as a function of execution time is illustrated for both models in Figure 2.2. Whether the curve for the logarithmic Poisson model crosses that for the basic model depends on its parameter values. Note that the expected number of failures for the logarithmic Poisson model is always infinite at infinite time. This number can be

FIGURE 2.2
Mean failures experienced versus execution time.

and usually is finite for the basic model during test, although it is usually infinite during the operational phase. The curve for the former model is logarithmic, hence the name. The curve for the latter is "negative" exponential, approaching a limit. Infinite failures can occur for the logarithmic Poisson model, even though the number of faults may be finite, because the model assumes decreasing effectiveness of the repair action, as explained in Musa, Iannino, and Okumoto (1987).

Let execution time be denoted by τ. We can write, for the basic model:

$$\mu(\tau) = \nu_0 \left[1 - \exp\left(-\frac{\lambda_0}{\nu_0} \tau \right) \right] . \tag{2.5}$$

Example 2.5. Let's again consider a program with an initial failure intensity of 10 failures/CPU hr and 100 total failures. We will look at the failures experienced after 10 and 100 CPU hr of execution. We have, for 10 CPU hr:

$$\mu(\tau) = \nu_0 \left[1 - \exp\left(-\frac{\lambda_0}{\nu_0} \tau \right) \right]$$

$$= 100 \left\{ 1 - \exp\left[-\frac{10}{100} (10) \right] \right\}$$

$$= 100[1 - \exp(-1)]$$

$$= 100(1 - 0.368)$$

$$= 100(0.632)$$

$$= 63 \text{ failures} .$$

For 100 CPU hr, we have:

$$\mu(\tau) = 100 \left\{ 1 - \exp\left[-\frac{10}{100} (100) \right] \right\}$$

$$= 100[1 - \exp(-10)]$$

$$= 100(1 - 0.0000454)$$

$$= 100 \text{ failures (almost)} . \qquad \blacksquare$$

For the logarithmic Poisson model, we have

$$\mu(\tau) = \frac{1}{\theta} \ln(\lambda_0 \theta \tau + 1) . \tag{2.6}$$

Example 2.6. Use the same parameters as Example 2.2. Let's find the number of failures experienced for the logarithmic Poisson model at 10 and 100 CPU hr of execution. We have:

$$\mu(\tau) = \frac{1}{\theta} \ln(\lambda_0 \theta \tau + 1)$$

$$= \frac{1}{0.02} \ln[(10)(0.02)(10) + 1]$$

$$= 50 \ln (2 + 1)$$

$$= 50 \ln 3$$

$$= 50(1.099)$$

$$= 55 \text{ failures}.$$

This is smaller than the number of failures experienced by the basic model at 10 CPU hr. At 100 CPU hr we have:

$$\mu(\tau) = \frac{1}{0.02} \ln \left[(10)(0.02)(100) + 1 \right]$$

$$= 50 \ln (20 + 1)$$

$$= 50 \ln 21$$

$$= 50(3.045)$$

$$= 152 \text{ failures}.$$

Note that we now have more failures than the basic model. In fact, the number exceeds the total failures that the basic model can experience. ∎

The failure intensity as a function of execution time for both models is shown in Figure 2.3. Again, the curves for the two models may or may not cross, depending on the parameter values. This relationship is useful for determining the present failure intensity at any given value of execution time. Compare Figure 2.3 with Figure 2.1. Since intervals between failures increase as failures are experienced, the curves of Figure 2.1 are stretched out to the right when plotted against execution time. For the same set of data, the failure intensity of the logarithmic Poisson model drops more rapidly than that of the basic model at first. Later, it

Basic model

Logarithmic Poisson model

Failure intensity λ

Execution time τ

**FIGURE 2.3
Failure intensity versus execution time.**

drops more slowly. At large values of execution time, the logarithmic Poisson model will have larger values of failure intensity than the basic model.

We have, for the basic model,

$$\lambda(\tau) = \lambda_0 \exp\left[-\frac{\lambda_0}{\nu_0}\tau\right] \tag{2.7}$$

Example 2.7. We will look at the failure intensities at 10 and 100 CPU hr, using the parameters of Example 2.1. We have, at 10 CPU hr:

$$\lambda(\tau) = \lambda_0 \exp\left[-\frac{\lambda_0}{\nu_0}\tau\right]$$

$$= 10 \exp\left[-\frac{10}{100}(10)\right]$$

$$= 10 \exp(-1)$$

$$= 10(0.368)$$

$$= 3.68 \text{ failures/CPU hr}.$$

At 100 CPU hr we have:

$$\lambda(\tau) = 10 \exp\left[-\frac{10}{100}(100)\right]$$

$$= 10 \exp(-10)$$

$$= 10(0.0000454)$$

$$= 0.000454 \text{ failure/CPU hr}. \qquad \blacksquare$$

We can write, for the logarithmic Poisson model,

$$\lambda(\tau) = \frac{\lambda_0}{\lambda_0\theta\tau + 1}. \tag{2.8}$$

Example 2.8. Consider the failure intensities for the logarithmic Poisson model at 10 CPU hr and 100 CPU hr, using the parameters of Example 2.2. We have for 10 CPU hr:

$$\lambda(\tau) = \frac{\lambda_0}{\lambda_0\theta\tau + 1}$$

$$= \frac{10}{10(0.02)(10) + 1}$$

$$= \frac{10}{2 + 1}$$

$$= \frac{10}{3}$$

$$= 3.33 \text{ failures/CPU hr.}$$

This is slightly lower than the corresponding failure intensity for the basic model. At 100 CPU hr we have:

$$\lambda(\tau) = \frac{10}{10(0.02)(100) + 1}$$

$$= \frac{10}{20 + 1}$$

$$= \frac{10}{21}$$

$$= 0.476 \text{ failure/CPU hr}.$$

The failure intensity at the higher execution time is larger for the logarithmic Poisson model. ∎

As we have seen, the execution time components of both models are characterized by two parameters. They are listed in Table 2.1. The significance of changes in their values is shown in Figures 2.4 to 2.7 with respect to mean failures experienced. Both models have initial failure intensity as one parameter. It affects the "scale" (overall vertical positioning) of the failure intensity curve with respect to mean failures experienced. The basic model has total failures (failures expected in infinite time) as the second parameter; the logarithmic model, failure intensity decay parameter. Both of these parameters relate to how fast the failure intensity changes. If initial failure intensity is held constant, a larger value for total failures means that failure intensity becomes smaller less rapidly with the number of failures experienced. A larger value for the failure intensity decay parameter means that failure intensity and the failure intensity decrements become smaller more rapidly with the number of failures experienced.

The significance of changes in parameter values for relationships between failure intensity and execution time is shown in Figures 2.8 through 2.11. They are a little more complicated than you might think at first look. The initial failure intensity affects the shape (nature of variation) of each curve as well as the scale. The shape depends on the quantity λ_0/ν_0 for the basic model, and $\lambda_0\theta$ for the

TABLE 2.1
Execution time component parameters

Parameter	Model	
	Basic	Logarithmic Poisson
Initial failure intensity	λ_0	λ_0

Failure intensity change:
   Total failures
   Failure intensity decay parameter
	
	ν_0
	—
		
		—
		θ

FIGURE 2.4
Variation of failure intensity versus mean failures experienced with initial failure intensity parameter — basic execution time model.

FIGURE 2.5
Variation of failure intensity versus mean failures experienced with initial failure intensity parameter — logarithmic Poisson execution time model.

FIGURE 2.6
Variation of failure intensity versus mean failures experienced with total failures parameter — basic execution time model.

41

FIGURE 2.7
Variation of failure intensity versus mean failures experienced with failure intensity decay parameter—logarithmic Poisson execution time model.

FIGURE 2.8
Variation of failure intensity versus execution time with initial failure intensity parameter—basic execution time model.

FIGURE 2.9
Variation of failure intensity versus execution time with initial failure intensity parameter—logarithmic Poisson execution time model.

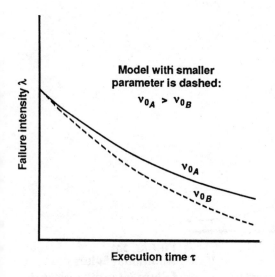

FIGURE 2.10
Variation of failure intensity versus execution time with total failures parameter—basic execution time model.

logarithmic model. Recall that λ_0 is initial failure intensity, ν_0 is total failures, and θ is the failure intensity decay parameter. If the shape quantities are held constant while λ_0 is varied, then the λ_0 variations affect only the scale of the curves.

DERIVED QUANTITIES. Assume that you have chosen a failure intensity objective for the software product being developed. Suppose some portion of the failures are being removed through correction of their associated faults. Then you can use the objective and the present value of failure intensity to determine the additional expected number of failures that must be experienced to reach that objective. The process is illustrated graphically in Figure 2.12. Equations describing the

FIGURE 2.11
Variation of failure intensity versus execution time with failure intensity decay parameter—logarithmic Poisson execution time model.

FIGURE 2.12
Additional failures to
failure intensity objective.

relationships in closed form may be derived for both models [see Musa, Iannino, and Okumoto (1987)] so that manual calculations can be performed. They are

$$\Delta\mu = \frac{\nu_0}{\lambda_0} (\lambda_P - \lambda_F) \tag{2.9}$$

for the basic model and

$$\Delta\mu = \frac{1}{\theta} \ln \frac{\lambda_P}{\lambda_F} \tag{2.10}$$

for the logarithmic Poisson model. The quantity $\Delta\mu$ is the expected number of failures to reach the failure intensity objective, λ_P is the present failure intensity, and λ_F is the failure intensity objective.

Example 2.9. For the basic model, we will determine the expected number of failures that will be experienced between a present failure intensity of 3.68 failures/CPU hr and an objective of 0.000454 failure/CPU hr. We will use the same parameter values as in Example 2.1. Thus:

$$\Delta\mu = \frac{\nu_0}{\lambda_0} (\lambda_P - \lambda_F)$$

$$= \frac{100}{10} (3.68 - 0.000454)$$

$$= 10 (3.68)$$

$$= 37 \text{ failures}.$$

Note that this result cross-checks with the results of Examples 2.5 and 2.7. ∎

Example 2.10. We will find, for the logarithmic Poisson model, the expected number of failures experienced between a present failure intensity of 3.33 failures/CPU hr and an objective of 0.476 failure/CPU hr. The parameter values will be the same as in Example 2.2. We have:

$$\Delta\mu = \frac{1}{\theta} \ln \frac{\lambda_P}{\lambda_F}$$

$$= \frac{1}{0.02} \ln \frac{3.33}{0.476}$$

$$= 50 \ln 6.996$$

$$= 50 \, (1.945)$$

$$= 97 \text{ failures}.$$

This result cross-checks with the results of Examples 2.6 and 2.8. ∎

Similarly, you can determine the additional execution time $\Delta\tau$ required to reach the failure intensity objective for either model. This is

$$\Delta\tau = \frac{\nu_0}{\lambda_0} \ln \frac{\lambda_P}{\lambda_F} \tag{2.11}$$

for the basic model and

$$\Delta\tau = \frac{1}{\theta} \left[\frac{1}{\lambda_F} - \frac{1}{\lambda_P} \right] \tag{2.12}$$

for the logarithmic Poisson model. This is illustrated in Figure 2.13.

Example 2.11. For the basic model, with the same parameter values used in Example 2.1, we will determine the execution time between a present failure intensity of 3.68 failures/CPU hr and an objective of 0.000454 failure/CPU hr. We have:

$$\Delta\tau = \frac{\nu_0}{\lambda_0} \ln \frac{\lambda_P}{\lambda_F}$$

$$= \frac{100}{10} \ln \frac{3.68}{0.000454}$$

$$= 10 \ln 8106$$

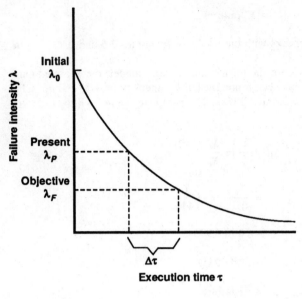

Failure Intensity λ

Initial λ_0

Present λ_P

Objective λ_F

$\Delta\tau$

Execution time τ

FIGURE 2.13
Additional execution time to failure intensity objective.

$$= 10\ (9)$$

$$= 90\ \text{CPU hr}.$$

This result checks with the results of Example 2.7. ∎

Example 2.12. For the logarithmic Poisson model, with the same parameter values used in Example 2.2, we will find the execution time between a present failure intensity of 3.33 failures/CPU hr and an objective of 0.476 failure/CPU hr. We have:

$$\Delta\tau = \frac{1}{\theta}\left[\frac{1}{\lambda_F} - \frac{1}{\lambda_P}\right]$$

$$= \frac{1}{0.02}\left[\frac{1}{0.476} - \frac{1}{3.33}\right]$$

$$= 50\ (2.10 - 0.30)$$

$$= 50\ (1.80)$$

$$= 90\ \text{CPU hr}.$$

The result checks with the results of Example 2.8. ∎

The foregoing quantities are of interest in themselves. The additional expected number of failures required to reach the failure intensity objective gives some idea of the failure correction workload. The additional execution time indicates the remaining amount of test required. However, even more importantly, they are both used in making estimates of the additional calendar time required to reach the failure intensity objective. More about that in the next section.

In most situations for the logarithmic Poisson model, an alternative formulation is also possible. The MTTF exists for this model in most circumstances (it does not for the basic model). We can set a MTTF objective instead of a failure intensity objective. The additional expected number of failures that must be experienced and the additional execution time required to reach that objective may be determined in terms of the present and objective MTTFs.

We will see later in this chapter that we can never determine the values of the parameters precisely. We will always have some range of uncertainty. It is expressed through confidence intervals, discussed in Section 2.2.2. This uncertainty results in corresponding uncertainty in the derived quantities described above. One can visualize the effects of confidence intervals for the parameters on confidence intervals for the derived quantities by thinking of the model curves being expanded to bands in Figures 2.12 and 2.13.

2.2.2 Parameter Determination

Model parameters may be divided into two categories, execution time component and calendar time component parameters. If you are not concerned with determining calendar time, resource expenditures, or costs, there is no need to be concerned with the calendar time component parameters.

For the two models just described, the values of two parameters must be determined for the execution time components. We need the value of initial failure intensity λ_0 in both cases, total failures experienced ν_0 for the basic execution time model, and failure intensity decay parameter θ for the logarithmic Poisson model. Initially, we can *predict* (determine before program execution) the parameter values for the basic model from characteristics of the program itself. There will be some degree of uncertainty associated with these predictions. Once a program has executed long enough so that failure data are available, we can *estimate* these parameters. Maximum likelihood estimation or other methods may be used. Maximum likelihood estimation yields that set of parameters that make it most likely that the observed data could have occurred. The accuracy with which they are known generally increases with the size of the sample of failures, for small and moderate size samples. The accuracy may be characterized by estimating confidence intervals. The confidence intervals represent that range of parameters that could possibly "explain" the data experienced, at some level of confidence (for example, 75 percent). Parameter determination procedures are described in detail in Chapter 5. Theoretical background is given in Musa, Iannino, and Okumoto (1987).

PREDICTION. Prediction of parameters is needed whenever system engineering studies are required in project phases before failure data are available. Procedures for predicting the values of the execution time component parameters are currently developed for the basic execution time model. They have not yet been developed for the logarithmic Poisson model. They are established from the size and perhaps other characteristics of the program and the average instruction execution rate of the computer on which the program is running. At present, the accuracy of prediction is limited because little work has been done in this area and only a small amount of data has been collected. However, since system engineering studies can be very significant in realizing substantial cost savings for a project, further work in this area is vital. Limited accuracy is not a handicap for studies in which only the *relative* values of quantities are important. Even where absolute quantities are needed, limited accuracy is usually preferable to making no study at all.

ESTIMATION. Estimation is generally accomplished either in subsystem or system test or in the operational phase. It is usually more accurate than prediction. Estimation is a statistical method that is based on either on the failure times or the number of failures per time interval (for example, failures per hour). The two formulations of the method are essentially equivalent theoretically. However, we are going to focus on the use of failure times. This approach often simplifies program implementation. There is no need to concern yourself with different intervals over which failures are counted. Furthermore, it is easy to convert failures per time interval into failure times and hence handle a mix of both kinds of data. This is simply done by randomly assigning the failures in the interval in which they are experienced. For example, if you have three failures in an hour, you would assign those three failures randomly within that time interval.

Estimation and the computation of derived quantities is straightforward, however, the calculations required are tedious. Consequently, it makes sense to develop computer programs to do the dirty work. We will discuss desirable characteristics of such programs in Chapter 5. However, their usefulness is illustrated in the following example.

> **Example 2.13.** A sample output from a software reliability program, taken during the system test phase of an actual project, is illustrated in Figure 2.14. Maximum likelihood estimates and 50, 75, 90, and 95 percent confidence intervals for each item are provided. The two confidence bounds are placed on either side of the maximum likelihood ("most likely") estimate in the figure. Clearly, the higher the confidence required, the larger the width of the interval. In practice, we have generally found that a reasonable compromise is to use 75 percent confidence intervals. The range of the present failure intensity is printed along with a range of projected completion dates based on the calendar time component. The dates are predictions of when a specified failure intensity objective will be reached. Note that failure intensities are specified as failures per thousand CPU hr. The expected number of additional failures that must be experienced $\Delta\mu$ and the additional execution time $\Delta\tau$ required to reach the failure intensity objective are given. The foregoing results are very useful for planning schedules, estimating status and progress, and determining when to terminate testing. In Figure 2.14 we have highlighted the maximum likelihood estimates and the 75 percent confidence interval of the quantities we have just been talking about. ∎

2.2.3 Operational Phase

If a program has been released and is operational, and no features are added or repairs made between releases, the failure intensity will be constant, as noted in

SOFTWARE RELIABILITY PREDICTION
BASIC MODEL
SYSTEM T2

BASED ON SAMPLE OF   54 TEST FAILURES
EXECUTION TIME IS   32.78 HR
FAILURE INTENSITY OBJECTIVE IS   .36e−01 FAILURES/CPU HR
CALENDAR TIME TO DATE IS   74 DAYS
PRESENT DATE   5/31/74

| | CONF. LIMITS | | | | MOST | | CONF. LIMITS | | |
	95%	90%	75%	50%	LIKELY	50%	75%	90%	95%
TOTAL FAILURES	55	55	55	55	56	57	58	60	61
FAILURE INTENSITIES (FAILURES/1000 CPU HR)									
INITIAL F.I.	4004	4258	4670	5077	5671	6282	6721	7183	7480
PRESENT F.I.	84.0	97.3	122.4	152.1	205.4	275.1	336.4	412.3	468.0

*** ADDITIONAL REQUIREMENTS TO MEET FAILURE INTENSITY OBJECTIVE ***

	95%	90%	75%	50%	MOST LIKELY	50%	75%	90%	95%
FAILURES	0	0	1	1	2	3	4	5	7
EXEC. TIME (CPU HR)	6.18	7.58	10.0	12.7	17.2	22.9	27.8	34.2	39.2
CAL. TIME (DAYS)	2.67	3.30	4.40	5.64	7.78	10.6	13.1	16.4	19.1
COMPLETION DATE	60574	60674	60774	61074	61274	61774	62074	62574	62874

FIGURE 2.14
Sample output—software reliability estimation program.

Chapter 1. Then both models, as nonhomogeneous Poisson processes, reduce to homogeneous Poisson processes with the failure intensity as a parameter. The number of failures in a given time period follows a Poisson distribution. The failure intervals follow an exponential distribution. The reliability R and failure intensity λ are related by

$$R(\tau) = \exp(-\lambda\tau) . \tag{2.13}$$

Note that the reliability is dependent not only on the failure intensity but also on the period of execution time. The reliability (probability of no failures in a period of execution time τ) is lower for longer time periods as is illustrated in Figure 2.15.

The operational phase of many programs consists of a series of releases. The reliability and failure intensity will then be step functions, with the levels of the quantities changing at each release. If the releases are frequent and the trend of failure intensity is decreasing, one can often approximate the step functions by one of the software reliability models we have presented. Alternatively, one may apply the software reliability models directly to reported unique failures (not counting repetitions). Note that the model now represents the failure intensity that will occur when the failures have been corrected. This approach is analogous to the one commonly taking place during system test of ignoring the failure correction delay, except that the delay is much longer here. Of course, if the failures are actually corrected in the field, then the operational phase should be handled just like the system test phase.

2.3   CALENDAR TIME COMPONENT

2.3.1   Description

The calendar time component relates execution time and calendar time by determining the calendar time to execution time ratio at any given point in time. The ratio is based on the constraints that are involved in applying resources to a pro-

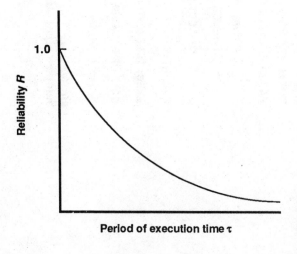

FIGURE 2.15
Reliability versus period of execution time.

ject. To obtain calendar time, you integrate this ratio with respect to execution time. The calendar time component is of greatest significance during phases where the software is being tested and repaired. During this period one can predict the dates at which various failure intensity objectives will be met. The calendar time component "exists" during periods in which repair is not occurring and failure intensity is constant. However, it reduces in that case to a constant ratio between calendar time and execution time.

In test, the rate of testing at any time is constrained by the failure identification or test team personnel, the failure correction or debugging personnel, or the computer time available.[3] The quantities of these resources available to a project are usually more or less established in its early stages. Increases are generally not feasible during the system test phase because of the long lead times required for training and computer procurement. At any given value of execution time, one of these resources will be limiting. The limiting resource will determine the rate at which execution time can be spent per unit calendar time. A test phase may consist of from one to three periods, each characterized by a different limiting resource.

The following is a common scenario. At the start of testing one identifies a large number of failures separated by short time intervals. Testing must be stopped from time to time to let the people who are fixing the faults keep up with the load. As testing progresses, the intervals between failures become longer and longer. The time of the failure correction personnel is no longer completely filled with failure correction work. The test team becomes the bottleneck. The effort required to run tests and analyze the results is occupying all their time. That paces the amount of testing done each day. Finally, at even longer intervals, the capacity of the computing facilities becomes limiting. This resource then determines how much testing is accomplished.

The calendar time component is based on a "debugging process" model. This model takes into account:

1. resources *used* in operating the program for a given execution time and processing an associated quantity of failures,
2. resource quantities *available,* and
3. the degree to which a resource can be *utilized* (due to bottlenecks) during the period in which it is limiting.

Table 2.2 will help in visualizing these different aspects of the resources, and the parameters that result.

RESOURCE USAGE. In Musa, Iannino, and Okumoto (1987) resource usage is shown to be linearly proportional to execution time and mean failures experienced.

---

[3]The calendar time component can readily be generalized to handle additional limiting resources.

TABLE 2.2
Calender time component resources and parameters

| Resources | Usage parameters— requirements per: | | Planned parameters | |
	CPU hr	Failure	Quantities available	Utilizations
Failure identification personnel	θ_I	μ_I	P_I	1
Failure correction personnel	0	μ_F	P_F	ρ_F
Computer time	θ_C	μ_C	P_C	ρ_C

Let χ_r be the usage of resource r. Then

$$\chi_r = \theta_r \, \tau + \mu_r \, \mu . \tag{2.14}$$

Note that θ_r is the resource usage per CPU hr. It is nonzero for failure identification personnel (θ_I) and computer time (θ_C). The quantity μ_r is the resource usage per failure. Be careful not to confuse it with mean failures experienced μ. It was deliberately chosen to be similar to suggest the connection between resource usage and failures experienced. It is nonzero for failure identification personnel (μ_I), failure correction personnel (μ_F), and computer time (μ_C).

Consider a test team that is running tests on a particular piece of software. If they conduct 2 hr of testing rather than 1, they will have twice the amount of work to be done. They will have approximately twice the amount of output to examine and they will spend twice as much time conducting the tests. The work effort related to failures experienced will be dependent on the number. A failure report will have to be written whenever a failure occurs. Some time will be needed to establish whether each suspected failure really is one, by checking the requirements. The test team may have to record some information, and perhaps make a couple of runs to get all the pertinent facts about the particular failure. Note that mean failures is used to estimate effort, so that mean resource requirements are obtained.

Example 2.14. Suppose the test team runs test cases for 8 CPU hr and identifies 20 failures. The effort required per hr of execution time is 6 person hr. Each failure requires 2 hr on the average to verify and determine its nature. The total failure identification effort required, using Equation (2.14), is

$$\chi_r = \theta_r \tau + \mu_r \mu$$

$$= 6(8) + 2(20)$$

$$= 48 + 40$$

$$= 88 \text{ person hr.} \qquad \blacksquare$$

For failure correction (unlike identification), resources required are dependent only on the mean failures experienced. However, computer time is used in both identification and correction of failures. Hence, computer time used will usually depend on both the amount of execution time and the number of failures.

Note that since "failures experienced" is a function of execution time, resource usage is actually a function of execution time only. The intermediate step of thinking in terms of failures experienced and execution time is useful in gaining physical insight into what is happening. Also, it permits data to be collected and fitted in a model-independent fashion, so that it has maximum applicability. Cumulative resource usage as a function of execution time is illustrated in Figure 2.16. In Example 2.14, if we eliminate failures experienced as the intermediate variable, we have an average of 11 person hr of effort used per hour of execution time. Alternatively, we may consider resource usage to be a function of failures experienced only. With execution time eliminated as a variable in the example, we have 4.4 person hr of effort used per failure.

Computer time required per unit execution time will normally be greater than 1. In addition to the execution time for the program under test, additional time will be required for the execution of such support programs as test drivers, recording routines, and data reduction packages.

Consider the change in resource usage per unit of execution time. This is shown in Figure 2.17. It can be obtained by differentiating Equation (2.14) with respect to execution time. We obtain

$$\frac{d\chi_r}{d\tau} = \theta_r + \mu_r\lambda \ . \tag{2.15}$$

Since the failure intensity decreases with testing, the effort used per hour of execution time tends to decrease with testing. It approaches the execution time coeffi-

FIGURE 2.16
Cumulative resource usage as a function of execution time.

FIGURE 2.17
Variation of resource usage per unit execution time with execution time.

cient of resource usage asymptotically as execution time increases. Let's now look at the change in resource usage per failure. This is shown in Figure 2.18. It can be obtained by differentiating Equation (2.14) with respect to failures. We have

$$\frac{d\chi_r}{d\mu} = \mu_r + \theta_r \frac{d\tau}{d\mu} . \tag{2.16}$$

Note that the execution time between failures tends to increase with testing. Thus, failure identification effort and computer time required "for each failure" tend to increase throughout the test period as well.

CALENDAR TIME TO EXECUTION TIME RELATIONSHIP. Resource quantities and utilizations are assumed to be constant for the period over which the model is

FIGURE 2.18
Variation of resource usage per failure with mean failures experienced.

being applied. This is a reasonable assumption, as increases are usually not feasible. Once a project is underway, there is a real limitation as to how fast personnel can be added without making the situation worse [Brooks (1975)]. Also, it's a well known fact that it's difficult to make substantial changes in computer resources rapidly. Orders for computers require a lead time and installation time is also long.

The instantaneous ratio of calendar time to execution time can be obtained by dividing the resource usage rate of the limiting resource by the constant quantity of resources available that can be utilized. Let t be calendar time. Then

$$\frac{dt}{d\tau} = \frac{1}{P_r \rho_r} \frac{d\chi_r}{d\tau} . \tag{2.17}$$

The quantity P_r represents resources available. Note that ρ_r is the utilization. The above ratio must be computed separately for each resource-limited period. Since χ_r is a function of τ, we now have a relationship between t and τ in each resource-limited period.

> **Example 2.15.** Consider our previous test team illustration in Example 2.14. Assume that failure identification personnel are the limiting resource. Recall that 88 person hr were required to test for 8 CPU hr and identify 20 failures. Note that 11 person hr of effort were used per hour of execution time, on the average. Suppose there are 2 members of the test team and both are fully utilized. Then the calendar time to execution time ratio, averaged over the period, is 5.5. We can compute the elapsed calendar time as 44 hr. Assuming a standard work week, this is slightly longer than a week. ∎

The form of the instantaneous calendar time to execution time ratio for any given limiting resource and either model is shown in Figure 2.19. It is readily obtained from Equations (2.15) and (2.17) as

$$\frac{dt}{d\tau} = \frac{\theta_r + \mu_r \lambda}{P_r \rho_r} . \tag{2.18}$$

The shape of this curve will parallel that of the failure intensity. The curve approaches an asymptote of $\theta_r / P_r \rho_r$. Note that the asymptote is 0 for the failure correction personnel resource. At any given time, the maximum of the ratios for the three limiting resources actually determines the rate at which calendar time is expended; this is illustrated in Figure 2.20. The maximum is plotted as a solid curve. When the curve for a resource is not maximum (not limiting), it is plotted dashed. Note the transition points *FI* and *IC*. Here, the calendar time to execution time ratios of two resources are equal and the limiting resource changes. The point *FC* is a potential but not true transition point. Neither resource *F* nor resource *C* is limiting near this point.

Let's look at the general shape of the plot of calendar time against execution time for both models (Figure 2.21). This curve is composed of segments, each of which represents a period in which a different resource is limiting. Each segment represents the integral of the instantaneous calendar time to execution time ratio with respect to execution time. This ratio always decreases with execution time,

FIGURE 2.19
Instantaneous calendar
time to execution time
ratio.

FIGURE 2.20
Calendar time to execu-
tion time ratio for different limiting resources.

FIGURE 2.21
Calendar time versus execution time.

hence the shape of the curve. The value of the ratio is continuous at the boundaries between different limiting resource periods. Hence the plot of calendar time against execution time is smooth with respect to these boundaries and the boundaries are not evident.

The calendar time component allows you to estimate the calendar time in days required to meet the failure intensity objective. The value of this interval is particularly useful to software managers and engineers. You may determine it from the additional execution time and additional number of failures needed to meet the objective that we found for the execution time component. Second, you now determine the date on which the failure intensity objective will be achieved. This is a simple variant of the first quantity that takes account of things like weekends and holidays. However, it is a useful quantity because it speaks in terms managers and engineers understand. If the foregoing prediction is not required, however, there is no need to be concerned with the calendar time component or the determination of its parameters. Note that uncertainty in determining model parameters will result in a corresponding uncertainty in the previous quantities.

2.3.2 Parameter Determination

There are two categories of parameters that must be established for the calendar time components of the two models. The parameters are the same and have the same values for both models. The categories are: planned and resource usage. Planned parameters are those that are established by managerial decisions on the project or by project conditions and policies. The decisions involve resource quantities. Resource quantity parameters include things such as the size of the test team and the number of failure correction personnel employed on the project. Conditions and policies affect the degree of resource utilization during the resource-limiting period for that resource. The resource usage parameters relate to the resources required for failure identification and correction. They are generally stated in terms of resources required per hour of execution time and per failure experienced. The resources are, as noted earlier in this chapter, failure identification personnel, failure correction personnel, and computer time. Note that computer usage is not the same quantity as execution time of test or operation. Computer usage includes the latter time, but also includes computer time devoted to collecting data related to a failure, debugging, demonstrating the fix, and performing regression testing.

Resource quantities available are readily ascertained from managers or project planners. Resource utilization expected is generally determined by formula or experience (Section 5.2.2). You can best establish resource usage parameter values at present by the collection of data for a particular project. Fit the data in a least squares fashion as described in Chapter 5. Some information on values of resource usage parameters is currently available (Section 5.2.3). It is hoped that ultimately these values can be determined for all software projects or for large classes of projects. It may eventually be unnecessary to actually collect and fit data. If you don't have information from a similar project available and cannot or do not wish to collect data on your own project, it is best to rely on experience. However, this is not the preferable approach. The values of the resource usage parameters may be related to such factors as:

1. batch debugging versus interactive debugging,
2. debugging aids available,
3. computer used,
4. language used, and
5. administrative and documentation overhead associated with corrections.

Herndon and Keenan (1978) have investigated some of these factors.

Uncertainties in determining the foregoing parameter values occur primarily for resource usage parameters. The range of uncertainty depends on a number of factors. The effects of these uncertainties on the prediction of the date for reaching the failure intensity objective can be established by calculating this date for different sets of values.

2.4 MODEL CHOICE

The choice of which of the two models to use in any given application depends on several factors. These are summarized in Table 2.3. If you desire to conduct studies or make reliability predictions before the program is executed and failure data taken, you will lean toward the basic model. The basic model would also be used when studying the effects of a new software engineering technology *if* this is done by looking at the effect of the new technology on faults. In that case, faults must be related to failure intensity. At present, only the basic model has this capability. If the size of the program is changing continually and substantially as fail-

TABLE 2.3
Choice between models

Purpose of application or existence of condition	Basic	Logarithmic Poisson
Studies or predictions before execution	X	
Studying effects of software engineering technology (through study of faults)	X	
Program size changing continually and substantially	X	
Highly nonuniform operational profile		X
Early predictive validity important		X

ure data is collected, then the basic model would again be the choice. This situation could occur due to design changes or to the program being integrated stage by stage. Moderate rates of program evolution do not affect the choice of model. Neither has been shown to be superior in the foregoing situation.

If the program is expected to be used with a decidedly nonuniform operational profile, the logarithmic Poisson model may be better. Note that efficiently run test phases generally employ input state (test case) selection without replacement. In this situation, as will be noted in Chapter 4, the test phase operational profile is, in effect, uniform. If high predictive validity is needed early in the period of execution, the logarithmic Poisson model will probably be preferable. The margin of superiority is greatest for small samples of failures (that is, after a short time of execution). For larger samples of failures, the superiority may be small, so that any other factors that exist should play the predominant role. The better predictive validity during early execution may occur primarily in the case of a highly nonuniform operational profile. The rapidly changing slope of failure intensity during this period can be fit better with the logarithmic Poisson than the basic model. This will be clear from Figure 2.1. In a number of circumstances, the choice between the two models may not be critical. In others, one may be preferable for just part of the period of application. One option may be to employ the basic model for pretest studies and estimates and periods of evolution. You would switch to the logarithmic Poisson model when integration is complete.

2.5 SUMMARY

The basic and logarithmic Poisson execution time models were selected for detailed exposition in this book. The basic model represents an arithmetic change of failure intensity with mean failures experienced; the logarithmic Poisson model, geometric. The two models have many advantages, and substantial practical experience has been gained with them. Modeling is initially performed in execution time. Results are then converted to calendar time. The determination of model parameters was discussed.

PROBLEMS

2.1 The same data have been fit with both the basic and logarithmic Poisson models. The parameters obtained are:

Basic	Logarithmic Poisson
λ_0 = 20 failures/CPU hr	λ_0 = 50 failures/CPU hr
ν_0 = 120 failures	θ = 0.025/failures

Note that the logarithmic Poisson usually has higher initial failure intensity. At first, recall that this falls off more rapidly than the failure intensity for the basic model, but finally it falls off more slowly. We will examine some consequences of this behavior.

First, determine the additional failures and additional execution time required to reach a failure intensity objective of 10 failures/CPU hr, using both models. Then repeat this for an objective of 1 failure/CPU hr. Assume in both cases that you start from the initial failure intensity.

2.2 Why do you speak of "failures that must be experienced to reach the failure intensity objective?" How will experiencing failures improve the failure intensity and permit an objective to be reached, unless the associated faults are corrected?

2.3 How can one determine the number of additional failures that must be experienced and removed to achieve a given reliability level (for an operating period of a specified duration)?

2.4 Does the ratio of calendar time to execution time approach 1 with increasing execution time?

2.5 Your basic model doesn't make sense. Suppose you have a program that runs for 1000 sec and has 100 evenly-spaced faults in it. After starting test, the first failure will occur at 10 sec. If you correct it and resume testing, the next failure will also occur after a 10 sec interval. This will continue right up to the last failure, which will also occur after a 10 sec interval. Where is the change in failure intensity that is supposed to occur as testing progresses?

THREE

APPLICATIONS

This chapter looks generally at how software reliability measurements can be used. The detailed procedures involved in application and some of the more advanced uses will be presented in Chapter 7.

It is convenient to classify applications into four groups, each of which we will treat in more detail:

1. system engineering,
2. project management during development and particularly test,
3. operational phase software management, and
4. evaluation of software engineering technologies.

Finally, we will discuss how to do overall planning for application of software reliability methods to projects. Table 3.1 summarizes some of the applications. It evaluates their potential value and current quality of results. Some applications are not presented until Chapter 7.

Software reliability measurement techniques are of great value in the evaluation of software engineering technology and in operational software management. The results of applying software reliability measurement to software project management are good but capable of improvement. Most of the project management applications relate to subsystem or system test phases. However, there is a reasonable possibility that they can be extended to the unit test phase.

The quality of the results of many of the studies in the system engineering phase is dependent on the quality of parameter prediction. The "fair" rating we have given these results may improve markedly if parameter prediction can be improved. In any case, the things that can be done now are beyond the pure research

TABLE 3.1
Summary and evaluation of applications

Development phase	Applications	Potential value of application	Current quality of results
System engineering	Product feasiblity studies	Very high	Fair−
	Trade-off studies	High+	Fair+
	Cost studies	High	Fair
	Scheduling studies	High+	Fair
	Reliability allocation	High−	Fair+
	Reliability specification	High−	Fair
Test	Status tracking	High	Good+
	Project completion estimation	High	Good−
	Redoing system engineering studies	High	Good
	Investigating management alternatives	High	Good
Operation	Reliability demonstration	High−	Excellent
	Change control	High	Excellent
	Preventive maintenance control	High−	Excellent
All	Evaluating software engineering technology	High−	Excellent

stage. We should be attempting practical applications. You should be judicious in doing so, of course. However, application to system engineering problems may be one of the most promising areas. Decisions are made at this time that can have great financial, schedule, and other impacts on a project. Hence one is in greatest need of quantitative tools at this stage. Do not undervalue making applications in this area, even though the techniques may not be totally perfected. The significance of the general comments we have just made should become clearer after you have explored the details of this chapter.

The fact that software reliability measurement is better developed for the later stages of the software life cycle is not a problem. About two-thirds of the total costs occur after release. On many projects system test represents 40 to 50 percent of prerelease costs. Thus 80 percent or more of total life cycle costs occur after the start of system test. Improved decision making in this period can indeed have an impact! On the other hand, some of this money is committed (even if not spent) somewhat earlier in the life cycle. Consequently, any guidance that can be given to early decisions (even if imprecise) can be of great value.

3.1 SYSTEM ENGINEERING

Let us consider some typical system engineering applications (this is not an exhaustive list):

1. specifying reliability to a designer,
2. estimating costs of failure for an operational system,

3. pricing a service,
4. helping establish the market window for a software product (or product containing software),
5. investigating trade-offs between reliability and resources, cost, and schedules,
6. selecting the failure intensity objective, and
7. determining the amount of system testing required.

Reliability specification may be used internally within an organization to give concrete guidance or direction to a design team vis-à-vis other desired characteristics of a software product. It may be used similarly with external organizations (for example, subcontractors). It can even be employed as a contractual requirement with legal standing. An example of what you might do here is to state that the reliability of the program delivered from a particular subcontractor must be 0.99 for 10 CPU hr of execution. You would also specify this in terms of the operational profile that one would use to make this measurement.

How do we go about determining the costs of failure for an operational system? This can involve restoration costs such as reloading the program and cleaning up the data base. Even if recovery is automated, there will be an interruption in service, resulting in lost revenue and possible lost customers, among other things. Hence there is some average amount of resources expended or revenue lost each time a failure occurs. We multiply this by the number of failures for the period being studied. Let's look at an example. Suppose we have a system that has a failure intensity of 0.025 failure/CPU hr. Now let's also assume that the system works for 40 CPU hr/week. Suppose it requires an average of 4 person hr/failure to do restoration, including travel, at a cost of $25/hr loaded salary. On the average we'll be getting 1 failure per week per system, each requiring 4 hr of work and costing $100. That's $400/month per system.

When pricing a service, we first compute failure costs as above. Then we add other costs and a reasonable rate of return, based on financial considerations and market conditions. Suppose in the example given that our other system costs are $500/month. We would price this particular service at $900/month plus some reasonable rate of return.

Failure intensity estimates can help determine the market window for a software product or product containing software. Most of you probably know that the market window is the time period within which you can introduce a new product and have it be profitable. The main concern is the "late" limit of the market window. That is, if you should introduce a product too late, your competitors may have captured most of your expected market share. They can now reduce prices because of their volume. It is extremely difficult for you to compete. For software products particularly, there is likely to be a trade-off between the time of introduction of a product and its reliability. If you introduce the product too early, it may be unreliable, gain a bad reputation, and hence not sell well. And, of course you don't want it to be late either.

Here is an example of the application of software reliability measurement to this problem. Suppose you expect your competitor to introduce a product on June 17. You look at the trade-off between reliability and product introduction by running simulations with a software reliability program. You find you have the option of beating out your competitor by introducing a product on May 15, about a month ahead, with 0.02 failure/CPU hr. On the other hand, you may decide that you will compete on reliability. You could introduce your product at the same time as your competitor on June 17. Then you would have a failure intensity of 0.001 failure/CPU hr. This reliability improvement comes from more testing. You may feel that the 0.001 failure/CPU hr you can attain on June 17 will be superior to anything your competitor will be putting out. In your judgment, this margin of quality may be important for your market. The simulation clarifies the alternatives so you can apply external factors to the decision.

Let us now consider the topic of making trade-offs between reliability and resources, costs, and schedules. We will speak in terms of a failure intensity objective rather than a reliability objective as the analysis is simpler. The two are alternative forms of each other. Details on trade-offs are presented in Section 7.2.3. The trade-offs are usually straightforward if the range of possible values of failure intensity objective is moderate. We then typically involve only one limiting resource. Increasing reliability is equivalent to reducing the failure intensity objective or increasing the ratio of initial failure intensity to failure intensity objective. An increase in this ratio is associated with an increase in the limiting resource usage required and hence an increase in project cost. If the quantity of the limiting resource available is fixed, then increasing the failure intensity ratio lengthens the schedule.

If the range of possible values of failure intensity objective is sufficiently large such that more than one limiting resource is involved, the situation becomes more complex. Resource usages, cost, and project duration all still increase with failure intensity ratio. Making more resources available can reduce schedule durations. However, each resource can only affect the duration of its associated limiting period. Thus the effect of adding resources is limited. Clearly, cost provides one possible basis for selecting the failure intensity objective. Other bases will be discussed in Chapter 7.

If we can establish the failure intensity objective and the initial failure intensity at the start of system test, the execution time required for system test can be determined. This can be seen in Figure 2.13. The relationships are given by Equations (2.11) and (2.12) for the basic and logarithmic Poisson execution time models, respectively. The calendar time component of the selected model can then be used to find the length of system test in terms of calendar time.

3.2 PROJECT MANAGEMENT

Some typical project management applications include:

1. progress monitoring,

2. scheduling, and

3. investigation of alternatives.

These applications occur during time periods when the program is being executed and at least some repair action is being taken on the failures. Most commonly, this is the system test period. Estimates are made from failure data, generally using one or more of the programs described in Chapter 5.

A plot from a representative project, using the basic execution time model, is shown in Figure 3.1. The plot is a project history of present failure intensity. It is useful for indicating progress toward the failure intensity objective. The solid center curve is the maximum likelihood estimate and the dashed outer curves delineate the bounds of the 75 percent confidence interval. The report of Figure 3.2 could have been used to evaluate progress. However, plotting the recent history of the present failure intensity (Figure 3.1) will make additional information available for managerial judgments.

Scheduling involves determining when a program will be ready for release. When will the failure intensity objective be met as the result of the failure intensity decreasing due to repair actions? The date can be obtained from the completion date line in the tabular report in Figure 3.2. It is January 29, with a 75 percent confidence interval of January 16 to February 15. Figure 3.3 is a plot of the history of project completion date predictions.

The investigation of alternatives is a reopening of the question of trade-offs made during system engineering. The methods of Section 7.2.3 apply, with the

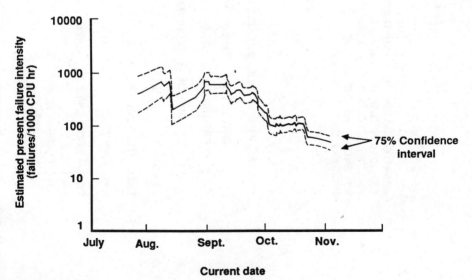

FIGURE 3.1
History of estimates of present failure intensity.

SOFTWARE RELIABILITY PREDICTION
BASIC MODEL
SYSTEM T1

BASED ON SAMPLE OF 136 TEST FAILURES
EXECUTION TIME IS   25.34 HR
FAILURE INTENSITY OBJECTIVE IS   .24e−02 FAILURES/CPU HR
CALENDAR TIME TO DATE IS 96 DAYS
PRESENT DATE   11/9/73

	CONF. LIMITS				MOST LIKELY		CONF. LIMITS		
	95%	90%	75%	50%		50%	75%	90%	95%
TOTAL FAILURES	139	139	140	141	142	144	145	147	149
FAILURE INTENSITIES (FAILURES/1000 CPU HR)									
INITIAL F.I.	953.0	988.1	1044	1098	1177	1258	1315	1376	1415
PRESENT F.I.	28.6	31.3	35.9	41.0	49.2	59.0	66.8	75.9	82.3

*** ADDITIONAL REQUIREMENTS TO MEET FAILURE INTENSITY OBJECTIVE ***

	CONF. LIMITS				MOST LIKELY		CONF. LIMITS		
	95%	90%	75%	50%		50%	75%	90%	95%
FAILURES	3	3	4	5	6	8	9	11	13
EXEC. TIME (CPU HR)	33.7	35.4	38.2	41.1	45.8	51.2	55.7	60.9	64.7
CAL. TIME (DAYS)	41.9	44.0	47.4	51.1	56.9	63.8	69.3	75.9	80.5
COMPLETION DATE	10874	11074	11674	12174	12974	20774	21574	22474	30474

FIGURE 3.2
Project status report.

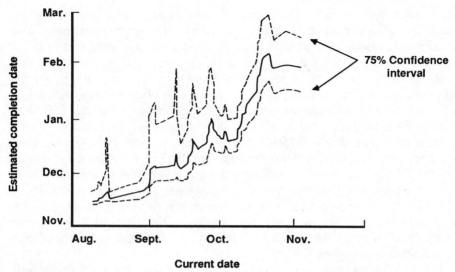

FIGURE 3.3
History of completion date predictions.

execution time parameters being estimated from failure data. An example has already been presented in Section 1.6.

3.3 MANAGEMENT OF OPERATIONAL PHASE

Failures continue to occur and new features (hence new code) continue to be added for virtually all software systems of any size during the operational phase. Usually the introduction of new features and fixes for discovered faults is handled by scheduled releases, perhaps on the order of months apart. In that case, we have a piecewise constant failure intensity. Each release has a failure intensity associated with it. The value of failure intensity changes when a new release is installed. In some situations, however, the incorporation of fault repairs occurs much more frequently, perhaps weekly or more often. Then the behavior of failure intensity looks more like that occurring during system test. Also, the manager of a particular operational installation may have discretion as to when a release with new features is installed. The failure intensity of the system exhibits a general stability about some value over the long term. However, there are many swings about this value. This behavior is generally due to the periodic incorporation of newly developed features that increase the failure intensity, followed by periods of fault removal, during which the failure intensity decreases.

In this situation, the manager is often faced with conflicting demands. He or she has some users and managers who are insisting that the new features that they value be introduced as soon as possible. On the other hand, there will be people who are running production programs, or other sorts of programs on which they're highly dependent, who insist that the reliability be as high as possible. They can't afford to have their functions interrupted. A good example of this would be the situation in a computation center that's also used by the payroll department. You may have some engineers who want changes made in the operating system to accommodate new things that they want to do. On the other hand, payroll is insistent that the operating system be as reliable as possible, since they have to get the checks out every week. The data processing manager is often caught in the middle of a tug of war between these conflicting interests. Suppose we let these interests slug it out and establish a level of service. This would be a failure intensity objective that is reasonable when all factors are taken into account. Once this has been established, the manager's job is vastly simplified, because he or she then controls the particular software system to maintain this particular level of service. This is done by freezing new feature changes to the system when the failure intensity level climbs above the objective. New features are introduced into the system only when the failure intensity is below the objective. The manager may use the amount of margin below the service objective as a guide to the size of the change to be permitted at any given time.

Figure 3.4 shows this sort of control, using data taken on a real operational software system. We have applied the basic execution time model, taking estimates of the parameters and then computing failure intensity at a number of points in time. The center line indicates the most likely value of the failure intensity estimate as a function of time. The dashed lines indicate the 75 percent confidence interval. A service objective of 0.05 failure/CPU hr is indicated. If the system is running 40 CPU hr/week, this means two failures per week. You will note periods of sharply rising failure intensity estimates where new features have been introduced into the system. You will also see the slow but steady drop during periods where the system is being debugged. Suppose we decide that we want to meet the service objective level with 75 percent confidence. Then every time the upper 75 percent confidence limit exceeds that level, we have a signal for stopping change to the system. And every time it drops below, we have an indication that now we can afford to make some changes. In actuality, you might first want to be sure that the failure intensity estimate drops an amount equal to the expected increment caused by the changes. Then the introduction of the changes would be allowed. In Chapter 7 we will consider how to estimate this increment.

3.4 EVALUATION OF SOFTWARE ENGINEERING TECHNOLOGIES

Many of you, either from reading the literature or attending conferences, have been bombarded by ideas, techniques, or tools for improving software productivity and software quality. Many ideas are presented with much fanfare but, unfortunately, not much solid evidence. We should be obtaining quantitative measures of the values of the techniques that are suggested. Obviously, improvement in productivity is one value. However, with today's emphasis on quality, improvement in reliability is very important also.

Software reliability measurements play an essential role in determining the value of new software engineering technologies, such as design methodologies,

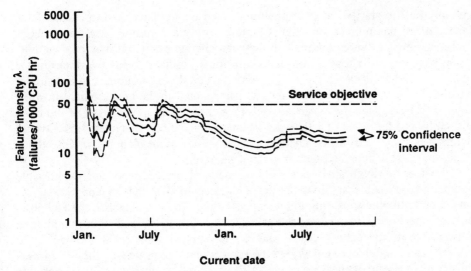

FIGURE 3.4
Failure intensity used for change management of operational software.

development tools, test methodologies, and inspections. Reliability and cost of a product are probably its two most important characteristics. Reliability is important in itself and it plays a major role in determining what the total cost of operating the product is. Thus it has a major effect on the customer. Any new software engineering technology should be considered at least in terms of its effects on reliability and cost.

The measurements of reliability in the operational phase of the software product are easily established by taking failure data. This should be done for software developed both with and without the new technology. The comparison should be made for releases occurring after the same amount of testing. An example of this might be to look at the technology of design inspections. We could collect data on failure intensities for releases occurring 100 CPU hr after the start of system test. We might obtain a result like "failure intensity is improved from 0.04 failure/CPU hr to 0.02 failure/CPU hr." In other words, we have cut in half the failure intensity experienced. This should be valuable in gaining an idea of the usefulness of design inspections. Suppose you compute the effect on operational phase cost of this failure intensity change. If you know the cost of the new technology, you now have a simple economic decision.

In doing the foregoing evaluation, it is important to establish confidence intervals. One must then see if the difference due to the new technology is significant in comparison with the uncertainty.

3.5 PLANNING FOR APPLICATION

Hopefully, the reader has at this point developed an interest in trying out the material presented in this book on an actual project. How should one go about it? It is probably best to start with some planning, even if the plans need to change later. Laner (1985) has pointed out that, "A plan is only a common base for changes. Everyone needs to know the plan so they can change easily." It may be desirable, if you have one or a few major customers for a product, to involve them in the planning of reliability objectives. The perceived quality of a product to a customer is usually higher when the customer has participated in the development in some way. In any case, the customer is likely to gain a better appreciation of the costs of quality and the trade-offs that can be made with other characteristics. Overall planning is presented in this chapter and implementation planning in Chapter 8. There are several steps involved in overall planning.

First, a thorough analysis should be made of project needs against possible applications. Possible applications are suggested in this chapter and Chapter 7. This is probably the most important step. It is important to establish the key problems engineers and managers are facing that might be helped with quantitative software reliability techniques. In making the analysis, one good approach is to poll managers and lead engineers on the project about their needs. Their responses will be most useful if they are made in the context of awareness of the possible applications. Another good method is to use a consultant who is knowledgeable in the possible applications to look at the situation in which the project finds itself. The needs should be scrutinized in the hard light of reality. Each activity that arises from a need will have a cost, and the expected benefit should justify that cost. You should be particularly skeptical of unplanned approaches like, "We'll collect data on everything and decide how to use it later."

Applications, such as those described in this chapter, are usually carried out in the context of a development project or in an operations organization. There are five roles that are commonly involved. Note that, depending on the organization concerned, a person may play one or more roles. The tasks usually associated with each role are presented in Table 3.2. Note that some tasks are divided between several roles. In practice, the details of this division must be clearly established.

The five roles are:

1. managers,
2. systems engineers,
3. quality assurance engineers,
4. test teams, and
5. debuggers.

The managers involved are the project or operations managers. They are most frequently at low or middle levels, but can be at relatively high levels for large projects. They are most commonly software managers, but large numbers are system managers, hardware managers, or data processing operations managers. Some of the functions they perform in which software reliability measurement can help are:

1. monitoring the status of projects that include software,
2. predicting the release date of software,

TABLE 3.2
Common tasks and possible assignments to roles in application of software reliability measurement.

Tasks	Managers	Systems engineers	Quality assurance engineers	Test team	Debuggers
			Roles		
System analysis & tailoring procedures to project		X			
Data collection					
Failures		X	X	X	
Resource usage			X	X	X
Parameter determination			X		
Run programs		X	X		
System studies		X			
Supervision	X				

3. judging when to allow software changes in operational systems,

4. deciding on what software engineering technologies to apply to a project, and

5. deciding whether to accept delivery of subcontracted software.

Managers must have sufficient background to make intelligent decisions in these areas *in the context of their projects or organizations*. They must be able to evaluate the information generated for them to aid such decisions. Managers, aided by systems engineers, choose and revise schedules, budgets, system and component reliability goals, and development resource quantities. Finally, they must supervise the people performing the other roles in the information-gathering and decision-making processes.

The systems engineers have primary responsibility for thoroughly understanding the nature of the system to which software reliability measurement is being applied. They adopt, adjust, and tune models and tailor processing rules and procedures to the system. They must define what a "failure" is for the system and continually interpret it as failure data is collected. They study trade-offs between reliability, resources, and schedules. They investigate different options for allocation of reliability between components of the system. They may estimate operational failure costs for the system. The results can be used for maintenance planning and pricing of service based on the system. They can develop information on different software engineering technology options for managers to consider for use on a project. Systems engineers may estimate the impact of a proposed design change on reliability. In general, systems engineers perform studies and interpret results for management.

The quality assurance engineers are responsible for developing the data collection procedures that are needed to measure software reliability for the project or organization. They oversee the collection of data and process the data to yield useful results. They receive some direction from the systems engineers and provide some direction for the test team and the debuggers. They identify initial parameter values with the help of the systems engineers. They collect and process resource expenditure and failure data, operating various software reliability programs in doing so. They test the achieved failure intensity for programs that are being validated. Note that they do not have to have the depth of understanding of the system that the systems engineers do.

Test team members and debuggers have relatively simple roles. The test team member must identify when a failure has occurred and record the execution time of occurrence and other pertinent data. The debugger records when correction of the failure is complete. For both roles, resource expenditures must be recorded. The relative simplicity of these functions does *not* imply that the persons performing them need not have much understanding of software reliability measurement. On the contrary! The data that the test team members and debuggers collect is the ultimate source of the information generated as input to decision making. The quality of this data is vitally dependent on the intelligence and understanding that they apply in interpreting the real world conditions and complexities that they encounter. They must assist in planning the process of data collection. They need to be able to recognize problems and communicate them to quality assurance engineers, systems engineers, and managers.

Once the analysis of needs has been made, you should develop a list of all the tasks that must be done. The list will arise out of a consideration of the applications to be implemented and the characteristics of the project. It will often be a subset of the tasks listed in Table 3.2. Then assign responsibilities for the tasks. Table 3.2 will provide helpful guidance in making the assignments.

You then should consider what tools will be needed. Probably the most important tools will be the computer programs described in Chapter 5. Tool selection will depend on the tasks to be done, the form of the input failure data, and the form desired for the output of the programs. Certain additional tools may be required such as least squares fit programs for handling resource usage data. The programs must be acquired and tested on the machines on which they are to be used.

Training must be planned for project personnel. Most will need a broad view of what is happening so that they can intelligently help collect data and interpret the results of data analysis. Preferably, this involves educating the entire or a major portion of the project to at least the level given by Part I of this book. We have used a 1-day course for this. In addition, anyone who is *actively* involved in collecting and processing data and interpreting results needs further training that includes at least Part II as well. An additional 2-day course, supplemented by reading from this book and familiarization with program tools, can achieve this objective. There will also probably be some project-specific information to be conveyed such as system configuration, special conditions, and data collection and processing procedures. This might involve doing something as simple as providing a memorandum or a sheet of instructions. ·

Finally, it should be appreciated that projects can ultimately help themselves by helping to advance the general state of software reliability knowledge. Planning should take this need into account. Collection of failure data for both test and operational phases will permit models to be tested over a wide variety of projects. More resource usage data is needed, along with knowledge of the project characteristics that affect it. If special problems are encountered, they need to be clearly identified so that researchers can address them. Close liaison between a project and a researcher can often be particularly productive.

3.6 SUMMARY

Software reliability measurements can be used to guide managerial and engineering decisions on projects involving software. They can also guide customers and users of systems that have software components in purchasing and operating these systems. They can help focus software engineering research and its application by determining those methods that are most effective in enhancing reliability. Before applying software measurement techniques, a prospective user should analyze needs and plan for the most effective implementation.

TWO

PRACTICAL APPLICATION

This part of the book assumes that the reader has already considered the advantages to be gained in using software reliability measurement. It also assumes that the reader understands the basics of software reliability models, as covered in Part I. Consequently, we will proceed directly to the "how to do it." Specifically, the reader will learn how to conduct studies to support managerial and engineering decisions. In doing this, it is necessary to learn how to tailor the approach and procedures to the project involved. The reader will gain general familiarity with the features that we have found useful in software reliability estimation programs. Finally, implementation planning for application to actual projects will be discussed.

The models applied will be the basic and logarithmic Poisson execution time models. However, the techniques described can be applied to other models with appropriate modification. We will consider the most general case and assume that the software system being studied is part of a larger system that involves hardware and possibly other software components.

The steps to be taken in the process of practical application, in approximate logical order, may be outlined as follows:

1. failure definition (Section 4.1),
2. system description and decomposition (Section 4.2),
3. test run selection (Section 4.3),
4. determination of parameters for both execution time and calendar time components of the model (Chapter 5),
5. performance of studies and computation of useful quantities (Chapter 7).

Step 4 is very involved because of many practical considerations for different systems and circumstances; the latter are covered in Chapter 6. The implementation planning of the effort is discussed in Chapter 8.

In general, steps 1, 2, and 5 are principally performed by systems engineers. Step 3 is the province of the test planners. Step 4 is primarily organized and directed by quality assurance engineers. However, managers, test team members, and debuggers all get involved to varying degrees in the different steps. Thus a good overall understanding of all steps by all parties is highly desirable.

SYSTEM DEFINITION

System definition is the first step in applying software reliability measurement and prediction. The definition of a system for reliability purposes has three principal aspects. The first of these is the specification of just what "failure" means for the system, and perhaps the categorizing and classification of failures. The second is the definition of the system configuration and its decomposition into components. The third is the interpretation of the system definition through test selection. In Chapter 5 we will discuss how the reliability parameters of the model(s) for the software part(s) of the system are established.

4.1 FAILURE DEFINITION

In this section we will determine what will be considered "failures" for the system whose reliability is being studied. The definition of failures sharpens the system definition by providing the perspective of what the system should *not* be doing. We will do this for various kinds of systems and circumstances. We will consider the classification and categorization of failures. Our discussions will apply to both software and hardware, unless otherwise noted.

Recall that a "failure" is a departure of operation from requirements, conveniently described for software in terms of the output state of a run. Note that "failure" implies operation of the system. A software failure must occur during execution of a program. Potential failures found by programmers as the result of design inspections, code reading, and other methods do not count.

A "fault" is a program defect that has caused or can potentially cause a failure [see Musa, Iannino, and Okumoto (1987) for a full discussion of failure and fault concepts]. Some projects have included documentation faults in the count of program faults. This is generally *incorrect*, because documentation does not directly affect the execution of the program. Documentation faults may well lead to operator or user failures, as the operators and users will receive incorrect information on the use of the program. However, users and operators should be considered as a separate system component with regard to failures and reliability.

"Requirements," in hardware as well as software systems, are somewhat subject to interpretation. They may be restricted to being explicit or may involve implicit needs as well. For legal purposes, requirements should be explicit. Also, explicit requirements generally result in lower development costs. They reduce the number of failures due to misunderstanding of customer requirements. Hence you want to make the requirements as explicit as possible. However, the explicit requirements never include all the requirements important to the customer because neither the customer nor designer understanding of customer needs is perfect. Hence, it may be reasonable to allow for implicit requirements. In effect these are faults of omission in the explicit requirements.

The exact nature of "requirements" is further delimited and interpreted by considering what variations in operational behavior are tolerable. In establishing requirements, you provide a *positive* specification of a system. In defining failures, you supply a *negative* specification. You describe what the system must not do. Engineers using software reliability concepts have found that this negative specification is an extremely valuable system engineering technique. It adds another dimension of communication with the customer.

The definition of failure is really project-specific and must be established in consultation with the customer. For example, you may define "failure" as a program crash requiring interruption of processing and program reload. On the other hand, a very small variation in operation (for example, an incorrect title on a report) may be considered as a failure. Systems engineers will generally find themselves involved in establishing the definition of failure for their project. They will also interpret the definition during test. This fact makes it desirable for the systems engineers to work closely with the system test team, perhaps even as members. They are likely to receive some direct questions from the test team about whether a certain behavior is a failure or not. Does it violate system requirements? Members of the test team can't always resolve exactly what the requirements are, hence the systems engineers are looked on as the final arbiters. However, it is also recommended that systems engineers review at least some fraction, if not all, of the trouble reports. They need to determine if the test teams are interpreting requirements correctly.

The process of establishing the requirements for a system involves a consideration of the environment the system will operate in, that is, the operational profile. Although you may not completely quantify this profile, you usually have a general idea of the input states that will be presented to the program and their relative frequencies. This information should be used in test planning, so that testing represents expected operational use or so that differing operational profiles are compensated for in estimating reliability. It should also be used in design. The designer should consider the possibility of unexpected input states occurring due to failure in some other system. It is necessary to provide an appropriate response that minimizes performance degradation, data corruption, or undesirable outputs. Systems that respond rationally to nonfunctional input states are said to be *robust*.

When comparing the output state that results from a particular run with the required output state, note that extraneous output variables can occur. Some of these may be significant in that they cause data corruption that ultimately leads to failure. Variables that are members of the input states of future runs can be unintentionally changed, resulting in unexpected input states for which the program was not designed. Hence there can be a tendency for the program failure intensity to increase as it operates. There is a particular danger of missing unwanted extraneous output variables and hence missing failures when testing is automated. Normally in automated testing, checks are run for only a fixed set of output variables. If extraneous output variables cause data corruption during test, the tester may lose control of input state selection unless the system data is reinitialized before each run. Such loss of control is not necessarily a bad thing. It may realistically represent the operational environment.

There are at least two techniques for dealing with data corruption. First, a system may be made data corruption tolerant. This is done by designing the system to behave rationally for the additional input states that can result from data corruption. Second, data correction can be employed. Simple data correction schemes employ reinitialization of all or part of the data. Reinitialization can be periodic or generated in response to detection of a problem by an auditing program. Reinitialization can result in a failure or some loss of capability over the short term. However, the total set of reinitializations that occur in a consistent approach to countering data corruption has a positive average effect on reliability over the long haul. The results are automatically incorporated when you estimate reliability based on failure data. Sophisticated data correction involves techniques of redundancy (error correcting codes, checksums, etc.). Such corrections are expensive, but they can prevent failure and loss of capability.

4.1.1 Classification

Failures usually differ in their impact on the operations of an organization. Therefore, you may wish to classify them by severity and come up with the failure intensity or reliability for each classification. This can be particularly true for critical systems such as nuclear power plants, where serious failures may be rare but have an enormous impact. You must be careful not to confuse failure severity with the complexity or subtlety of the fault, and the difficulty and effort required to identify and correct it. The cost of repairing a fault is usually small with relation to the operational cost impact of the failure. Failure severity classification results in a slight effect on the data requirements, since you must determine and note the classification.

At least three classification criteria are in common use: cost impact, human life impact, and service impact. Cost impact is particularly applicable to any sys-

TABLE 4.1
Failure severity classification—service impact example

Class	Service impact
A	Basic service interruption
B	Basic service degradation
C	Inconvenience, correction not deferrable
D	Minor tolerable effects, correction deferrable

tem that is operating in the business world. What does this failure cost in terms of repair, recovery, lost business, and disruption? Human life impact is appropriate for nuclear power plants, air traffic control systems, military systems, or any kind of a system where safety or defense is paramount. Service impact might be appropriate for an interactive data processing service or a telephone switching system. It would probably be preferable to use the criterion of cost impact for systems such as this, but you may have situations where the cost impact is difficult to quantify. Also, service impact may be more relevant to the user. An example of service impact classification is given in Table 4.1 [Bardsley (1984)]. The most severe or Class A failure is one in which basic service is interrupted. An example of this would be the inability of a telephone switching system to process calls. Class B failures involve degradation of basic service. In the same system, excessive waits for dial tone would be considered Class B. Class C failures cause inconvenience, but not degradation of basic service. For example, suppose that an enhanced service such as call forwarding malfunctions. Class D failures are those that have effects that are minor and tolerable, such that repair can be deferred. An example would be slightly mistimed ringing.

An important question that must be answered with regard to any type of impact, but particularly cost impact, is "impact to whom?" A developer who delivers a product but has little continuing responsibility for it will have one viewpoint. A developer who will use the product to provide a service will have a different view. Experience indicates that it is generally best to establish your severity classes on the basis of orders of magnitude of the criterion being measured, since the measurement usually can't be that precise. Even when you use cost impact, many quantities such as lost business or good will are difficult to quantify and hence approximate.

In practice, severity classifications of failures are often made by more than one person. Consequently, to avoid variability in results, it is desirable to have objective (quantitative, if possible) rather than subjective classification criteria. Even if the judgment of the quantitative criteria is prone to error, their existence enhances the likelihood of understanding and reducing differences.

There appear to be three principal approaches to handling severity classifications in estimating reliability and related quantities:

1. Classify the failures and estimate failure intensity and other quantities separately for each class.
2. Classify the failures, but lump the data together, weighting the time intervals between failures of different classes according to the severity of the failure class.
3. Classify the failures, but ignore severity in estimating the overall failure intensity. Develop failure intensities for.each failure class by multiplying the overall failure intensity by the proportion of failures occurring in each class.

The first method is the most precise approach, but it suffers from the problem of dividing the sample of failures into several groups. Consequently, the time required to build up a reasonable sample size for good statistical estimation is longer. It is much later during the project that you get the information that you want with reasonable accuracy. The second method does not have the drawback of the small sample sizes that the first does, but the resultant "weighted present failure intensity" has little physical significance. For example, what would be the meaning of "failure intensity weighted by dollars?" Consequently, reliability and other quantities computed from this failure intensity would also have little meaning. The third approach appears to be the best. It takes advantage of the largest possible sample size. The validity of this procedure depends on the proportion of failures in each class remaining constant with time. It appears that most projects have this experience. For example, on the Space Shuttle Ground System, failures were classified into critical, major, and minor severities [Misra (1983)]. There were only 4 critical failures. Hence, we will look at critical and major failures taken together. The proportions of these failures to total failures are 0.33, 0.36, 0.38, and 0.36 at the four "quarter" points of the data collected.

Example 4.1. Consider a system whose failures will be classified by cost impact. The overall failure intensity, determined by estimation from *all* failure data, is 0.1 failure/hr. The number of failures in each class is shown, and the class failure intensities have been calculated.

Class	Failure cost impact range	Failures observed	Class failure intensity (failure/hr)
A	>$100,000	10	0.01
B	$10,000–$100,000	20	0.02
C	$1,000–$10,000	40	0.04
D	<$1,000	30	0.03

∎

Sometimes it is useful to work with *categories* of failures to focus attention on particular aspects of reliability. Also, many systems that would appear to have requirements of ultrahigh reliability actually have these requirements only for certain categories of failures. Failure categorization makes it possible for the reliability goals of these systems to be achieved at costs that are economic and with schedules that are reasonable.

One example of the foregoing is illustrated by the area of *software safety* [Leveson (1986)]. We consider a software safety failure to be any software system behavior that involves risk to human life, risk of injury, or risk of equipment damage. We can determine a "safety" failure intensity, based on failures of this category. In one sense, software safety imposes less stringent requirements than software reliability. We do not consider all departures from requirements as failures, but only those departures that have output states that are unacceptable because they are unsafe.

Another example is that of the electronic switching system for telecommunications. Ultrahigh reliability requirements are specified for the category of failures that would effectively prevent all communication in the area served by the system. The categories of failures that would delay some communication or interrupt some communication in progress are related to less stringent requirements.

4.1.2   Counting

Sometimes you must give careful consideration as to whether and how to count certain failures.

First, you may deliberately decide not to repair the fault causing a failure. The failure impact may not be severe. The cost of distributing the fix may be high. There can be schedule pressures. A *deliberate* decision not to fix a fault is really a redefinition of the system requirements. You are now saying that the associated failure(s) can be accepted. Hence, they should not be counted.

Second, people often ask how to handle repeated identical failures. By "identical" we mean that when the same run is made, the same deviation of program behavior from requirements occurs. These can occur at the same site or at different sites. They occur because the fault underlying the failure has not yet been repaired. Repeated failures primarily arise during the operational period. Since one principle of efficient testing is to avoid repeating the same input states, failure recurrences in test should be rare. The delay in correction can be the result of the normal delay involved in identifying and correcting the fault. Alternatively, it may result from a deliberate policy of holding the installation of repairs for a later software release.

The effect is illustrated in Figure 4.1. Instantaneous failure correction yields the failure intensity curve shown by the solid line. The dashed line indicates the actual failure intensity curve that results from delaying the installation of fault repairs until the next release. The failure intensity estimates that are made in the presence of such recurrences are accurate. However, they are higher than the failure intensity estimates that would be obtained if the failure recurrences were not counted. The offset of the curve to the right is due to the delay between failure identification and the associated fault correction. The discontinuous, stepped effect results from the grouping of fault corrections into releases. The horizontal length of the steps varies with the delay time for installation of the fault repairs.

FIGURE 4.1
Actual failure intensity compared to instant repair failure intensity.

The vertical height of the steps varies with the number of fault repairs being delayed and their effect on failure intensity.

When we do not count recurrences, we obtain a failure intensity estimate based on unknown remaining faults (the solid line) rather than all remaining faults (the dashed line). This is a better indicator of progress and status if repair action is going on. An analogy would be a checking account. You are more interested in knowing the amount of uncommitted funds (balance minus outstanding checks) than the actual balance. Thus, if you are in the test phase, it is probably best *not* to count the recurrences. Since testing is in practice a fairly centralized and controlled activity, it is generally not difficult to recognize repeated failures of the same type.

On the other hand, in the operational phase, it probably is best to count *all* failures, including repetitions of the same type. Repairs are generally made back at the test site and batched and delivered in a new release. Therefore, the failure intensity will be constant for the duration of the present release. A release may remain in operation for a period of a few weeks to 2 or 3 years. It makes sense to measure what is actually being experienced over the life of the release. It is generally not practical to try to identify and "eliminate" repetitions anyway. Operational personnel generally have less system knowledge than testers and may not recognize the repetitions. Furthermore, the system is usually installed at multiple sites. Communication between sites is usually not good enough for most of the repetitions to be jointly identified. Finally, documentation of the failures is usually not thorough enough for the "elimination" to be done back at the central site with high confidence.

Suppose you want to obtain data during test on the effect of different operational profiles on failure intensity. Then the counting of repeated failures during test will be significant. Testing must be partitioned, and the selection of input states for each partition must be representative of the corresponding operational profile. Alternatively, the test and operational profiles could differ, if enough information were available to permit adjustment of the results.

Third, some failures may result from defects in the *tools* used to design and develop a system. This is not a common occurrence. It can occur when tools are developed in parallel with or only slightly ahead of the systems they are to be used on. Examples are compilers (for software) or computer-aided design/computer-aided manufacturing (CAD/CAM) systems (for hardware). Consider the final use of the tool for the product before delivery. If the tool is then expected to be reliable, do not count these failures when making estimates of failure intensity or reliability. If it will probably still be unreliable, you may wish to make your estimates twice. The tool-caused failures should be included in one and excluded in the other. You will then have a range of failure intensities or reliabilities. The extreme values will represent a reliable tool and an unreliable one.

Fourth, there may be some question of what a failure is in fault-tolerant systems. Fault-tolerant systems include design features (either hardware or software, but frequently software) that counter the effects of hardware or software faults. They are called *hardware-fault-tolerant* or *software-fault-tolerant* in accordance with the faults they defend against. In interpreting failure for a fault-tolerant system, note that we are always concerned with variations of *external* and not internal behavior from requirements. Thus, an internal component failure may occur but be counteracted by fault-tolerant features of the system. In that case, there is no system failure. On the other hand, a malfunction of a fault-tolerant feature that affects program output *will* represent a system failure. A fault-tolerant feature is a requirement that a system defend against certain faults. Another view of a fault-tolerant system is that it is a system that is insensitive to defects, physical defects if hardware-fault-tolerant and design defects if software-fault-tolerant. Note that this fault-tolerance is purchased at a cost. Usually fault-tolerant software contains extra code. Two common fault-tolerant techniques applied to software are audits and recovery blocks.[1] The extra code induces additional faults into the system that must be found and removed, increasing the development time and costs.

Data in a system can degrade with time as they are affected by failures. Once a fault causes a failure to occur, further deviations from required behavior on the same run due to data degradation *are not counted as additional failures*. Sometimes a fault acting during a run causes a data item that can be an input to other runs to be degraded. The effect is that each later run is made with a different input state than what it otherwise would have been. One frequent attribute of software-fault-tolerant systems is that they constrain what the outputs resulting from all or some of such "degraded" input states can be. Thus, such systems are, in effect, more tightly and broadly specified than are systems without such tolerance. Finally, failures identified during subsystem test should usually not be com-

---

[1]For a thorough survey of this topic, see Anderson and Lee (1981). A method of reliability modeling of recovery blocks is given in Laprie (1984).

bined with those found during system test. The exception would be if subsystem test is viewed as a stage in the evolution of the overall system. Then appropriate techniques for evolving systems are applied (Chapter 6).

4.2 SYSTEM CONFIGURATION

The next step in the practical application of software reliability modeling is to gain a full understanding of the hardware-software system whose reliability is to be studied. You need to know exactly what is included in the system. Ordinarily you will be concerned with the deliverable product, and not tools or "scaffolding" unless they are part of the delivered product. Sometimes tools introduce faults into a system (for example, a compiler). You may want to account for this phenomenon, as noted in Section 4.1.

The system should be divided into a set of components, each of whose reliabilities is known or is easy to estimate or measure. We then deal with the relationships between the reliabilities of components and the reliability of the system. One uses these relationships to predict or evaluate system reliabilities from component reliabilities and to allocate or budget a system's reliability to its components.

4.2.1 Components and Operational Modes

Division into components is often dependent on the physical nature of the system or the nature of previously collected data. For example, what sets of similar elements of known reliabilities exist? However, other important considerations are the need to track a particular component for project management purposes and the amount of effort required for data collection. Tracking many separate components can be expensive, although the cost probably increases somewhat less than linearly with the number of components. Further, an excessive number of components results in a division of the failure sample among the components to the extent that accuracy suffers. If a system is integrated in stages, the code included in each stage may suggest the best way to divide the system into components.

The determination of what constitutes a software component requires a clear understanding of the term "program" in the definition for software reliability. A *program* is defined as a set of complete machine instructions (operations with operands specified) that executes within a single computer and relates to the accomplishment of some major function. In any particular situation, the identification of the specific program(s) in question is important. Many other definitions such as "input state," "output state," "failure," and "execution time" are dependent on the delineation of exactly what is included in the program. For example, an application program may or may not be considered separately from the operating system with which it runs. That depends on the objectives and method of analysis adopted for the study being undertaken.

Some systems operate in several different *operational modes*, or characteristic operational profiles. The proportion of time spent in each mode varies from installation to installation, or as a function of time. Here it may be desirable to determine the reliability for each mode, so that the different overall reliabilities at different installations can be determined. An example of the foregoing is a telephone switching system, which may operate in either a business customer mode or a residential customer mode. This is illustrated in Figure 4.2, with operational mode A representing the business customer mode and operational mode B, the residential customer mode. Operational mode A has a wide variety of types of calls such as conference calls, credit card calls, and international calls. Operational mode B has fewer of the special calls, hence the operational profile shows more of a peak. At any given site, the proportions of time devoted to the two modes will vary. Further, a given installation may operate primarily in the business customer mode in the daytime and the residential customer mode at night.

It may be possible to determine the different reliabilities for different operational modes by analysis of the effect of operational profile on reliability. However, different operational modes are often associated with the employment of different parts of the system. For example, at one installation, only certain functions are implemented. At another, a set of different functions is implemented. If so, it will probably be easiest to use this information to divide the system into components and analyze the different operational modes as different combinations of components.

Note that when we have different operational modes, we do increase the data requirements. When we record data, we must record the operational mode in which the data are being taken. Alternatively, if operational modes are correlated with components, we must record component information with all our failure data.

Example 4.2. The program for a space vehicle has two operational modes, prelaunch checkout and flight. In the prelaunch checkout mode, the system uses a

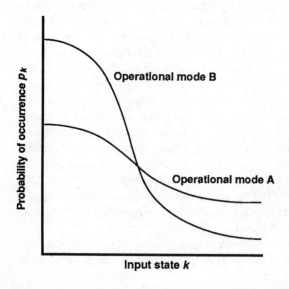

FIGURE 4.2
System with different operational modes.

driver, a functional component that performs all the in-flight tasks, and a display module. The display module interfaces with the astronaut and tells him or her what is going on. The flight mode uses only the functional and display modules. Let us assume that the driver module is going to be developed by a separate contractor. How should you analyze this system?

There may be more than one answer to this situation, since much engineering judgment is involved. However, the solution that many people would choose is to define two subsystems. One subsystem would consist of the driver and the other, of the functional and display modules. You now have a situation where the prelaunch checkout mode uses subsystems A and B and the flight mode uses just subsystem B. Thus, you have things set up in such a way that you can apply combinatorics to get the appropriate reliabilities for each of these different operational modes. You also have the driver module isolated by itself. That is probably desirable since it is being delivered by a subcontractor. You will want to know the reliability of the code that this subcontractor is delivering to you. Furthermore, you will want the contractor to be collecting data on this module. It is probably better to have that data collected separately, with the subcontractor using his own procedures, than to try to have a mixed multicompany data collection system.

Why not three subsystems? This would be satisfactory, but the factor that pushes us to two subsystems is simply economy and simplicity of data collection. ∎

For the purposes of this chapter, we will assume that component reliabilities can be determined. Literature on the reliability of hardware components is extensive [see, for example, Shooman (1986)]. Reliability of software components was initially discussed in Chapter 2 and is developed in more detail in many other chapters.

Since we have divided the overall system into hardware and software components, it is necessary to be able to attribute a failure to a particular component. Although experience indicates that perhaps 95 percent or more of failures can be readily classified on examination as software or non-software (hardware, operator, etc.), occasionally the choice is not certain. Then we recommend that you classify a failure as non-software if it doesn't recur when you run the program with all software and known non-software inputs exactly the same.

Recall from Chapter 1 that "requirements" should be interpreted very broadly. There are cases where the requirements that must be met by a system include performance figures, such as response time for a specified load. Thus, system reliability depends not only on our conventional concept of reliability, based on failures of functionality, but also reliability based on failures of performance. For example, it may be required that response time under a certain load be less than 0.2 sec. Determination of the frequency the system fails to meet such an objective depends on an analysis of performance which may involve load studies and queueing theory. A convenient way to handle systems of this kind is to consider the performance requirement as a pseudocomponent. This component would have a "reliability" equal to the probability with which the performance requirement is met (see Figure 4.3). Note that this approach implicitly assumes that performance is independent of the "conventional reliability" of the system. This may not be precisely true, but it is adequate as an approximation. The performance analysis is

FIGURE 4.3
Use of pseudocomponent to represent performance.

then conducted separately and the probability that the performance requirement is met is calculated. This reliability of performance is combined with the conventional reliability of the actual system to determine the system reliability with performance requirements accounted for.

There are two basic types of system relationships considered in the combinatorial analysis of reliability, concurrent and sequential. *Concurrent* systems consist of components that function at the same time, for example, a computer and its operating system. *Sequential* systems consist of components that function at different times, with only one component functioning at a time. An example of a sequential system is a set of software routines that function as a subsystem, with only one routine executing at a time. Strictly speaking, software components executing on the same processor do so sequentially, although they may have the appearance of being concurrent. They can generally be analyzed as a concurrent system, however, as will be shown in Example 4.4. Further, it is often more convenient to do so.

4.2.2   Concurrent Systems

The most general approach to analyzing concurrent systems is known as Failure Modes and Effects Analysis [Lawson (1983)]. It provides for the consideration of different types of failures and usually involves a complex, computerized analysis. It generally proceeds forward from components to the system. It is often preceded by fault tree analysis. This analysis works backward from the system to the components, with the purpose of determining which combinations of component failures can lead to system failures. Fault tree analysis based on the existence or nonexistence of a specific fault is feasible but probably not practical for software. If you knew what the specific fault was, you would fix it. However, fault tree analysis at the module level can identify the modules that are most critical. These modules must operate properly for critical functions of the system to work. Hence they need the most attention. This may be of particular value for analysis of safety of critical systems. Note, however, that a given module can have a range of faults, some of which may be catastrophic in effect and others negligible. Thus we are only identifying criticality in an average sense.

If it is assumed that all failures are of the same type or if we conduct a separate analysis for each type, then the problem is considerably simplified. Further, many systems can be described in terms of certain types of combinations for which simple combinatoric rules hold. The simplest types of combinations are AND and OR.

AND-OR CONFIGURATION. The AND-OR configuration of components with independent failures represents many common situations and it is easy to analyze. Hence, it is one of the most useful. It consists solely of subconfigurations of two types, AND and OR. It can be identified from its event diagram or event expression. Sometimes the subconfigurations are called *series* or *parallel* systems, respectively, based on electrical circuit analogies to the event diagram.

The *event diagram* is an analog of an electrical circuit with each component represented as a switch (see Figure 4.4). If the component is functioning, the switch is viewed as being closed and if not functioning, as open. System success occurs if there is a continuous path through the configuration. An AND-OR configuration exists if each component appears only once on the diagram and the diagram is composed solely of components in parallel and in series.

The *event expression* is the Boolean expression that relates the event of system success to the events of component successes. An AND-OR configuration exists if the event expression contains only ANDs and ORs and component success events appear only once. For example, in the AND-OR configuration of Figure 4.4, we have the event expression $S = (A + B + C)DE$, where S represents system success.

An example of a configuration that is *not* AND-OR is a set of three components, any two of which must be functioning for the system to function.

The following combinatoric rules apply, based on the failures in Q_P different components being independent of each other.

1. If *all* Q_P components must function successfully for system success (AND condition), or the failure of any of the Q_P components will cause system failure, the system reliability R is given by

$$R = \prod_{k=1}^{Q_P} R_k, \tag{4.1}$$

   where R_k are the component reliabilities.
2. If successful functioning of *any* of Q_P components will result in system suc-

S = (A + B + C) DE   S = System success

FIGURE 4.4
Event diagram for AND-OR configuration.

cess (OR condition), or the failure of all Q_P components is required for system failure, the system reliability is given by

$$R = 1 - \prod_{k=1}^{Q_P} (1 - R_k) . \tag{4.2}$$

This formula is derived from the principle that the overall failure probability is equal to the product of the individual failure probabilities.

Suppose we have Q_P components with constant failure intensities. Their reliabilities are measured over a common calendar time period. Assume that *all* must function successfully for system success. Then the system failure intensity λ is given by

$$\lambda = \sum_{k=1}^{Q_P} \lambda_k , \tag{4.3}$$

where λ_k are the component failure intensities.

K-OUT-OF-N STRUCTURE. Let us consider a system with Q_P components. At least Q_E components must operate for the system to work. Such a system is commonly said to have a *k-out-of-n structure* (in our notation, it is Q_E-out-of-Q_P). The reliability evaluation of such a system is, in general, difficult, except for the case where all the component reliabilities are the same.

If it is assumed that all components have the same reliability R_0 the system reliability R is given by

$$R = \sum_{k=Q_E}^{Q_P} \binom{Q_P}{k} R_0^k (1 - R_0)^{Q_P - k} , \tag{4.4}$$

which is a partial sum of the binomial probabilities.

Note that a Q_E-out-of-Q_P structure reduces to an AND structure when all the components must be operating (that is, $Q_E = Q_P$). Thus, the system reliability is obtained from Equation (4.4) for $Q_E = Q_P$ as

$$R = R_0^{Q_P} . \tag{4.5}$$

If at least one component must be operating (that is, $Q_E = 1$), the structure becomes an OR structure. The system reliability is obtained as

$$R = \sum_{k=1}^{Q_P} \binom{Q_P}{k} R_0^k (1 - R_0)^{Q_P - k}$$

$$= 1 - (1 - R_0)^{Q_P} . \tag{4.6}$$

The last equation was obtained using the fact that the sum of all the binomial probabilities is one.

TIME BASIS. Implicit in the rules for combining reliabilities of software and hardware components is the assumption that the reliabilities are all based on the same calendar time period. Since hardware component reliabilities are commonly stated with respect to operating time, we actually want to work with reliabilities based on the same clock time period. After combination of component reliabilities, the resultant system reliability will be established in terms of the same clock time period.

Software reliabilities are usually stated in terms of periods of execution time. Hence, before combining software and hardware components, conversion of software reliabilities will be necessary. To do this, it will be most convenient to convert reliability R of each software component to failure intensity. We will use the notation λ_τ to distinguish this failure intensity as being with respect to execution time. We use the equation

$$\lambda_\tau = -\frac{1}{\tau} \ln R, \tag{4.7}$$

obtained from Equation (2.13), where τ is the execution time period for which the reliability was specified. Note that combinatoric analyses are generally done for some specified state of the software (for example, at release to the field). Hence reliability change is not occurring, and Equation (4.7) is valid. This does not rule out the possibility of looking at the combination at several different points in time.

Let ρ_C be the average utilization by the program of the machine it runs on. Assume that this average utilization, taken over a period comparable to the failure intervals, does not vary significantly. Such is often the case. Then the failure intensity with respect to clock time λ_t is given by

$$\lambda_t = \rho_C \lambda_\tau. \tag{4.8}$$

Note that the failure intensity with respect to clock time is always the same or lower than that with respect to execution time, since $\rho_C \leq 1$. Utilization can be measured by recording processor clock (CPU) time expended in a given clock time interval. Many operating systems have the capability to do this readily. If the computer is running continuously, then Equation (4.8) also yields calendar time.

Once the failure intensities with respect to the "reference" period of clock time are established for all components, we can compute the corresponding reliabilities. We have

$$R = \exp(-\lambda_t t). \tag{4.9}$$

Note that the system failure intensity λ_t for an AND combination of Q_P software components, using Equations (4.3) and (4.8), is

$$\lambda_t = \sum_{k=1}^{Q_P} \rho_{C_k} \lambda_{\tau_k}. \tag{4.10}$$

The quantity ρ_{C_k} is the utilization of the machine on which it runs by software component k. The quantity λ_{τ_k} is the failure intensity with respect to execution time of the same component.

Adjustment of failure intensities and hence reliabilities when a program is moved to a different machine is readily done. Suppose a program is moved from computer 1 of average instruction execution rate r_1 to computer 2 of average instruction execution rate r_2. Then the failure intensity λ_2 on computer 2 is given by

$$\lambda_2 = \frac{r_2}{r_1}\lambda_1, \qquad (4.11)$$

where λ_1 is the failure intensity on computer 1.

Example 4.3. This example will illustrate some of the foregoing points. Consider a system made up of two software components, 1 and 2, as illustrated in the event diagram of Figure 4.5. Both operate concurrently, and both must operate without failure for the system to operate without failure. Assume that all hardware components have reliability 1. The components have reliabilities, respectively, of 0.670 and 0.527 for a period of 8 hr of execution time. It will be seen from Equation (4.7) that these correspond to failure intensities of 5 failures/100 CPU hr and 8 failures/100 CPU hr, respectively.

Consider the case where both software components run on the same machine, each taking up half the execution time. Then, using Equation (4.8), we get failure intensities with respect to clock time of 2.5 failures/100 hr and 4 failures/100 hr, respectively. The corresponding reliabilities for 8 hr of clock time are 0.819 and 0.726. System reliability for this period is thus 0.595. Alternatively, you can add the failure intensities with respect to clock time from both components, yielding 6.5 failures/100 hrs, and use Equation (4.9) to obtain 0.595 for system reliability. Note from Equation (4.10) that the system failure intensity with respect to clock time can also be obtained directly. Each component failure intensity is weighted by the average utilization of the machine by that component. Here we obtain $0.5(0.05 + 0.08) = 0.065$ failure/hr as the system failure intensity with respect to clock time.

If software components run on *different* machines, we have a different situation. Assume that both machines have the same average instruction execution rate and are fully utilized by these components. Each software component experiences a greater amount of execution time and thus more failures in the same amount of clock time. Thus, failure intensities in clock time are now higher: 5 failures/100 hr and 8 failures/100 hr. Corresponding reliabilities are, for 8 hr of clock time, 0.670 and 0.527, and system reliability is 0.353. ∎

INDEPENDENCE OF SOFTWARE FAILURES IN REDUNDANT PROGRAMS.

The rules for combination of AND-OR and k-out-of-n component structures assume that failures in the different components are independent of each other. This means that there can be no failures that result from the same cause. [For a survey of the topic of common-cause failures, see Watson (1981).] Reliability is often increased in hardware systems by providing redundant components. It is hence

1   **2**

$R_1 = 0.670$ $R_2 = 0.527$

FIGURE 4.5
Event diagram for system with two AND software components.

tempting to apply the same principle to software, but usually *it does not work*. The causes of failure associated with physically individual but functionally identical hardware components are frequently independent of each other. This is not true for software, because copies of a program are identical not only with respect to function but also with respect to the faults that can cause failures.

There is a possible exception. If programs are developed in separate versions by separate teams, following the same requirements, there is some possibility that many of the faults introduced may be independent of each other. Experiments in multiversion programming [for example, Knight and Leveson (1986)] seem to indicate that failures in different versions are clearly not completely independent of each other. They do not appear to all be common either, however. The amount of correlation remains to be determined. Hence multiversion programming may well improve the reliability level, but not to the extent totally independent components would. Having totally independent components may be cost effective for critical modules of systems with ultrahigh reliability requirements, such as nuclear power reactors, air traffic control, and space missions. Typical failure intensity requirements for such systems are in the range of 10^{-7} to 10^{-9} failure/CPU hr.

CASE STUDY 4.1
HANDLING REDUNDANT SOFTWARE
IN SYSTEM RELIABILITY CALCULATIONS

Suppose a chain of department stores wants to set up a computerized transaction processing system. They set a reliability objective of 0.90 for an 8-hr shift. Several different system configurations are being considered. We will take a look at each of these and in the process determine the reliability required of the transaction processor software to meet the overall reliability objective. The cost of each alternative will also be considered. In addition, several of the proposed system configurations illustrate some important points about "redundant" software.

Each configuration is composed of a front-end processor (FEP) whose job is to assign incoming transactions to one or more transaction processors (TP). The load is such that the utilization of one TP is 0.4. FEP utilization is 1. The FEP has an 8-hr reliability of $R_{fh} = 0.99$ for its hardware and $R_{fs} = 0.95$ for its software. The 8-hr reliability of the TP hardware is $R_{th} = 0.98$. These reliabilities can be related to failure intensities by using Equation (4.10). Table 4.2 summarizes the reliabilities and failure intensities for these components.

The reliability of the TP software is to be determined. The cost of developing this software is shown in Figure 4.6 as a function of the failure intensity (expressed in terms of execution time). As is seen, the cost increases as the delivered failure intensity decreases. The transaction processor hardware costs $250,000 per unit.

In computing costs, we will ignore constant factors and calculate software development cost plus any hardware costs beyond a single transaction processor

TABLE 4.2
Summary of component reliabilities

Component	8-hr reliability	Failure intensity (failures/hr)
FEP hardware (fh)	0.99	0.00126
FEP software (fs)	0.95	0.00641
TP hardware (th)	0.98	0.00253

system. For the purposes of this study each of the following configurations is said to have failed if the processing of any transaction is incorrect or made impossible for any reason.

ALTERNATIVE A

The first alternative is a single transaction processor being fed by a front-end processor, as shown in Figure 4.7(a). In this situation, the event diagram is as shown in Figure 4.8(a), where we have denoted the unknown TP software reliability as R_x. Applying the formula for AND events, Equation (4.1), we have for the system reliability $(0.99)(0.95)(0.98) R_x = 0.922 R_x$. Setting this equal to our objective and solving for R_x results in $R_x = 0.976$. Since it is known that the utilization of the TP will be 0.4, an 8 hr shift corresponds to 3.2 hr of execution time. Using Equation (4.9), we can write

FIGURE 4.6
TP software development cost as a function of failure intensity.

FIGURE 4.7
Different system configurations. (*a*) Alternative A. (*b*) Alternatives B, C, and D.

$$R_x = \exp(-3.2\lambda_x), \qquad (4.12)$$

where λ_x is the failure intensity of the TP software expressed in execution time. Solving, $\lambda_x = 0.0076$ failure/CPU hr. The cost of developing this software, from Figure 4.6, is about $940,000. This is also the "total" cost.

ALTERNATIVE B

The second alternative is an attempt to save some of the TP software development costs. We try to trade off a lower component reliability (higher failure intensity) with the greater expense of added redundancy. The proposed processor configuration is shown in Figure 4.7(b). The front-end processor assigns every incoming transaction to each processor, that is, each transaction will get processed twice. Successful system operation occurs if either transaction processor correctly processes the transaction. The event diagram for this case is shown in Figure 4.8(b). It is not difficult to apply our AND-OR rules to determine the overall system reliability, that is, $(0.99)(0.95) \{ - [1 - (0.98)R_x]^2 \}$. Setting this equal to the system reliability objective and solving, $R_x = 0.809$. This translates into a failure intensity of $\lambda_x = 0.0662$ failure/CPU hr. This latter figure is almost 10 times less stringent than that required by the first alternative. The software development cost is about $290,000. An additional cost of $250,000 will be incurred because of the second TP, giving a very attractive total cost of $540,000. *But this is wrong!* We have fallen into a common trap, as we shall see below.

A failure in one TP software component would also occur in the other since they are identical. Both copies contain identical faults. Since the software components are not independent of each other in regard to failure behavior, software redundancy does not improve reliability. *This is a commonly occurring and very important point for software components.*

In hardware reliability theory where multiple components fail due to a single cause, a *common-cause* failure is said to have occurred. This can be easily extended to software components. A straightforward method to incorporate these common-cause failures in our analysis is given in Dhillon (1983). Define γ as the fraction of component failures that are common-cause. Each component's failure

FIGURE 4.8
Event diagrams. (*a*) Alternative A. (*b*) Alternative B. (*c*) Alternative B (corrected). (*d*) Alternative C.

FIGURE 4.9
Event diagram for common-cause model.

intensity λ is the sum of an independent failure intensity $(1 - \gamma)\lambda$ and a common-cause failure intensity $\gamma\lambda$.

Suppose two components subject to common-cause failures are in a parallel configuration. The event diagram is shown in Figure 4.9. Our model will yield as the system reliability $[1 - (1 - R^{1-\gamma})^2] R^\gamma$. The overall effect of common-cause failures is displayed in Figure 4.10. Shown in this figure is the percent increase in reliability achieved using two independently developed components instead of a single component as a function of the fraction of common-cause failures. The reliability of a single component is given by R. Thus, when all failures are common-cause, $\gamma = 1$ and there is no improvement in system reliability. When there are no common-cause failures, $\gamma = 0$ and maximum improvement $[100(1 - R)$ percent] is achieved.

Now, let us apply the common-cause model to the configuration of Figure 4.7(b). Here $\gamma = 1$, that is, all TP software failures are common-cause and the model for the TP software degenerates into a single component with reliability R_x. The correct event diagram is shown in Figure 4.8(c). Solving for R_x results in a value of 0.957 (or $\lambda_x = 0.0137$ failure/CPU hr), which represents some but not

FIGURE 4.10
Effect of common-cause failures on reliability.

the significant reduction in reliability requirement hoped for. The software development cost now is $780,000 as opposed to the incorrect value of $290,000. Total cost is $1,030,000.

ALTERNATIVE C

The store's third approach, one that is potentially expensive, is to have two completely separate development teams produce two independent versions of the TP software. We assume that each copy of the software has attained the same reliability. The system operates just like the previous alternative, that is, a front-end processor is used to assign every incoming transaction to *each* processor. System success is obtained if either transaction processor correctly processes the transaction. The event diagram using our common-cause model is shown in Figure 4.8(d). The system reliability is $(0.99)\,(0.95)\,\{\,1 - [\,1 - (0.98)\,R_x^{1-\gamma}]^2\}R_x^{\gamma}$. If there are no common-cause failures then $\gamma = 0$ and R_x becomes 0.809 ($\lambda_x = 0.0662$ failure/CPU hr). This is, of course, the value of R_x we determined in our original analysis of alternative B. However, chances are that γ is relatively large, that is, similar errors are made by each team. If $\gamma = 0.5$, then $R_x = 0.922$ ($\lambda_x = 0.0254$ failure/CPU hr).

If $\gamma = 0$ the development cost for the TP software will be about $580,000 ($290,000 for each copy of the software). Similarly, if $\gamma = 0.5$ the software development cost will be about $1,150,000. As with alternative B an additional $250,000 will be incurred for the second unit of TP hardware. Total cost will be $830,000 or $1,400,000, depending on the value of γ.

ALTERNATIVE D

The final and most difficult alternative to analyze is a dual transaction processor with the front-end processor assigning transactions to the *next* transaction processor that becomes available. Each transaction is only processed once. This type of parallel system is sometimes referred to as a *shared load* system [Kapur and Lamberson (1977)]. In normal operation, each TP equally shares the load. Upon failure of the hardware component of one TP, the surviving processor must sustain an increased load, which can be limited by the capacity of the processor. Thus, the failure intensity, measured in clock time, of the software component of the surviving processor will increase. The failure intensity expressed in execution time will remain unaltered.

A system transition diagram is shown in Figure 4.11. Three states can be identified. State S represents a fully operational system, that is, both TPs are functioning. State P represents a partially operational system, that is, the hardware component of one TP has failed. State F represents the failed system. The indicated failure intensities represent the rates at which the system goes from one state to another.

We need to make two assumptions before giving an expression for system reliability. These are:

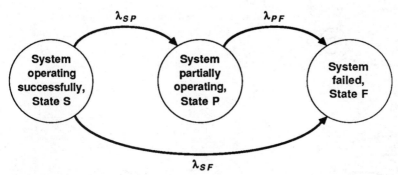

FIGURE 4.11
System transition diagram.

1. System failures are statistically independent.
2. Both TP hardware components cannot fail simultaneously.

Given these assumptions it can be shown [Dhillon (1983)] that the system reliability, defined as the probability of being in state S or P, is given by

$$R(t) = \exp[- (\lambda_{SP} + \lambda_{SF})t]$$

$$+ \frac{\lambda_{SP}}{\lambda_{SP} + \lambda_{SF} - \lambda_{PF}} \left\{ \exp(- \lambda_{PF}t) - \exp[- (\lambda_{SP} + \lambda_{SF})t] \right\}. \quad (4.13)$$

What remains to be done is to determine the values of λ_{SP}, λ_{SF}, and λ_{PF}. The system goes from operating normally to operating partially if one TP hardware component fails but not both. The transition diagram for the transition from state S to state P is shown in Figure 4.12(a). Thus, $\lambda_{SP} = 2 \lambda_{th}$. The system goes from normal operation to a failed state if the FEP hardware or software fails or if either TP software component fails. The transition diagram for the transition from state S to state F is shown in Figure 4.12(b). Let ρ_{C_0} be the utilization of a TP when the system is operating normally. Then, from Equation (4.8), the failure intensity of the TP software expressed in calendar time is $\rho_{C_0}\lambda_x$. Thus, $\lambda_{SF} = \lambda_{fh} + \lambda_{fs} + 2\rho_{C_0}\lambda_x$. Finally, the system goes from operating partially to a failed state if the FEP hardware or software fails, the TP software fails, or the remaining unit of TP hardware fails. The transition diagram for the transition from state P to state F is shown in Figure 4.12(c). Let ρ_{C_1} be the utilization of the TP hardware when only one processor is operating. Then, $\lambda_{PF} = \lambda_{fh} + \lambda_{fs} + \lambda_{th} + \rho_{C_1}\lambda_x$.

The system reliability for an 8-hr shift can be found by substituting the values of λ_{SP}, λ_{SF}, and λ_{PF} into $R(t)$ with $t = 8$. Carrying this out and making use of relationships such as $\exp(-8\lambda_{th}) = R_{th}$ results in

$$R_{th}^2 R_{fh} R_{fs} R_x^2 + \frac{2\lambda_{th} R_{th} R_{ts} R_{fh}}{\lambda_{th} + (2\rho_{C_0} - \rho_{C_1})\lambda_x} \left[R_x^{\frac{\rho_{C_1}}{\rho_{C_0}}} - R_{th} R_x^2 \right]. \quad (4.14)$$

(a)

(b)

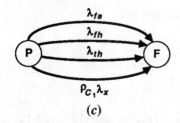

(c)

FIGURE 4.12
Transition diagrams for alternative D. (*a*)
Transition from state S to state P. (*b*) Transition
from state S to state F. (*c*) Transition from state
P to state F.

Since ρ_{C_1} is the utilization for a single processor doing the work that was previously done by two processors, its value is given by min $(2\rho_{C_0}, 1)$. Note that ρ_{C_1} cannot exceed 1. Thus, if $\rho_{C_0} = 0.6$ and one TP fails, the remaining processor will be worked to the limit. In fact, the responsiveness of the system to the user may be intolerable at this point. This may be outweighed by the fact that system availability is more critical.

In our store example $\rho_{C_0} = 0.2$ and $\rho_{C_1} = 0.4$. If the system is operating partially, it is equivalent to alternative A. Solving for the TP software reliability results in $R_x = 0.978$. This value is actually somewhat larger than R_x for alternative A! It seems we have wasted a TP for nothing. Actually, since the utilization of each processor is half of the utilization in alternative A, the required failure intensity with respect to execution time for the TP software is correspondingly larger. In fact, it is $\lambda_x = 0.0139$ failure/CPU hr. The software development cost will be about \$770,000. Total cost will be \$1,020,000.

SUMMARY

Several examples were presented that illustrated the important concepts of common-cause failures and shared-load systems. The development of system reliability figures when these conditions are present was also shown. For our specific examples the results are summarized in Table 4.3. These should not be taken to endorse any particular configuration over another. The value of γ may be difficult to

TABLE 4.3
Summary of results for each alternative

Alternative	Failure intensity (failures/CPU hr)	Cost (millions of dollars)
A	0.0076	0.94
B	0.0137	1.03
C ($\gamma = 0$)	0.0662	0.83
C ($\gamma = 0.5$)	0.0254	1.40
D	0.0139	1.02

quantify a priori. If it is only moderately large, then alternative C will cost a great deal in comparison to the other alternatives. Other factors, such as the cost of of slow response time to the users of the system, were not considered. If this is a major factor, then alternative D has a distinct advantage.

4.2.3 Sequential Systems

We will consider the case of a series sequential system, illustrated in Figure 4.13. The satisfactory operation of the system is dependent on the satisfactory functioning of each component *when it is active*. This type of system is characteristic of most software. It does not include the case of software with recovery features. In such software, one routine can cause recovery from a failure experienced in another routine and hence effectively cancel it out.

Littlewood (1976) has developed a model for such systems. The model assumes that the system consists of Q_P components among which control is switched randomly according to transition probabilities that depend only on the two components involved. Typically a component is a segment or branch of a program. Thus, it would consist of a sequence of instructions without branches or loops. The branching and looping structure is expressed by the transition probabilities. Failures for the kth component are assumed to occur in accordance with a Poisson process with failure intensity λ_k. If the λ_k are small, then the system failure process is Poisson with failure intensity λ given by

$$\lambda = \frac{\displaystyle\sum_{k=1}^{Q_P} \sum_{l=1}^{Q_P} \rho_k p_{kl} \mu_{kl} \lambda_k}{\displaystyle\sum_{k=1}^{Q_P} \sum_{l=1}^{Q_P} \rho_k p_{kl} \mu_{kl}}. \tag{4.15}$$

Transition probability P_{kl}

Component k Component l

FIGURE 4.13
Sequential system.

The transition probability from component k to component l is given by p_{kl}. The quantity μ_{kl} is the mean duration (sojourn time) spent in component k before switching to component l. Note that no assumption regarding the probability distribution of the sojourn times has to be made. The ρ_k are the probabilities of control residing in each component. They are given by

$$\rho_k = \sum_{l=1}^{Q_P} \rho_l p_{lk} , \qquad (4.16)$$

where the sum of all ρ_k must be 1.

Let us try to understand the two foregoing equations conceptually. Note that Equation (4.16) states that the probability of control residing in a target component is equal to the sum of the probabilities of control residing in each component *and* switching to the target component. Now consider Equation (4.15). Note in the numerator that $\mu_{kl}\lambda_k$ represents the average number of failures experienced in component k in the case where there is a transition to component l. Now $\rho_k p_{kl}$ is the probability of control residing in component k and switching to component l. Thus for each term in the numerator we have the number of failures experienced in a particular situation multiplied by the probability of being in that situation. Since the double sum covers all possible situations, the numerator is the total number of failures experienced. Each term of the denominator represents the average time spent in component k when a switch to component l occurs, multiplied by the probability of being in that situation. Thus the denominator represents total time elapsed. Note that the transition between components is assumed to be instantaneous. Hence Equation (4.15) yields total failures divided by total time, or overall failure intensity.

It is possible to generalize Equation (4.15) to handle the possibility of failures occurring during transition [Littlewood (1979)]. This would be done by replacing $\mu_{kl}\lambda_k$ in the numerator by $\mu_{kl}\lambda_k + q_{kl}$, where q_{kl} is the probability of a failure occurring during the transition from component k to component l. Usually failures during transition are erroneous transitions. You should not also count these situations as transitions in their own right.

The application of sequential system formulas requires knowledge of transition probabilities p_{kl}, sojourn times μ_{kl}, and component failure intensities λ_k. Transition probabilities and sojourn times can be determined most accurately by instrumenting the program to measure them. Many software development environments have execution trace facilities that could be modified to collect the foregoing statistics. Before execution, you would have to predict these quantities from knowledge of software system functions (the expected operational profile) and software system architecture. Component failure intensities can be determined by estimation if the program can be executed. To do this, failures and execution times would have to be separated by component. Prior to execution, component failure intensities would be predicted from component characteristics, especially size.

It will be seen that practical measurement and analysis problems increase rapidly with the number of components involved. Hence, the formulas given are most useful *in practice* when the number of components is small. However, they are a valuable conceptual tool independent of the number of components.

Note that when two software components execute on the same processor, a sequential configuration exists. However, this type of analysis is complex. The combination can generally be analyzed as a concurrent configuration, provided that the "dwell time" in each component is small compared to the interval between failures. Here the transfer of control is so rapid that it appears as if the components were operating concurrently. However, each component is operating in a slowed-down fashion since it is only operating part of the time. Analysis as a concurrent configuration is much simpler. This is illustrated by the following example, a sequential configuration analysis of the system presented in Example 4.3.

Example 4.4. The system of Example 4.3 may be viewed as consisting of components 1 and 2. Each component has a transition probability of 0.5 to itself and 0.5 to the other component. The state transition diagram is shown in Figure 4.14. The steady state probabilities of execution in the components are given by, using Equation (4.16):

$$\rho_1 = \rho_1 p_{11} + \rho_2 p_{21} = 0.5(\rho_1 + \rho_2) \,, \tag{4.17}$$

$$\rho_2 = \rho_1 p_{12} + \rho_2 p_{22} = 0.5(\rho_1 + \rho_2) \,. \tag{4.18}$$

Thus, since $\rho_1 + \rho_2 = 1$,

$$\rho_1 = \rho_2 = 0.5 \,. \tag{4.19}$$

In Example 4.3 the overall time spent in the two components is equal. For simplicity we will assume that this results from dwell times in each component that are equal and independent of the component from which control is transferred. Then Equation (4.15) becomes

$$\lambda = \frac{\rho_1 p_{11}\lambda_1 + \rho_1 p_{12}\lambda_1 + \rho_2 p_{21}\lambda_2 + \rho_2 p_{22}\lambda_2}{\rho_1 p_{11} + \rho_1 p_{12} + \rho_2 p_{21} + \rho_2 p_{22}}$$

$$= \frac{\lambda_1 + \lambda_2}{2} \,. \tag{4.20}$$

Note that this is the same result as obtained in Example 4.3. ∎

4.2.4 Simplified Approach for Distributed Systems

The concurrent system combinatoric approach represents a straightforward approach for handling distributed computing systems. However, it has certain practical disadvantages. First, data collection is complicated. Failure data must be kept separated by component and the failure intensity of each component must be tracked separately. Second, execution times must be measured on each machine and referred to a common base. Third, the process of setting failure intensity objectives is made more difficult, since the overall system failure intensity objective

FIGURE 4.14
State transition diagram
for system with two
software components.

must be allocated among the components. Finally, computation of calendar time to overall failure intensity objective for the system is complicated, since each component must be considered and then results for the overall system derived.

A simplified approach is possible if:

1. It is only desired to track system and not component reliability behavior.
2. The system fails if any software component fails.
3. The ratios of execution time intervals between each component and an arbitrarily chosen reference component are constant, for intervals of size comparable to the failure intervals.

Constant ratios of execution times among software components imply that the various processors in the system work together in some approximately synchronous manner.

This approach permits the software components to be considered as *one* software system. A failure in any component is also a system failure, hence the union of the sets of component failures is identical with the set of system failures. Even though the components may be executing on different machines with different average instruction execution rates, they are running together synchronously (on the average). You measure failures with respect to the execution time of a reference component, and all failure intervals are determined on that basis. The total system execution time will be proportional to that of the reference component. The foregoing does *not* imply that the hardware components can be lumped together.

Consider the example of the bank data network given in Case Study 1.1. It is likely that the firm hired by the bank will use different processors for the front-end processor and system controller. This, coupled with the fact that the functions and hence the software differ between processors, would lead to the disadvantages described previously if the full combinatoric approach were taken.

Instead, we will take the simplified approach. Let the average instruction execution rates of the front-end processor and system controller be r_F and r_S, respectively. The utilization of the front-end processor is ρ_{C_F} and that of the system controller is ρ_{C_S}. In a given period of clock time the execution time τ_S of the system controller is related to the execution time τ_F of the front-end processor by

$$\tau_S = \frac{\rho_{C_S}}{\rho_{C_F}} \tau_F .$$

(4.21)

We will consider the front-end processor as the reference. An execution time τ_S on the system controller is equivalent to an execution time of $(r_S/r_F)\tau_S$ on the front-end processor. Hence the execution time of the system controller referred to the front-end processor, using Equation (4.21), is $(r_S/r_F)(\rho_{C_S}/\rho_{C_F})\,\tau_F$. Then the total execution time, referred to the front-end processor, is

$$\tau_F\left(1 + \frac{r_S}{r_F}\frac{\rho_{C_S}}{\rho_{C_F}}\right).$$

Note that the factor in parentheses can be determined from measurements of r_F, r_S, ρ_{C_S}, and ρ_{C_F} made at one time. For our example, this factor is taken to be 3.63. Table 4.4 shows the first few operating execution times of the front-end processor between software failures (which may occur anywhere) and the resulting system failure intervals.

In some complex systems, it may be impractical to determine all the execution time ratios among the various software components. There may be another measure that is representative of the total software workload of the system. The measure should be proportional to the sum of all instructions executed in all system processors. The average proportionality factor, when averaged over a time comparable to the failure intervals, should be approximately constant. Then this measure can be used as an approximation to execution time. One example of such a measure is the number of scheduling messages flowing in the distributed system. The scheduling messages represent the assignment of tasks to processors. If the average task size in instructions, where the average is taken over a time comparable to a failure interval, is constant, then the measure approximates execution time.

4.2.5 Standby Redundant Systems

Redundant systems, such as OR systems discussed in Section 4.2.2, represent one approach to improving system reliability. A standby redundant system is another

TABLE 4.4
Failure data for distributed system example

Failure number	Front-end processor execution time	System failure interval[1]
1	148	537
2	1	4
3	1631	5920
4	1422	5162
⋮	⋮	⋮

[1] System failure time = 3.63 × FEP execution time

method that is frequently used to achieve high reliability. Spare parts and back-up systems are examples of standby redundancy.

Consider a system that has Q_P components, where only one component is in operation. If the operating component fails, then another component is brought into operation. Time to system failure is therefore a sum of operation times of Q_P components. Suppose that all components have a constant failure intensity of λ. Then, the distribution of time to system failure is given by the sum of Q_P exponential random variables, which is a Gamma distribution with the shape parameter Q_P and the scale parameter λ. Hence, the reliability function of the standby redundant system is given by

$$R(t) = \exp(-\lambda t) \sum_{i=0}^{Q_P-1} \frac{(\lambda t)^i}{i!}. \tag{4.22}$$

4.2.6 Procedure for Analyzing System Configuration

Let us now summarize the procedure for analyzing the system configuration. If the system has different operational modes, this question must be addressed first. Assuming that this question has been settled, you must determine what kind of a system you have from a combinatorial viewpoint. The two principal kinds to consider are the concurrently functioning system and the sequentially functioning system. If you have a concurrently functioning system, you will develop an event diagram to describe the system. If you have a sequentially functioning system, you will use a transition diagram.

Now you have to determine the different components that you are going to track. In making your reliability predictions and estimates, there are in general four principal things to consider. First, you may want to consider your operating modes. If operating modes are correlated with components, this could influence the division into components. Second, you should address the question of system evolution, which is covered in Chapter 6. Sometimes you have systems that are integrated as major blocks or major subsystems. If that is the situation, you may want to track the reliability of these separately, because this will be the most appropriate approach to handling the evolution. The third thing to consider is that your project may have particular needs for tracking the reliabilities of certain components. For example, certain components may be critical from either a cost, schedule, or development risk point of view. The three initial factors that we talked about here are all factors that tend to drive you in the direction of more components. The fourth and countervailing factor is the complexity and difficulty of data collection and the possible loss of statistical significance when failure samples are divided among many components. Thus, you must reach a trade-off here. Finally, if you have a distributed system, you can handle the analysis of system configuration in a simplified fashion under certain conditions.

4.3   TEST RUN SELECTION

A set of requirements for a software system only achieve true validity when the performance of the system designed to satisfy them has been verified. Thus, verification is an aspect of system definition. Although there are many approaches to verification, sooner or later the system must be tested. To the best of our knowledge, there currently is no economically viable or perhaps even technically feasible methodology that *guarantees* that user requirements for useful program products can be met without test. The quality and efficiency of testing depend largely on how the test runs are selected. Hence testing must be carefully planned. Of course, there are other considerations such as adequacy of data recorded, and quality of data reduction and diagnostic tools available. But the foregoing are to little avail if test selection is poorly done.

4.3.1   Selection Strategy

Input state selection during test can, of course, be deterministic, since the tester and not the external environment is in control. Test selection is *deterministic* if each test case and its order in the test sequence is specified with certainty. It is *random* if more than one test case is possible at any point, and each test case has a probability of occurrence at that point associated with it. Estimated reliability status can be manipulated almost at will by picking the "right" input states. You must, of course, have previously executed the run corresponding to that input state, so you know whether a failure occurs. Completely arbitrary selection of input states is undesirable, however, from the viewpoints of test realism, optimum testing strategy, and characterization of reliability status.

   The optimum test strategy at any point during test is the one that yields the greatest reduction in operational failure "cost" per unit of test cost. "Cost" usually is economic, but it can represent human life lost, service degradation, or other operational impacts. Test cost at any given level of failure intensity is primarily affected by execution time. The operational cost of failures is, on the average, proportional to the failure intensity. Hence, the optimum average test strategy will be to select input states in a way that will reduce failure intensity most rapidly with respect to execution time. Suppose we select input states randomly with probabilities equal to those that occur during operation. Then, on the average, the first executions of the input states will occur in the order of their occurrence probabilities. Hence, failures associated with the most frequently occurring input states tend to be found and removed first, reducing the failure intensity the most rapidly. Note that this approach also yields a failure intensity at each point in test that would be equal to that experienced in operation if the program were released at that time. This is because the operational profiles would be the same. You will recall that our test selection strategy is based on average operational cost of failures. Sometimes it may be possible to identify particular input states which, if faulty, would lead to exceptionally costly failures. In that case, it might be wise to test them first. This situation might occur for life-critical systems. Fault tree analysis can be useful in identifying the critical input states.

You must be careful to have the entire input space open to selection at all times. This does not mean that every input state must be selected at least once. That is usually impossible to accomplish in any reasonable length of time. However, sometimes testers concentrate on one part of the input space and then move to another. This approach is likely to yield misleading software reliability figures and *late, unpleasant* surprises about problem areas in the software. Following a fixed, deterministic sequence of testing is particularly dangerous if different functions tend to each have their own code. Then you obtain no information at all about the condition of certain parts of the software until late in test. It may then be too late to take expeditious corrective action. Sometimes the localization of input selection mentioned is unavoidable when the system is integrated in phases. In that case, however, the special techniques for handling evolving systems described in Chapter 6 should be employed. They may reduce, but probably not eliminate, the reliability figure errors caused by localization.

Testing can be more efficient if one recognizes that once an input state has been selected, it does not have to be repeated. Sometimes this is referred to as *test selection without replacement*, a reference to classic sampling problems in statistics. Repetition should not be necessary, because any failure that would occur would be observed and corrected on the first execution of the input state. This is the principle behind the concept of test compression, discussed in Chapter 6. If repetition is prevented, failure intensities should be adjusted as described there. When test selection without replacement occurs, we in effect obtain a uniform operational profile in test. However, the sequence of input states selected will be, on the average, in the order of their occurrence probabilities. In practice, some repetitions of input states are made. These are known as *regression tests*. Regression testing is necessary because the principle of "first execution fault removal" is not totally met in practice. It depends on the program being stable (no changes), all failures being observed, and all corrections being perfectly carried out.

Some testers criticize random selection of input states as being inefficient. This may be because they have taken advantage of test selection without replacement when selecting tests deterministically but not when choosing them randomly. Such an approach leads to an obviously unfair basis of comparison. Recent studies [Duran and Ntafos (1984)] have shown that random testing is an effective strategy for many programs, both for minimizing test cost and finding faults. This is seen both from direct measures and the fact that random testing performs well with respect to branch and path coverage. Often, it is superior to *partition testing* or dividing input space into sections (partitions) and taking one input state from each section. Note that path testing is a special case of partition testing, since input space can be partitioned by program structure as well as function. Partitions have the effect of forcing a certain planned diversity on testing. A recent study [Currit, Dyer, and Mills (1986) interpreting data of Adams (1980)] points to the superiority of random testing. It shows that random testing based on the operational profile would have been 30 times more effective than structural testing for nine large

IBM products. Structural testing is testing based on knowledge of a program's structure. It is oriented toward executing as many different program branches or paths as possible.

The tester who is trying to truly represent the operational phase by random selection is not constrained in selection by the correlations between input states that can occur during operation. This is because input states can be set by manual intervention. As long as the operational period is sufficiently long such that input state selection probabilities can be characterized by the steady state, random testing using these probabilities but independent selection will be representative of the operational environment.

Testers often pick input states to test that they think are fault-prone. These states may lie at the boundaries of the expected range of inputs or appear to be ones that the designers may not have considered. This strategy is seductive, because the likelihood of finding a fault and enjoying the resultant satisfactions *is* frequently higher. However, often these input states do not occur with high probability in the operation of the program. Consequently, the strategy is inefficient when evaluated against the proper objective of reducing failure intensity rapidly. Do not confuse the inappropriate strategy of specially selecting input states that may be fault prone but infrequently executed with the good strategy of specially selecting input states that may have severe costs associated with them *if* faulty.

It could conceivably be worthwhile to try to identify frequently occurring input states that are fault-prone. This is much more difficult than picking rarely occurring ones. There is no proven way to do this now. There is great risk that overconfidence of a tester in ignoring certain input states could lead to disaster. The risk is akin to that of betting your life savings on a "sure thing" in the stock market.

There is some indication that some *modules* may be more fault-prone than others. The fault-proneness may relate to the function implemented, the development methodology employed, or the capability of the designer. However, single modules usually do not correspond to single input states. Virtually any program product with any substantial function will be quite complex in the pattern of modules executed during a run. Consequently, we cannot take advantage of the possible existence of fault-prone modules in predicting fault-prone input states.

It has been suggested [Budd et al. (1979)] that *mutation testing* may be an efficient approach to identifying fault-prone input states. It is based on the concept that certain patterns of faults are likely to occur, and that these result in certain types of mutations in a program. You then try to design tests so that they are most efficient in stimulating the failures connected with these mutations. Work in this area has generally concentrated on designing the tests, given that the particular types of mutations occur. Further studies of the error process in software engineering are necessary to establish mutation patterns. If mutation testing is to be cost effective, the patterns identified must represent types of faults that will occur even though designers are aware of their likelihood and are taking precautions against them. It is not at all clear that this is the case.

We have implicitly assumed that test selection is primarily a question of selecting individual input states. In some circumstances, it may be important to select sequences of input states. One such circumstance is that of systems in which there is substantial undetected corruption of data. This would typically occur for systems that access and modify large and complex data bases such as those used by CAD/CAM systems. A run may function quite properly except for an erroneous change in the data base. We may not consider that a failure has occurred, since the immediate function meets customer needs. Or, if data corruption is specified as a violation of a requirement, we may not be able to completely examine the many dimensions of the output state and detect the failure. As a result, it may be desirable to include sequences of runs in test to uncover failures that would result from data corruption. Unfortunately, this approach has its own problems. The number of sequences is so large that it is difficult to enumerate them and/or establish their probabilities of occurrence. A compromise test plan involving some sequence testing may be feasible.

4.3.2   Equivalence Partitioning

Equivalence partitioning is a useful technique that can increase the efficiency of testing. The key to the technique lies in the fact that many input states are very similar to one another, differing in only a few aspects. For example, two deposit transactions in a banking program may differ only in the amount of the deposit. If one functions correctly, it is extremely (but not perfectly!) likely that the other will also. One can perform a grouping or *equivalence partitioning* [Cox (1981) and Myers (1979)] of the input space. You select only one input state from each group, with a probability equal to the total probability of occurrence of all states in the group. This drastically reduces the number of input states that you must select from and speeds up testing, since input states that are unlikely to expose new failures are not executed. This increase in testing efficiency is achieved with added risk, however, in that the ignored states may indeed be associated with failures, which are then missed. In reality, the practicality of limited time available for test often forces an implied equivalence partitioning. The test phase may consist of a few hundred or few thousand test cases, but the input space may be much larger.

Equivalence partitioning may be performed on the basis of either functional similarity or structural coverage. More attention has been paid to the latter approach. The basic philosophy of the structural coverage approach is to select input states to most rapidly "cover" the program in some fashion, avoiding redundant coverage. In order of increasing capability to find potential failures, you may cover the execution of all instructions, all segments or branches, or all paths. Note that the coverage of all paths still does not insure that all failures are found, since failures may be data-dependent. Structural testing at the path level is very lengthy because loops vastly increase the possible number of paths (each additional iteration represents one or more additional paths). In practice, it is usually feasible to test only some random sample of paths. Studies by Howden (1980) suggest that overall, structural testing is not as effective as functional testing in uncovering faults. However, each method finds certain faults more effectively than the other. Incidentally, Howden's work also shows that static analysis is more effective than testing for finding about half the faults. It may be difficult to take into account the various frequencies with which input states (functions) can be executed. Relating structural elements executed to input states can be complicated from a practical point of view. The use of equivalence partitioning does not require any adjustment to failure intensity figures. The failure intensity figures obtained in test will directly reflect and incorporate the more rapid reduction obtained through this technique.

One way to lessen the risk inherent in equivalence partitioning is to select a new input state within an input state group whenever a regression test must be performed for that group. If the test fails, you will not know whether the failure is due to poor partitioning or the introduction of a new fault due to program change. There is even a very minor risk that a newly introduced fault would be detected by a run with the initial input state but not by another run in the same partition group. The foregoing effects are very small, however, compared with the overall advantage gained.

4.4 SUMMARY

The definition of "failure" really involves the thorough elucidation of system requirements. This elucidation comes about because of the different perspective taken when thinking about failures and their varying impacts on the use of a system.

The way in which we think about the configuration of a system is strongly influenced both by the analytical tools available to us and the purposes of our analysis. Both must be clearly understood before attempting to establish a system decomposition. Finally, the reliability figures obtained for a system during test are dependent on the tests selected. Hence, this process is very important.

PROBLEMS

4.1 A computing center has a reliability objective of 0.90 for an 8-hr shift for its interactive service. The system requirement is simply that service be provided, regardless of the response time involved. All reliabilities are measured with respect to this shift. It has a dual processor configuration fed by a front-end processor, as shown in Figure 4.15. The front-end processor has a reliability of 0.99 and its operating system, 0.95. The reliability of each mainframe processor is 0.98. What must the reliability of the mainframe operating system be to meet the overall reliability objective?

4.2 Figure 4.16 represents the event diagram for a time-sharing system running on a multiprocessor machine with two processors. The time-sharing system runs under a general purpose operating system, and both run on both processors. The reliabilities of the hardware for a 10-hr prime shift are labeled. The operating and time-sharing sys-

FIGURE 4.15
Computing center configuration.

FIGURE 4.16
Event diagram for interactive computing service.

tems have failure intensities measured in *execution time* of 0.05 and 0.025 failure/
CPU hr, respectively. Each runs about 20 percent of the time and the other 60 percent
of the processor capacity is used by application programs. Find the prime shift reliability of the entire extended machine (reliability of application programs is not
considered).

4.3 We are working with a compiler that is not fully debugged. Consequently, we often
find that a failure is the result of incorrect compilation rather than erroneous programming. Should we account for this in any way?

4.4 When you experience a failure in testing, can you continue testing or must you restart from scratch? If the former, how do you account for the fact that degraded data
may cause another failure?

4.5 Would complex or subtle faults be more likely to be uncovered toward the end of the
test period?

4.6 We find in testing that we tend to locate the most severe failures first and the failures
with less impact later. Note that "severity of failure" is not the same thing as "complexity of fault" in that severity relates to impact on the user. Does this affect the application of the theory?

4.7 If a program and its associated data are reloaded, won't this affect the length of the
failure interval just afterward, since degraded data will be cleaned up by the reload?

4.8 Are there cases where it is difficult to determine whether a failure is due to hardware
or software?

4.9 What is the difference between hardware-fault-tolerance, software-fault-tolerance,
and robustness?

4.10 Does the reliability of test drivers have an impact on a software reliability model?

4.11 Do we have different failure types when the same software is run on two different
machines and fails in the same way on the same runs?

4.12 Derive Equation (4.3).

4.13 Can a deficiency in performance of a software component (for example, excessive response time at a given traffic level) be a failure?

4.14 Many operating systems can recover from certain kinds of software malfunctions and
continue to process work. Are these malfunctions failures?

4.15 You define "failure" as an unacceptable departure of program operation from program requirements. Does this rule out the possibility of failures resulting from requirement faults?

4.16 How do you handle multiple failures resulting from the same fault on a single run
during test?

4.17 How do you handle failures found by unit test that continues in parallel with system
test?

FIVE

PARAMETER DETERMINATION

We have defined the system we are working with in Chapter 4. We must now determine the parameters for the model(s) of the software part(s) of the system. The determination of parameters was first discussed in Chapter 2. In this chapter, we will deepen our understanding of this process, particularly with respect to its practical aspects. A summary of methods for the determination is presented in Table 5.1. Finally, we will discuss some of the features of programs we have found helpful in experience with estimating parameters and computing other useful quantities. In Chapter 6 we will look at a number of project-specific techniques.

5.1 EXECUTION TIME COMPONENT

You will recall that execution time component parameters for the basic model can be determined by prediction from characteristics of the software and the development process. This can be done before any execution of the software. Once the software is executed and failure data is available, the parameters can be estimated statistically from the data. The parameters are summarized in Table 2.1.

5.1.1 Prediction

The basic execution time model has two parameters we must predict, total failures ν_0 that would be experienced in infinite time and initial failure intensity λ_0.

5.1.1.1 TOTAL FAILURES. The net number of faults removed is only a portion of the failures experienced, expressed by the fault reduction factor B. Thus the total

TABLE 5.1
Method of parameter determination

Parameter	Method				
	Prediction	Estimation	Identification	Formula and/or experience	Data
Execution time component					
Basic model	X	X			
Logarithmic Poisson model		X			
Calendar time component (both models)					
Planned					
Resource quantity			X		
Resource utilization				X	
Resource usage					X

failures ν_0 may be estimated, before test, from the number of inherent faults ω_0 and the fault reduction factor B, since

$$\nu_0 = \frac{\omega_0}{B}.$$ (5.1)

Faults. You can theoretically determine the number of inherent faults in coded programs by an empirical method, variously called "fault seeding," "error seeding," or "bebugging" [Gilb (1977), Rudner (1977), Basin (1973), and Mills (1972)]. Introduce artificial faults into the program in some suitable random fashion, unknown to the people who will be trying to find program faults. It is assumed that these seeded faults are equivalent to the inherent faults in the program in terms of difficulty of detection. Inspect the code and count separately the inherent and seeded faults discovered. The proportion of seeded faults found to total seeded faults is noted. You can then predict the number of inherent faults in the program. The reasoning is based on the concept that with equal difficulty of discovery, the same proportions of both types of faults will have been uncovered at any point in time.

For example, suppose that 100 faults are seeded into a program that contains an unknown number of inherent faults. After a period of debugging, 20 seeded and 10 inherent faults have been discovered. The seeded faults discovered represent 20 percent of the total number of seeded faults. We assume that 20 percent of the inherent faults have been discovered also. Therefore, the total number of inherent faults must be 50. Actually, the situation is a bit more complex than this. We are dealing with random samples, and we are estimating the number of inherent faults and its confidence interval.

Unfortunately, it has proved difficult to implement seeding in practice. It is not easy to introduce artificial faults that are equivalent to inherent faults in difficulty of discovery. It is generally *much* easier to find the seeded faults. Consequently, the number of inherent faults is usually underestimated with this technique. Hence, we usually determine the number of faults from program characteristics.

It has long been assumed that the size of a program has the most effect on the number of inherent faults it contains. At least several researchers [Feuer and Fowlkes (1979), Motley and Brooks (1977), Thayer (1976), and Akiyama (1971)] have verified this hypothesis. It appears that for *modules*, there may be a constant inherent fault component unrelated to size [Shen et al. (1985)], although its existence is in dispute [Card, Church, and Agresti (1986)]. A possible source of this component is interface faults, which are likely to be size-independent [Basili and Perricone (1984)]. In any case, we are interested in estimating the number of inherent faults in *systems*, usually of appreciable size, or in increments to systems. The constant inherent fault component for modules should not be significant in either of these situations.

Inherent fault density. Data can be collected on average inherent fault densities (faults per instruction) at the start of various phases of testing. These data will permit the number of inherent faults ω_0 to be estimated by simply multiplying predicted inherent fault density by program size. Implicit in this approach is the assumption that the number of inherent faults is linearly related to program size. The validity of this assumption is supported by Basili and Hutchens (1983) and strongly backed by Takahashi and Kamayachi (1985). The latter found less than 0.03 correlation between inherent fault density and program size over 30 projects, ranging from 4K to 130K lines of developed (new or modified) code. The Basili and Hutchens study also presented evidence to indicate uniform inherent fault distribution across the code. Metrics based only on specific parts of the code were less effective in predicting the number of inherent faults.

Experience has indicated that inherent fault quantities are more closely correlated with source than object instructions. Hence we count *deliverable executable source instructions* developed during the project. Thus, we do not count drivers or support programs. Data statements, declarations, and comments are not counted. When the project involves program changes rather than program creation, we do not count instructions/statements that are left alone or deleted. The incidence of inherent faults associated with such statements is much less than that associated with those that are created or modified. In studies of mathematically oriented FORTRAN routines for space applications, 98 percent of the modules that were reused without change were fault-free. In practice, the number of *instructions* is highly correlated with the number of *lines* of code. As the latter is easier to count, it is most often used.

A summary of available data on the density of inherent faults found in different phases of a number of projects is presented in Table 5.2. The data vary in quality because of differences in the care with which the terms were defined and the data were collected. Individual references are presented so that the user of these data may investigate them. Possibly, one might make better predictions than those

TABLE 5.2
Density of faults found during different life cycle phases for various projects

Reference	System identifier	Developed code (K source lines)	Faults/K source lines	Phases[1]
Basili and Perricone (1984)		90	44.1[2]	C, UT, SS, S
Stover (1977)		4.0	71.3	C, UT, SS, S
Albin and Ferreol (1982)		27.6	21.0[2]	C, UT, SS, S
Boehm (1981)		2	75	C, UT, SS, S
Rubey, Dana, and Biché (1975)	multiple[3]	9	113	C, UT, SS, S
Ostrand and Weyuker (1982)		10	16.0	UT, SS, S
Akiyama (1971)		17.1	20.3	UT, SS, S
Schafer et al. (1979)	4	115.3	36.2	SS, S
Mendis (1981)		28	4.6	S
Motley and Brooks (1977)	S	181	19.5	S
	T	115	17.4	S
Akiyama (1971)		17.1	3.2	S
Schafer et al. (1979)	1	120	17.0	S
	2	610	12.8	S
	3	96.9	3.78	S
	7	1317	2.69	S
	14	32.2	15.6	S
	15	32.4	13.8	S
	16	123.7	10.8	S
Angus, Bowen, and VanDenBerg (1983)		330	10.6	S
Weiss (1981)	SEL 1	46.5	3.87	S
	SEL 2	31.1	3.83	S
	SEL 3	78.6	3.91	S
	ARF	21.8	6.56	S
Bendick (1976)	1	217	4.8	S
	2	31.5	9.8	S
	4	32	5.2	S
	5	73	5.1	S
	6	36	3.6	S
Endres (1975)	DOS/VS	86	6.0	S
Rubey, Dana, and Biché (1975)	multiple[4]	18.3	4.5	S
Walston and Felix (1977)	multiple[5]	20	3.1	S
Inglis et al. (1986)	multiple[6]	-	4.20	S
Inglis et al. (1986)	multiple[7]	-	1.44	OP
Walston and Felix (1977)	multiple[8]	103	1.4	OP
Schafer et al. (1979)	5	115.3	3.9	OP

[1]Phases: C = coding, UT = unit test, SS = subsystem test, S = system test, OP = operation

[2]Likely to be low because of way data were collected.

[3]Average of 12 systems, with size ranging from 3 to 16 K source lines and faults from 13 to 320 faults/K source lines.

[4]Average of 8 systems, with size ranging from 1.5 to 27 K source lines and faults from 1.7 to 20 faults/K source lines.

[5]Data from 46 systems. Median size is 20 K source lines and lower and upper quartiles are 10 and 59 K source lines. Median fault density is 3.1 faults/K source lines and lower and upper quartiles are 0.8 and 8.0 faults/K source lines.

[6]Carefully defined data from 55 systems, with fault density ranging from 0.01 to 80.39 faults/K source lines. Sizes extended from 4.1 to 564.9 K source lines of developed code.

[7]Carefully defined data from 50 systems, with fault density ranging from 0 to 10.95 faults/K source lines. Average time in operational phase is 11 months, ranging from 0 to 41 months. Sizes ran from 4.1 to 523.8 K source lines of developed code.

[8]Data from between 3 to 11 projects (exact number not reported). Median size is 103 K source lines and lower and upper quartiles are 56 and 474 source lines. Median period of operation is 18 months; lower and upper quartiles are 11 and 31 months. Median code changed is 4 percent. Median fault density is 1.4 faults/K source lines and lower and upper quartiles are 0.2 and 2.9 faults/K source lines.

obtained from averages if one matched product and development process characteristics with those of the recorded projects.

There are three likely sources of error in these data:

1. The data usually are taken for all faults repaired, not just inherent faults. Thus, they include the repair of faults that were themselves spawned in the repair process. This factor results in estimates that are probably about 1 to 7 percent high, as we will discuss shortly.
2. The data generally represent corrections reported rather than faults repaired. Some faults will be repaired by means of multiple corrections, each correction representing a partial fault repair. This factor results in estimates that are high by some unknown amount.
3. Data collection does not usually continue until all faults are repaired. Hence estimates are low, probably by not more than 15 percent and perhaps around 8 percent.

Although the effects of these error sources are not well known at present, there appears to be substantial cancellation between them. Hence the net error can probably be ignored.

When data are specified for the coding phase, they include all semantic but no syntactic faults. *Semantic faults* are defects arising from programmer error in communicating the *meaning* of what is to be done. An example would be specifying the wrong variable for an operation. *Syntactic faults* result from errors in following the rules of the language in which the program is written. For example, one might not establish the end of a loop properly. Syntactic faults are generally discovered by the compiler or assembler. They usually must be removed before successful compilation or assembly can occur. Semantic faults are hence the faults that are left after successful compilation or assembly. Coding phase inherent faults represent inherent faults found by inspection, since inherent faults found in unit test are noted separately. Subsystem test represents that phase in which developers, working individually or as a team, perform tests that involve more than one unit or module but not the entire system. Testing is generally functional rather than structural in system test. It is usually performed by an independent test team. Ordinarily, the code is under configuration control and a formal failure reporting system is in use. Operation is, of course, the phase after release to the customer. The number of inherent faults found in a phase varies with the length of the phase. Of all life-cycle phases, the operational phase exhibits the greatest variation in length. Hence we potentially have the most severe problem in specifying these data. One possibility would be to define a period such as 2 years after release as the duration for which inherent fault data should be collected. A standard period has not been defined for the data presented here. Fortunately, the proportion of inherent faults found during operation is small compared to that of other phases, so the effect of any variation is considerably moderated.

If we average the data presented in Table 5.2, we obtain the results shown in Table 5.3. The data for the subsystem and system test phases combined are proba-

TABLE 5.3
Means and ranges of fault density data

Phase (or group of phases)	Number of systems providing data	Faults/K source lines	
		Range	Average
C, UT, SS, S	16	13–320	98.0
UT, SS, S	2	16.0–20.3	18.2
SS, S	1	36.2	36.2
S	131	0.01–80.4	4.53
OP	51	0–11.0	1.48

bly unreliable. The data for the system test phase are probably good, since they represent 131 projects. Although operational phase data come from 51 systems, there is some variation due to the length of the phase. If a standard is established for this, the variation will be reduced. The average value will probably not change by more than 1 fault/K lines. In Table 5.4, we have estimated mean inherent fault density remaining at the beginning of several different life-cycle phases. The difference in inherent fault density between the start of coding and the start of unit test is believed to be due to desk checking and code inspections.

Possibly, measures of program complexity can improve the prediction of number of inherent faults. Complexity measures form an active current research area. However, most of the complexity metrics developed to date show a high correlation with program size. They provide little improvement over just program size alone in predicting inherent faults remaining at the start of system test [Sunohara et al. (1981)]. The metrics considered were:

1. McCabe's cyclomatic number [McCabe (1976)],
2. Halstead's effort [Halstead (1977)],
3. a statement count weighted by data references and branches from each statement, and
4. a data flow metric.

TABLE 5.4
Mean fault density remaining at beginning of various phases

Phase	Faults/K source lines
Coding (after compilation/assembly)	99.5
Unit test	19.7
System test	6.01
Operation	1.48

Typical coefficients of determination relating program size and inherent faults range between 0.5 and 0.6, so there is room for predictability improvement. The foregoing conclusions are supported by similar findings by Basili and Hutchens (1983) and Gremillion (1984).

Takahashi and Kamayachi (1985) have studied the effects of other factors on improving inherent fault prediction, based on data taken for 30 projects. After normalizing the inherent fault data by program size (the most important predictive factor) to obtain inherent fault density, they found three significant additional factors:

1. specification change activity, measured in pages of specification changes per K lines of code,
2. average programmer skill, measured in years, and
3. thoroughness of design documentation, measured in pages of developed (new plus modified) design documents per K lines of code.

Greater specification change activity increases the inherent fault density. Greater programmer skill and more thorough design documentation decrease inherent fault density. The effect of all three factors accounts for about 60 percent of the variation in inherent fault density experienced for the projects. In another study [Basili and Hutchens (1983)], it has been shown that use of a disciplined development methodology in a team setting reduces inherent fault density. Most of this current research on inherent fault density has been empirical. At this point, adding insight coming from studies of human problem-solving activity to this empiricism may result in inherent fault density models with greater predictability.

Belady and Lehman (1976) have observed a growing "unstructuredness" in systems that undergo a series of releases. The unstructuredness probably results from several factors such as:

1. different people modifying or repairing the system,
2. the tendency of modifications and repairs to be made locally and cheaply, degrading the global conceptual integrity of the system, and
3. deficiencies in documenting modifications.

It appears likely that the inherent fault density of developed code in multirelease systems will increase from release to release, unless deliberate system restructuring activities are undertaken. We are not aware of presently existing data that indicate the magnitude of the foregoing effect.

The inherent fault density at the start of system test will probably show the least variation from project to project. Earlier measurements will be subject to uncertainties in determining the size of the program until it is well developed and at least partially tested. Later measurements will reflect the fact that reliability goals of different projects vary, hence there will be considerable variation in remaining inherent fault density at release to the field.

Several researchers [for example, Jones (1986)] have raised the issue of the validity of counting instructions or lines of code. However, this question has arisen in the context of *productivity*. This may well be a valid concern, because a software engineer can write a lengthy program and appear more productive, while providing no more function than the more concise designer. This is much less of a problem regarding reliability, since we are only interested in predicting the number of faults introduced. This relates to human error processes and thus appears to be strongly related to the amount of design work done. Hence, a longer program with the same function probably *will* have a larger number of inherent faults. Whatever the disadvantages of instructions or lines of code, they comprise, when clearly defined, an objective, readily determinable metric. It is a metric that can be fully automated. Finally, despite much effort, no one has been able to develop another metric that is consistently superior.

Fault reduction factor. The fault reduction factor B is the ratio of *net* fault reduction to failures experienced as time of operation approaches infinity. Expected values are taken for both the faults and the failures. If this weren't done, the result would depend on the particular realization of input states executed rather than the operational profile. The *total* number of faults corrected is frequently larger than the net number. As a simple example, 100 failures may occur for a system. Let us assume that insufficient information is available to permit the faults that caused 2 of them to be found. However, 98 faults are removed. In the correction process, assume that 5 new faults are spawned. The *total* number of faults corrected is 98 but the *net* number is 93. The fault reduction factor B would be 0.93.

A long period of operation is necessary for obtaining a good count of faults corrected. Correction actions are often only partial in nature. A fault may be repaired only for certain input states [see Musa, Iannino, and Okumoto (1987)]. The factors that must be considered in estimating B are:

1. the degree to which relationships between failures that are the product of the same underlying fault are recognized,
2. detectability (the proportion of failures whose faults can be found, which depends on the amount of information recorded about the failure),
3. the extent to which code inspection independent of test is performed,
4. the degree to which relationships between faults are discerned, and
5. the extent to which new faults are spawned during fault correction.

The proportion of failures whose faults can be identified depends on the amount of information recorded about the failures. It is close to 1 during test phases, although variable during operation. Since we are ordinarily applying B in the period before operation, the latter situation is generally not significant. Independent code inspection during test does not occur for most projects. The first, fourth, and fifth factors probably will not vary much from project to project. There is evidence [Miyamoto (1975) and Musa (1975)] that the fifth one does not. Thus, there is a good possibility that a project-independent value of B can be found, although the value is not known at present.

Some data are currently available that indicate the values of B that typically result from just new fault spawning alone. This is shown in Table 5.5. The range of values is 0.925 to 0.993 and the average is 0.955.

5.1.1.2 INITIAL FAILURE INTENSITY. The initial failure intensity parameter λ_0 may be predicted from

$$\lambda_0 = fK\omega_0. \qquad (5.2)$$

The quantity f is the linear execution frequency of the program. This is the average instruction execution rate r divided by the number of *object* instructions I in the program,

$$f = \frac{r}{I}. \qquad (5.3)$$

The linear execution frequency is the number of times the program would be executed per unit time if it had no branches or loops. Then it would simply execute all instructions in a linear sequence. If the size of the program has been measured in source instructions I_S, an estimate of the number of object instructions I can be made by multiplying by the average expansion ratio Q_X. For a table of approximate expansion ratios, see Jones (1986), p. 49. The fault exposure ratio K relates failure intensity to "fault velocity." The fault velocity $f\omega_0$ is the average rate at which faults in the program would pass by if the program were executed linearly. The concept of fault velocity is illustrated in Figure 5.1.

Fault exposure ratio. The fault exposure ratio K represents the fraction of time that the "passage" results in a failure. It accounts for the following facts:

1. Programs are not generally executed in "straight line" fashion, but have many loops and branches.

TABLE 5.5
Values of fault reduction factor B due to faults spawned while correcting other faults

Reference	System	System size (K source lines)	B
Basili and Perricone (1984)		90	0.94
Weiss (1981)	SEL 1	50.9	0.98
	SEL 2	75.4	>0.925
	SEL 3	85.4	0.952
	ARF	21.8	0.993
Fries (1977)		120	0.939

Instructions with faults are shaded

Linear execution

FIGURE 5.1
Concept of fault velocity.

2. The machine state varies and hence the fault associated with an instruction may or may not be exposed at one particular execution of the instruction.

The effect of machine state in exposing a fault is illustrated in Figure 5.2. Note that when X has a value larger than 25, the faulty program executes correctly by performing A. It also executes correctly by performing B if X is 20 or less. A failure occurs, exposing the fault of the incorrect conditional statement, only if X is larger than 20 but less than or equal to 25. Since faults such as this can cover narrow ranges of data, it is no surprise that K can be small.

At present, K must be determined from a similar program. It may be possible in the future to relate K to program structure in some way. Another possibility is that the range of values of K over different software systems may be small, allowing an average value to be used without excessive error. This could be due to program dynamic structure averaging out in some fashion for programs of any size. The small range would require that the average "structuredness" or decision density not vary from one large program to another. This appears to be the case. It has been shown that cyclomatic complexity, a measure of the number of decisions in a program, is highly correlated with program size [Basili and Hutchens (1983)]. It may be possible to more accurately determine a value for K as a function of some program characteristic. Values of K for several different systems are given in Table 5.6. The systems are described in Table 13.1, except for systems P7, P9, P10, and P15. Systems P7 and P9 are identical copies of an operating system running in different environments. System P10 is a different operating system and P15 is a large real-time system. For details, see Musa (1979), systems SS1A, SS1C, SS4, and 14C, respectively. The average value of K is 4.20×10^{-7} failures/fault and the values cover a total range of 7.5 to 1. It will be seen from the values of K that intervals between failures typically represent cycling through the program a large number of times.

Correct program	Faulty program
IF x > 25	IF x > 20 ---- Fault
THEN A	THEN A
ELSE B	ELSE B

FIGURE 5.2
Effect of machine state in exposing a fault.

TABLE 5.6
Fault exposure ratio
on different projects

System designator	K ($\times 10^{-7}$)
T1	1.87
T2	2.15
T3	4.11
T4	10.6
T5	4.2
T6	3.97
P7	4.43
P9	5.64
P10	1.41
P15	2.09
T16	3.03
T19	4.54
T20	6.5

To evaluate K for other projects for which data may be available, we require only four items of information:

1. a set of failure data sufficient to permit $B\phi = \lambda_0/\nu_0$ to be estimated,
2. the fault reduction factor B,
3. program size in object instructions, and
4. average instruction execution rate.

Care must be taken to insure that the failure data are true execution time data or that appropriate adjustments are performed to make them so. You can find execution time intervals from clock time intervals by multiplying the clock time intervals by the average computer utilization ρ_C. If failure intervals are from the test phase, they must be adjusted to the operational phase by multiplying by the testing compression factor (Chapter 6). Data in the form of failures per time interval are adjusted by dividing by the average computer utilization and the testing compression factor. Estimation of the quantity λ_0/ν_0 of the basic execution time model is now done. The linear execution frequency f is computed from the average instruction execution rate and program size. The value of K can now be determined from Equations (5.1) and (5.2) as

$$K = \frac{1}{Bf} \frac{\lambda_0}{\nu_0}. \tag{5.4}$$

Example 5.1. A health insurance claim processing program, involving 50,000 deliverable executable source instructions, has just been turned over to the system test group. Previous experience in this development environment for similar programs indicates a fault density of 6 faults/1000 delivered executable source instructions. The fault reduction factor is 1. We have a fault exposure ratio of 2×10^{-7} failure/fault. The code expansion ratio (object instructions per source instruction) is 4. The instruction execution rate of the target machine is 3.33 million object instructions/CPU sec. If we apply the basic execution time model, what values of the total failures and initial failure intensity parameters can we expect?

We compute the inherent faults ω_0 from

$$\omega_0 = \omega_I \Delta I \; . \tag{5.5}$$

Note that ΔI is the number of developed source instructions and ω_I is the fault density. Thus

$$\omega_0 = \left[\frac{6 \text{ faults}}{1000 \text{ inst}} \right] (50{,}000 \text{ inst})$$

$$= 300 \text{ faults}.$$

From Equation (5.1) we have

$$\nu_0 = \frac{\omega_0}{B}$$

$$= \frac{300}{1}$$

$$= 300 \text{ failures}.$$

Now

$$I = I_S Q_X \; , \tag{5.6}$$

where Q_X is the code expansion ratio. Thus

$$I = (50{,}000 \text{ inst}) \, (4)$$

$$= 200{,}000 \text{ inst}.$$

The linear execution frequency f is

$$f = \frac{r}{I}$$

$$= \frac{3.33 \times 10^6 \text{ inst/CPU sec}}{0.2 \times 10^6 \text{ inst}}$$

$$= 16.7 \text{ cycles/CPU sec}.$$

Using Equation (5.2) we have

$$\lambda_0 = f K \omega_0$$

$$= (16.7 \text{ cycles/CPU sec}) (2 \times 10^{-7} \text{ failure/fault}) (300 \text{ faults})$$

$$= 10^{-3} \text{ failures/CPU sec}. \qquad \blacksquare$$

5.1.2   Estimation

We can use estimation to determine the execution time component parameters of either the basic or logarithmic Poisson execution time models as execution progresses. For the basic model, estimation can be used to refine the values established by prediction. We will use maximum likelihood estimation, although other methods are also possible [see Musa, Iannino, and Okumoto (1987)]. It is most efficient to use a program to do the calculations. Hence, we will not discuss them in detail but will take a graphical view.

The essential data required for estimation are the failure times or failures per time interval (grouped data) experienced during execution. The process is illustrated schematically for the basic model in Figure 5.3. A set of failure intensities has been plotted against execution time. They represent number of failures in a time interval divided by that time interval. The basic execution time model provides the basis for plotting the dashed line of anticipated failure intensity against execution time. Two parameters determine this line, the initial failure intensity λ_0 and the total expected failures ν_0. The first parameter is represented by the vertical axis intercept. Values of the parameters are chosen to maximize the likelihood of occurrence of the set of failure intensities that have been experienced. In an approximate sense, the curve is being fit to the data indicated. Some derived quantities are also illustrated on the plot.

FIGURE 5.3
Conceptual view of parameter estimation.

The foregoing parameters were selected to describe the basic model because they had the most immediate connection with the characteristics of the product and the development process. We can also define a parameter ϕ, the per-fault hazard rate, given by

$$\phi = \frac{\lambda_0}{\omega_0}. \tag{5.7}$$

The quantity ω_0 is the number of faults inherent in the code. Note that the decrement in failure intensity per failure is given by $\lambda_0/\nu_0 = B\phi$, where B is the fault reduction factor or ratio of net fault reduction to failures experienced. We can describe the model in terms of ν_0 and $B\phi$. This alternative formulation of the model simplifies parameter estimation. Conversion between different parameters is readily accomplished.

Since estimation of the parameters is a statistical process, you will also wish to determine confidence intervals. The curve should now be viewed as a band. The width increases with the magnitude of the confidence interval. A 90 percent confidence interval requires a wider band than a 75 percent one. The confidence interval for λ_0 is given by the range of vertical axis intercepts.

The process of estimating the parameters of the logarithmic Poisson model, initial failure intensity λ_0 and failure intensity decay parameter θ, is analogous.

To obtain some idea of the accuracy with which model parameters are being estimated, look at plots of the estimates as functions of execution time. The values should be constant if the program is stable except for repairs. A confidence interval estimated late in the period of execution will be a reasonable approximation to the range of values in which the parameter actually lies. Hence, a confidence interval estimated earlier can be compared with it to check the quality of the estimation.

Example 5.2. We will look at how use of calendar time as the basis for modeling can lead to results that are not useful. In Figure 5.3, we have an increasing spacing of failures or decreasing failure intensity in execution time, as more and more faults are removed. For execution time, you will obtain a finite estimate for total failures. Assume that the project is in the failure-correction-personnel-limited phase. This resource can handle, on the average, a fixed number of failures per day. Therefore, testing will be paced such that failures will have an approximately constant spacing or constant failure intensity in calendar time. This is shown in Figure 5.4. With no trend in the failure intensities, the estimate of total failures is undefined or infinite. It is not possible to predict when various failure intensity objectives will be reached, as it is when failure intensity is expressed in execution time. ∎

During the initial use of estimation, accuracy can be low (generally indicated by large confidence intervals) because of the small failure samples available. Note that accuracy is primarily related to number of failures in the sample. If data are in the form of failures per interval, you can have an adequate sample size even though the number of intervals may be small. We can sometimes improve accuracy by taking a weighted average of previous parameter predictions along with parameter estimates. The weights would be functions of the sample

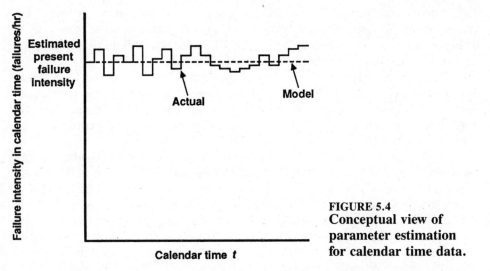

FIGURE 5.4
Conceptual view of parameter estimation for calendar time data.

size. It is probably best that the weights for the estimates be zero until the estimates have an accuracy within an order of magnitude of that of the predictions. We would then set the relative weights proportional to the relative estimated accuracies. The weights for the predictions would be set to zero when the estimates become superior in accuracy by about an order of magnitude. Adjust the confidence intervals as well as the parameter values proper by this technique.

The refinement of parameters raises many practical issues relating to the collection of failure data. Project-specific techniques are discussed in Chapter 6. We will cover general data collection planning and procedures in Chapter 8.

GROUPED FAILURE DATA. Many projects collect grouped failure data (failures in some time interval) rather than individual failure times or intervals. This is slightly easier to do, involving somewhat less data collection effort, particularly if the time interval is a natural unit like a day. The disadvantage is decreased accuracy in estimating parameters, which we will examine. We will treat this topic in more detail in the Discussion at the end of this chapter. A summary is given here of grouping for fixed time periods. We will consider both the basic and logarithmic Poisson execution time models. Estimation of the parameter that affects the rate of failure intensity reduction is examined in each case ($B\phi$ or $\lambda_0\theta$, respectively). The initial failure intensities and all derived quantities depend on the foregoing parameters and their accuracies in the cases of both models. Note that the study is based on a representative rather than an exhaustive set of parameter values. The accuracy depends on the parameter values. Hence, our results will convey general effects rather than precise behavior.

The effect of grouping will be quantified by comparing the observed information in the grouped data to that in the failure time data. Observed information affects the accuracy of the estimates. More information leads to greater accuracy. Let I_g be the ratio of the observed information in the grouped data to that in the failure time data. Values of I_g which are less than 1 show that our estimates are more variable for grouped data. Values of I_g greater than 1 indicate otherwise. It is *expected* that I_g will generally be less than 1 since there will inevitably be some loss of information in neglecting the actual failure times.

Results are presented in Tables 5.7 and 5.8 for the basic and logarithmic Poisson models. Note that the quality of the estimates for the basic model is excellent if the number of groups is, say, 10 or more. Quality of estimates for the logarithmic Poisson model is markedly inferior. It does not even become satisfactory until there are at least 200 groups or so.

If data have been gathered in grouped form, there are situations where it may be desirable to convert them to failure times or failure intervals. The most realistic method for doing this is to assign the failure times randomly within the interval in which the data have been collected. We use a uniform distribution, which reflects the fact that we have no knowledge that would favor assignment to any particular part of the collection interval. Let us consider the error introduced into the estimation of the parameter $B\phi$ or $\lambda_0\theta$. The amount of error will vary with the values of the parameters. We will consider representative cases, illustrated in Tables 5.9 (simulated data) and 5.10 (real project data). Randomization does not cause errors in estimation of $B\phi$ or $\lambda_0\theta$ greater than about 15 percent for either model, even when there are as few as five groups.

5.2 CALENDAR TIME COMPONENT

Parameters have the same values for the calendar time component of both the basic and logarithmic Poisson execution time models. Refer to Table 2.2 to obtain

TABLE 5.7
Values of I_g for equal time groupings for the basic execution time model

Number of failures	Number of groups	I_g
100	4	0.899
	8	0.969
	15	0.992
	29	0.995
	48	0.999
	72	0.999
50	5	0.941
	11	0.992
	21	0.997
	42	0.999
25	8	0.987
	16	0.999
	32	1.002

TABLE 5.8
Values of I_g for equal time groupings for the logarithmic Poisson execution time model

Number of groups	I_g
10	0.118
19	0.163
47	0.104
94	0.411
156	0.538
312	1.032

a good overview of these parameters. Usually, the failure correction personnel resource has the greatest effect on calendar time prediction. This is particularly true for a system released to the field with moderate failure intensity.

Only the computer time and failure identification personnel resources can be simultaneously limiting. It is not a frequent occurrence, since it is required that

$$\frac{\mu_C}{\mu_I} = \frac{\theta_C}{\theta_I} = \frac{P_C \rho_C}{P_I} \tag{5.8}$$

for the situation to occur. When two resources are simultaneously limiting, the ratios of calendar time to execution time for both resources are identical. Hence either can be used to compute calendar time.

On some projects, separate failure identification and failure correction personnel are not used. Each person does both jobs. If these resources are thus com-

ABLE 5.9
Results of randomizing grouped data for some simulated data sets

Model group	Number of failures	Number of groups	Maximum likelihood estimate of $B\phi$ or $\lambda_0\theta$ using		
			Original data	Randomly converted data	Uniformly converted data
Exponential	100	4	0.293×10^{-4}	0.266×10^{-4}	0.257×10^{-4}
($B\phi = 0.3 \times 10^{-4}$)		15	0.287×10^{-4}	0.284×10^{-4}	0.275×10^{-4}
	50	5	0.347×10^{-4}	0.401×10^{-4}	0.268×10^{-4}
		11	0.327×10^{-4}	0.326×10^{-4}	0.265×10^{-4}
Geometric	100	10	0.283×10^{-3}	0.253×10^{-3}	0.244×10^{-3}
($\lambda_0\theta = 0.25 \times 10^{-3}$)		20	0.307×10^{-3}	0.301×10^{-3}	0.321×10^{-3}
	50	10	0.246×10^{-3}	0.241×10^{-3}	0.210×10^{-3}
		20	0.249×10^{-3}	0.257×10^{-3}	0.213×10^{-3}

TABLE 5.10
Results of randomizing grouped data for systems T38 and T39

Model group	System	Maximum likelihood estimate of $B\phi$ or $\lambda_0\theta$ using		
		Original data	Randomly converted data	Uniformly converted data
Exponential	T38	0.105×10^{-1}	0.122×10^{-1}	0.089×10^{-1}
	T39	0.664×10^{-6}	0.661×10^{-6}	0.641×10^{-6}
Geometric	T38	0.207×10^{-1}	0.227×10^{-1}	0.170×10^{-1}
	T39	0.377×10^{-5}	0.354×10^{-5}	0.341×10^{-5}

bined, you must merge them and the resource requirements as far as the calendar time model is concerned.

The question may arise of the effect of deviations in the values of calendar time component parameters from the values we have predicted for them. Deviations are most likely to occur for the resource usage parameters, since we may be using values taken from another project or averages over a group of projects. The effect can be determined by doing a sensitivity study. One chooses parameter values on either side of the estimated values in accordance with the range of variation expected. The resultant calendar time, resource use, and cost variations can then be determined. It is usually easiest to do this with a simple simulation, but there may be times when an analytic study is possible.

5.2.1 Interpretation of Resource Definitions

Failure identification involves the activity of testing, the determination of what failures have occurred, and the documentation of the nature of the failures. Failure correction starts from the point where failures are identified. It includes fault identification, which is the determination of the fault that caused the failure, and fault correction. The process ends when the fault has been corrected. The person performing the fix must prove through appropriate testing, to the satisfaction of the test team, that the input state that previously caused the failure no longer does so. It may also be necessary to run certain regression tests to show that the fix, to a reasonable degree of confidence, did not adversely affect other input states. The failure correction activity includes the task of program change documentation *if* required to be completed during test rather than after.

Computer time is the measure that is used for allocating computer resources; it is not necessarily the same as execution time. In a dedicated facility that is allocated to a single user at a time, it may be clock time. Frequently, it is the residence time of the program in the machine (perhaps divided by the number of programs in the case of multiprogramming).

The key concept in determining what resource quantities should be counted under special conditions that may exist on different projects is the idea of a resource being *limiting*. Does the resource limit the pace at which test and failure correction for the program can proceed? For example, support staff such as programming librarians and technical writers are not counted because they do not directly constitute a limiting resource. Of course, the amount of support available may affect the environment in which the project operates, so that the *resource usage parameters* (μ_C, μ_F, μ_I, θ_C, θ_I) may be a function of the support level. That is, a higher level of support may reduce the amount of work done by the failure identification and failure correction personnel.

The failure identification activity usually includes the generation of trouble reports. This task must be performed by failure identification personnel for each failure before other activities related to the failure can take place and is thus limiting. Tasks associated with test planning and test case development are usually (but not always) completed before the test effort and not included. Including the foregoing tasks improperly in making resource usage estimates can lead to appreciable error because of their substantial size. One large project [Angus, Bowen, and VanDenBerg (1983)] reported 15 percent of test activity devoted to test planning and 35 percent to test case development. Only 50 percent was used for test conduct and analysis and could be considered limiting.

Test planning or replanning or test procedure debugging may be performed by failure identification personnel *as part of the test effort*. Often they require work proportional to the amount of testing (execution time) or the number of failures or both. We adjust the debug environment parameters μ_I (failure identification work per failure) and θ_I (failure identification work per unit execution time) to reflect this fact. At other times, the work is not proportional to these factors but does require effort by failure identification personnel. Then the number available should be reduced to reflect the time taken by these tasks.

As another example of interpretation of limiting resources, one project created test cases by recording data in the field and then processing them. The rate at which the cases could be generated was limited, and this paced the testing effort. The project determined the execution time associated with the tests that could be generated per week. The available computer time was then set at the minimum of the actual and foregoing values.

Generally a problem review board is not a limiting resource in the sense that failure identification or correction personnel are. Ordinarily you wouldn't halt testing so that the review board could catch up on a backlog of problems. The board causes a fixed delay that should be added to the total test period. Visualize test as a pipeline of a fixed length that represents the amount of processing done on each failure. A certain number of failures must be corrected or flow through the pipe before the failure intensity objective is reached. One determines calendar time primarily by flow rate through the pipe and number of failures processed. Limiting resources appear as bottlenecks that slow the flow. The problem review board appears as an added fixed length of pipe. You should add the *maximum* expected delay.

5.2.2 Planned Parameters

The planned parameters of the calendar time component of the model are easily determined. These parameters consist of resource quantities available and their utilizations. They are:

P_C: available computer time (measured in terms of prescribed work periods),

P_F: number of available failure correction personnel,

P_I: number of available failure identification personnel,

ρ_C: computer utilization factor during the computer-limited period, and

ρ_F: failure correction personnel utilization factor during the failure-correction-personnel-limited period.

RESOURCE QUANTITIES. The project manager is usually faced with the task of determining the proper resource quantities. This is really a system engineering problem of trade-offs between reliability, schedules, and resources, as described in Chapter 7. We obtain the resource quantities available by identification (that is, asking the person responsible). Note that "available" is not the same thing as "used." Personnel are simply counted, regardless of the length or time of their working hours. These two factors are considered only:

1. in counting computer time available, because computer time is measured in terms of prescribed work periods,
2. in converting calendar time hours to calendar time days, and
3. in converting calendar time days to dates.

The parameter P_C represents available computer time in terms of prescribed work periods. For example, if available computer time per week is 80 hr and the prescribed work week is 40 hr, then $P_C = 2$. This unit was chosen so that computer resources would be stated in the same units as personnel.

The prescribed work period represents "available time" or the total amount of time that the average member of the project can work *upon request*. In general, you establish available time by company policy or the practical consideration of the maximum time one can reasonably request a person to work. Normally, any one person will not work at the limit for an extended period, but it can happen. "Available" also implies reasonably short notice. It does not imply that the project member must be standing by for the available time. It *does* imply, for example, that he or she must be able to work 2 hr overtime sometime before the next day, when requested at 4 P.M. It also implies that the persons involved are not partially allocated to other tasks that take priority over the limiting resource activity. If they are, that time (in terms of prescribed work periods) must be subtracted from the number of persons available.

To calculate available computer time, determine the number of hours the computer is ready for use from a policy viewpoint. For example, although a computer may be available 24 hr/day, 7 days/week from a physical viewpoint, it may be operated for only 2 shifts on 6 days. Determine the maximum part of this time that *can* be allocated to your project, though you may not use all the time unless pressed. Subtract unavailable periods such as maintenance time, down time, and file backup time. The result is hours of availability, which should be expressed in terms of prescribed work periods. Consider the effect of work hours and procedures on availability. For example, suppose that all work to be done on the computer is interactive. If the machine is operated for 16 hr/day but personnel work one shift of 8 hr, availability is really only 8 hr. Availability in this case could be expanded to 16 hr by dividing personnel into 2 shifts or staggering their work hours in various ways. Alternatively, use of the machine for 8 hr in a noninteractive mode would accomplish the same objective. The calculation is normally made on a weekly basis, with the prescribed work period equal to the product of the workday and the workweek. The workday is the average hr per day personnel are available to work. The workweek is the average days per week personnel are available to work.

We obtain the best estimate of the number of failure correction personnel P_F by counting the number of programmers available who were occupied full time in coding the units of the system under test. The parameter P_I represents the number of members of the test team. This is the number of personnel familiar with system requirements and test plans and available for executing tests, verifying proper operation of the system, and identifying departures from proper operation.

We assume that each person involved in failure identification can run and examine the results from any test that is made. Failure correction personnel are assumed to work only on failures that have been attributed to their respective design areas. A person who can and does work at either failure identification or failure correction, depending on where staff is required, should be included in *both* counts. This does not represent duplication, at least to a first approximation, because only one resource at a time can be limiting. Inaccuracy arises only if there aren't enough people to perform the nonlimiting function.

Personnel who are not being fully utilized may be assigned other tasks without violating the assumptions of the calendar time component of the model. However, they must be *available* for their primary task when needed. For example, failure correction personnel may be transferred to other projects in the latter stages of a project. Infrequent but priority demands will be made on them for correction of failures on the original project. Availability may be taken care of with "suitable" replacements, suitable meaning having the same skill level and experience with respect to the project as the original personnel.

When programs are executed at multiple sites, some adjustments are necessary. Add personnel and computer resources P_F, P_I, and P_C for all sites. Note that in making this addition, we are implicitly assuming that the *location* of the resources is unimportant. This is generally true if the failure identification personnel are reasonably well distributed among the sites. If they can be redistributed when necessary, or if they can run tests remotely, then it is also true. It is correct to add P_C's from computers of different power, since the power differences are accounted for by adjusting execution times. The parameters μ_F, μ_I and θ_C will normally be the same for all sites.

RESOURCE UTILIZATIONS. Resource utilizations are generally estimated from formula or practical experience. We are interested in their maximum practical values for the limiting period of the resource. This is not necessarily the same as the values that may actually occur.

The resource utilization of failure identification personnel ρ_I is 1. It is not restricted by any queueing constraints.

The computer utilization factor ρ_C is often either implicitly or explicitly controlled to maintain satisfactory turnaround time. If testing is scheduled and organized, and there are few unpredictable demands for computer time, the computer utilization factor may approach 1. However, even in a scheduled testing situation, demands for computer time for failure correction often occur at unpredictable times. The most likely situation is one in which the demand for computer time is dependent on many complex factors. Thus it is essentially unpredictable and can best be modeled as being random. One approach to controlling utilization is to provide sufficient hardware to maintain the utilization at an economic optimum. We minimize the sum of computing costs and and wait time (for response) costs of software engineers. When utilization is high, response is poor and salary costs (due to waiting) will be high, although direct computing costs will be low. When utilization is low, response will be excellent and salary costs will drop. However, direct computing costs will be high. The minimum overall cost will occur at some intermediate value. This approach is described in more detail in Musa, Iannino, and Okumoto (1987).

The resource utilization to be selected for failure correction is based on preventing an excessive backlog of failures awaiting correction from building up in any area of code. Such a backlog might hamper further testing in that area. Note that the area of code will generally be associated with a particular person responsible. We compute the failure correction personnel utilization factor ρ_F using

$$\rho_F = (1 - P_{m_Q}^{1/P_F})^{1/m_Q}, \tag{5.9}$$

where P_{m_Q} is the probability that the number of failures awaiting correction by any debugger does not equal or exceed m_Q. In Figure 5.5, curves of utilization are plotted against number of failure correction personnel for various values of queue length. The plot is constructed such that 90 percent of the queues that occur are less than the specified value. Data taken on projects T1, T2, T3, and T4 (projects described in Table 13.1) showed that the 90 percent points for queue lengths occurred at 7, 4, 5, and 5 failures, respectively. Thus it appears reasonable for the present to assume that the failure queue length is controlled so that it does not equal or exceed 5 with probability 0.9. The control is not usually conscious. However, the test team generally has some sense of the backlog of failures and paces testing accordingly. The queue lengths that you observe have a fair amount of consistency, as indicated. It may be possible to refine the values with more knowledge of the effect of backed-up failures on the debugging process. The foregoing computation can be incorporated in software reliability estimation programs.

The foregoing relationship assumes that the assignment of failures for correction can be modeled by random assignment among all failure correction person-

FIGURE 5.5
Failure correction personnel utilization.

nel. This is a reasonable approximation if each programmer has code in the part of the system that is being tested. If this is not the case, it may still be possible to handle the situation with an appropriate correction. For example, we can adjust the number of failure correction personnel to the average number to whom failures can be assigned. One common case in which the foregoing situation occurs is that of a program that is highly modular in terms of function. Such a program is often tested in a modular fashion so that only some of the failure correction personnel are involved at any given time. Note, however, that it is possible to tolerate a somewhat longer failure queue for each programmer because a backlog of failures has less effect on another function. Hence, the actual effect on calendar time may not be large.

5.2.3 Resource Usage Parameters

The resource usage parameters describe resource usage as a function of execution time and failures experienced. They are:

θ_C: average computer time expended per unit execution time,

θ_I: average failure identification work expended per unit execution time,

μ_C: average computer time required per failure,

μ_F: average failure correction work required per failure, and

μ_I: average failure identification work required per failure.

The values of the resource usage parameters of the calendar time model represent *average* values of resource expenditure. They appear to be dependent on the factors of programmer skill level, level of task difficulty, and development environment. By "environment" we are referring to characteristics such as batch debugging versus interactive debugging, debugging aids available, computer used, language used, and administrative and documentation overhead associated with corrections. The values are accurate if measured for the project on which they are used, and there are no major changes in the factors after the measurements are taken. Values from another project can be applicable if it is similar to the project on which they will be used in the foregoing three aspects. If both projects are of reasonable size, differences in the first two factors tend to become small, and applicability is dependent primarily on the similarity of development environment. This averaging effect has been noticed on projects as small as 5 programmers and 5000 instructions. When there is a marked difference in, say, programmer skill level between two small projects, it still may be possible to apply parameter values from one project to the other. One estimates appropriate multiplicative factors. If failure correction is not done on the test machine (and there is sufficient time for it on another machine), the parameter μ_C will be 0.

ESTIMATION FROM DATA. The resource usage parameters may be evaluated by collecting data on failure identification work, failure correction work, and computer usage at various values of execution time. We also record failures experienced. Then we fit the data with a transformation of the resource usage model expressed in incremental terms,

$$\frac{\Delta \chi_r}{\Delta \tau} = \theta_r + \mu_r \, \frac{\Delta m (\tau)}{\Delta \tau} , \qquad (5.10)$$

using a least squares criterion. Note that $\Delta \chi_r$ represents usage of the generic resource r. The subscript r becomes C for computer time, F for failure correction work, or I for failure identification work. The quantity $\Delta \tau$ is execution time; Δm, failures identified (for resource I), corrected (for F), or an average of the two (for C). Note that Δm and $\Delta \tau$ are not independent of each other, since they are related through the execution time component of the model.

A relatively painless approach to collection of the data for the estimation of the resource usage parameters μ_C, μ_F, μ_I, θ_C, and θ_I is to obtain weekly resource expenditure totals from each person involved in testing. It is also possible to collect data on a per-failure basis. This will be more accurate but will require much more data collection effort. Note that time spent in proving suspected failures false is included in either approach and thus will be apportioned among real failures. In cases where only one person is identifying the failures, the data gathered will be individual-dependent unless we average data for several "one identifier" projects involving different persons. The least squares fit to Equation (5.10) is unweighted. We treat all data points equally. Usually measurements made of the parameters will represent net times. The measures must be increased by a suitable overhead factor to account for overhead such as vacations, holidays, absences, training, and administrative activities. A common value is 1.67. This is based on typical figures of 15 percent for vacations, holidays, and absences and 25 percent for training and administrative activities.

If you can obtain better estimates of the resource usage parameters as the test period proceeds, you should use them. A "jump change" may occur in many of the quantities being computed as a result, but the quantities should henceforth be more accurate.

DELPHI AND OTHER ESTIMATION METHODS. If determination from data is not feasible, a "Delphi" survey of the members of the project may be useful. The Delphi survey involves taking an average of informed judgments. It appears to work best when periods of full communication between participants alternate with independently developed judgments [Boehm (1981)]. A coordinator should explain the purpose of the survey, define all the parameters carefully, and make sure everyone understands what they involve. This is best done in a meeting, so questions can be asked. Then each person writes down *independently* his or her best estimates of what the parameters should be, based on experience and careful consideration. The coordinator summarizes and presents the distribution of estimates for each parameter. The group discusses the results, focusing on the reasons for any wide variations in estimates. Then another round of independent estimation ensues, usually resulting in less variation. The process continues until little further convergence occurs. The mean of the estimates is used for each parameter value. These estimates are often surprisingly reasonable! It appears that people can estimate work time best in direct hours expended (that is, *you* should compute and apply overhead factors).

It appears likely that some or all of the resource usage parameters will prove to be constant over wide varieties or classes of projects. As more data are collected, we may gain a deeper understanding of what ranges of values these parameters can have and on what factors they are dependent. This knowledge should make it possible to establish appropriate parameter values from previously collected data for projects with similar characteristics. It may not be necessary to collect data for the project in question.

We currently have some data available for the failure correction work per failure μ_F. The data are illustrated in Table 5.11. Two components of this work are recorded. *Fault identification* is the work to diagnose the fault, given the identified failure. *Fault correction* is the work to design, install, and test the fix for a known fault. We also have total failure correction work. All the values except the Musa and Iannino ones come from data collected on a per-failure basis. The latter values were obtained from resource expenditure data [Musa (1979)] that were recorded weekly, along with number of failures and execution time. The data were fit by Iannino, using Equation (5.10) in a least squares sense. The systems on which the Musa data were taken are described in Musa, Iannino, and Okumoto (1987). The values are net, without provision for any overhead factor. Means are given, and also means adjusted by an overhead factor of 1.67.

TABLE 5.11
Failure correction effort per failure (in system test unless noted)

Reference	System	Fault identification (person hr)	Fault correction (person hr)	Failure correction (person hr)
Ostrand and Weyuker (1982)				5.5[1]
Weiss (1981)	SEL 1	4	1.8	5.8
	SEL 2	4	3	7
	SEL 3	1	2	3
Presson (1981)	A1	3.3	2.6	5.9[2]
	A2	2.4	2.4	4.8[2]
	B1	3.5	3.1	6.6
	B2	4.5	3.3	7.8[3]
	C	2.9	2.2	5.1
Musa, Iannino,	T1			4.42
and Okumoto (1987)	T2			6.88
	T3			0.58
	T4			0.68
Shooman and Bolsky (1975)		2.46	1.98	4.44
Mean value (system test)				4.54
Mean value with overhead (system test)				7.58

[1]For unit test and system test

[2]First and second halves of system test for same project

[3]Test prior to system test

There are also some values available for the other resource expenditures, failure identification effort and computer time. These values also come from data of Musa (1979), fit by Equation (5.10) in a least squares sense. They are given in Tables 5.12 and 5.13, respectively, along with the means. The values for the failure identification work parameters with an overhead factor of 1.67 are given also. Note that all four systems in each table were run on a computer with an average instruction execution rate of 280,000 object instructions/CPU sec. The failure

TABLE 5.12
Failure identification effort (in person hr)

Reference	System designator	Effort per CPU hr component[1]	Effort per failure component
Musa (1979)	T1	9.92	0.23
	T2	3.24	3.89
	T3	4.77	0.53
	T4	5.70	0.24
	Mean value	5.91	1.22
	Mean value with overhead	9.87	2.04

[1]Based on machine with instruction processing rate of 280,000 object instructions/CPU sec.

TABLE 5.13
Computer time (in CPU hr) used in failure identification and correction

Reference	System designator	Computer time per CPU hr component	Computer time per failure component[1]
Musa (1979)	T1	4.80	1.56
	T2	1.73	1.73
	T3	1.06	0.38
	T4	2.13	0.63
	Mean value	2.43	1.08

[1]Based on machine with instruction processing rate of 280,000 object instructions/CPU sec.

identification work per CPU hr may be a function of the computer on which the application is run, but this is not known for certain at present. The computer time per failure probably will be less for faster machines. It may be inversely proportional to the average instruction execution rate, as the function that has to be performed per failure may be almost constant.

SPECIAL CONSIDERATIONS. Poor computer turnaround time can affect the pace at which failures are corrected. Suppose that the total nonproductive wait time involved in correcting each failure is substantial in comparison with average failure work time required per failure. Then μ_F should be increased by the ratio of failure correction work plus wait time to failure correction work time. Note that there is usually only one approach to the machine for each failure identification. Hence, turnaround time has little effect on that process.[1]

If the fault reduction factor B is substantially different from 1, then it may be necessary to adjust the μ_C and μ_F parameters that would ordinarily be employed by multiplying by B. This is done because resources required for the repair work tend to be most closely related to the number of faults removed. However, for practicality they are measured in terms of failures experienced.

5.3 SUPPORTING COMPUTER PROGRAMS — RECOMMENDED FEATURES AND USE

5.3.1 Features

Experience with many projects and their needs over more than 10 years has indicated at least four computer programs that are useful in the *application* of software

---

[1]Shooman and Bolsky (1975) have collected data that indicate an average of 0.61 runs per failure for failure identification and 1.35 runs per failure for failure correction.

reliability measurement and prediction. This experience, and the construction and use of various versions of these programs, has led to some considerations regarding the *features* of these programs. The features are discussed here, and the *design*, in Appendix F. Of course, there are additional programs that may be useful for research purposes, but we are not discussing them.

The programs should be designed as a compatible set so that they can function with each other. When they have the same inputs, the formats should be identical. Human interfaces should be as similar as possible, using the same commands, command formats, and input variable names. The programs should allow for data input as failure times or grouped data (failures per time interval) to accommodate the varying practices of different projects. Failure times are preferred, because they retain the most information and are therefore most likely to yield accurate estimates and predictions. In any case, it is easy to convert from one form to the other. In general, programs of this kind can be used for any project phase in which the program is executing and experiencing failures. Also, they can ordinarily be used for hardware as well as software. Failure trends and predictions are not usually dependent on the source of the failures.

One program [Musa, Hamilton, and Hollander (1983) and Musa and Hollander (1983)] has been found to be essential. We shall call it a *tabular program* because of the form of its output. This program accepts failure intervals and calendar time component parameters as inputs. The output is a snapshot of status for a software system at a point in time. The program should estimate execution time component parameters for either the basic or logarithmic Poisson execution time models. It computes present failure intensity. It also computes the additional failures, execution time, and calendar time required to reach whatever failure intensity objective the user may specify. The date of reaching this objective is also computed. The foregoing quantities and their 50, 75, 90, and 95 percent confidence intervals are computed for whichever model has been selected. The output is illustrated in Figure 5.6. Various control variables provide the capability to select different program options and input a title. Defaults are taken if they are not specified. The program includes the capability to adjust failure times for evolving programs (Section 6.3) and can both use the resulting intervals for computation and output them to other programs. When this capability is used, information on total code and developed code at each failure is required.

Although not as essential, it is very useful to have a plotting program as well, since it provides a running history of a project and can highlight trends. It plots the data that would be obtained by running the tabular program again and again as the failure intervals available for estimation increase one at a time. This program has the same inputs as the tabular program. In addition, it has a set of plot control variables (with defaults) to let you select the plots you desire and the detailed format of the plots. You should be able to plot any of the quantities that are computed for the table of the tabular program. They can be plotted against either execution time, calendar time, date, or number of failures. It is also often useful to be able to plot total execution time. This is the time from start of execution to time predicted for meeting the failure intensity objective. The usefulness of

SOFTWARE RELIABILITY PREDICTION
LOG POISSON MODEL
SYSTEM T2

BASED ON SAMPLE OF   54 TEST FAILURES
EXECUTION TIME IS   32.78 HR
FAILURE INTENSITY OBJECTIVE IS .36e-01 FAILURES/CPU HR
CALENDAR TIME TO DATE IS   74 DAYS
PRESENT DATE   5/31/74

	CONF. LIMITS				MOST LIKELY	CONF. LIMITS			
	95%	90%	75%	50%		50%	75%	90%	95%
FAILURE INTENSITY DECAY	.0426	.0456	.0503	.0548	.0611	.0675	.0720	.0767	.0796
FAILURE INTENSITIES (FAILURES/1000 CPU HR)									
INITIAL F.I.	6440	7185	8563	10172	13054	16856	20260	24600	27873
PRESENT F.I.	377.8	391.5	415.0	440.1	480.5	527.9	566.5	611.8	643.8

*** ADDITIONAL REQUIREMENTS TO MEET FAILURE INTENSITY OBJECTIVE ***

	95%	90%	75%	50%	MOST LIKELY	50%	75%	90%	95%
FAILURES	30	31	34	37	42	49	55	62	68
EXEC. TIME (CPU HR)	315.5	329.0	352.3	377.8	420.2	472.5	517.2	573.1	614.9
CAL. TIME (DAYS)	142.1	148.4	159.2	171.0	190.8	215.2	236.1	262.3	281.9
COMPLETION DATE	121874	122674	11075	12875	22375	33175	42975	60375	63075

FIGURE 5.6
Sample project status report as generated by program.

this plot is described in Section 6.3. To avoid clutter on the plot, you should be able to determine whether confidence intervals should be plotted, and if so, which ones. A capability to "window" and blow up on a separate page any section of the plot you want to examine on a more detailed basis is frequently valuable. Early values of quantities plotted can sometimes be noisy. Consequently, it should be possible to select the point at which plotting starts to reduce excessive clutter. Finally, you should have some control over the labeling of the plot and be able to furnish an appropriate title. A sample plot is shown in Figure 5.7. This program should also be able to adjust failure times for evolving programs.

A simulation program is useful for system studies. It permits various parameters to be varied so that "what if" questions can be answered. It performs a function equivalent to that of running the tabular program repetitively, with different values of parameters. The results are most readily interpretable if plotted. For example, you can look at the effect of changes in failure intensity objective on program release date (that is, date of meeting the failure intensity objective). It is possible to either estimate the execution time component parameters from failure intervals or input them as parameters that can be varied.

A failure log conversion program has frequently proved to be helpful. Such a program processes failure information as recorded in failure logs or trouble reports and converts it to failure intervals. It handles time uncertainties (Section 6.2.2) and multiple copies of programs (Section 6.2.3), including those running on machines with different instruction execution rates. It can also sort out data from different subsystems that have been recorded together, weighting each time interval by its utilization. This program functions independently of the particular software reliability model being used. The output can be used as the input to any of the foregoing programs. Sometimes the failure intervals needed for input to the foregoing programs have been recorded directly and no adjustment is necessary. Then you do not need to run the log conversion program.

Many projects record or could record (with minor modifications) failure data in their software change management systems. A direct link between such a system and software reliability estimation programs through a failure log conversion program may be very advantageous for a project.

Finally, you may wish to have a standard least squares fit package. This will be needed if you determine resource usage parameters by collecting data.

5.3.2   Interpretation of Results and Special Problems

The 75 percent confidence interval has been found from experience to be the most useful from the manager's viewpoint. However, the 50, 90, and 95 percent confidence intervals contribute some added insight. The 75 percent interval provides a level of confidence comparable to that with which many other managerial decisions are made. Higher levels of confidence result in intervals for many quantities that are too large to be useful.

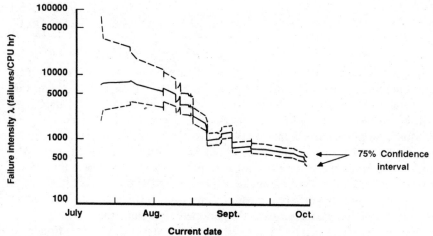

FIGURE 5.7
Sample plot of history of present failure intensity estimates.

To obtain an estimate of total remaining failures rather than failures to reach the failure intensity objective, set the failure intensity objective to zero.

Sometimes you may wish to determine the present failure intensity of a program that is released to the field with some faults not corrected. This, of course, depends on the particular faults that are not corrected. However, a first approximation to the present failure intensity may be obtained by running the software reliability estimation program with a number of the latest failure intervals removed. This number should correspond to the faults outstanding.

Occasionally, you may not be able to obtain a good estimate of the confidence interval for the completion date of a project. This may occur because the confidence interval for total failures has an upper bound of infinity. The estimation algorithm may not be able to discern a trend in failure intervals with high confidence. Here, other available information may be used to estimate an upper bound for the 75 percent confidence interval for total failures. One possibility is faults found per 1000 lines of delivered executable source code from system test onward. This information is applied to find additional failures required to achieve the failure intensity objective. To obtain the completion date bound to a first approximation, use linear interpolation or extrapolation between two additional failures-completion date pairs for different confidence bounds in the tabular output from the software reliability estimation program.

5.4 DISCUSSION: FAILURE GROUPING AND RANDOMIZATION

We will use two case studies to look more closely at the effects of the grouping of and the randomization of data.

CASE STUDY 5.1
EFFECT OF GROUPING DATA

Failure data are often available only in grouped form. Here we wish to compare the relative precision with which model parameters are estimated when using failure time data to the estimates obtained using the equivalent grouped data. Our focus will be on the basic and logarithmic Poisson execution time models.

In Musa, Iannino, and Okumoto (1987) it is shown that maximum likelihood inference for the basic execution time model is centered around the parameter representing the product $B\phi$. For the logarithmic Poisson execution time model, inference is centered around the parameter representing the product $\lambda_0\theta$. Although $B\phi$ and $\lambda_0\theta$ have somewhat different meanings, they both affect the rate of reduction in failure intensity. The rate increases as the parameter increases in both cases. Since all the other model parameters and derived quantities depend on our estimates of these two parameters and their associated accuracies, our study will focus on them.

The simplest way to do the comparison is via simulation (analytic results being too difficult to obtain). A sequence of failure time data can easily be generated according to a known model. It can then be converted into grouped data in many ways depending on how we define the duration of each group. Two of these ways, studied here, are fixed time per group and equal number of failures per group.

BASIC EXECUTION TIME MODEL

A sequence consisting of 100 failure times from the model defined by

$$\mu(t) = 150\{1 - \exp[-(0.3 \times 10^{-4})t]\},$$

where $\mu(t)$ is the mean number of failures in time t and $B\phi = 0.3 \times 10^{-4}$/sec, is used as our illustrative example. Table 5.7 contains the values of I_g resulting from various equal time groupings and several different sample sizes. It is apparent from an examination of this table that grouping has minimal effect when there is a moderate amount of failure data on hand. When grouping is based on an equal number of failures per group the results shown in Table 5.14 are obtained. The results are almost as good as before. Of the two types of groupings it appears that equal length is to be preferred, but equal number groups are acceptable in practice.

LOGARITHMIC POISSON EXECUTION TIME MODEL

Data for the illustrative example used in this section were generated from the model specified by

$$\mu(t) = 20 \ln[1 + (0.25 \times 10^{-3})t],$$

where $\lambda_0\theta = 0.25 \times 10^{-3}$/sec.

TABLE 5.14
Value of I_g for equal number of failures per group for the basic execution time model

	Number of failures	
	100	50
Number of groups	I_g	I_g
5	0.901	0.94
10	0.975	0.977
15	0.957	0.984
20	0.984	0.989

Consider first grouping based on an equal amount of time per group. Results analogous to those given in Table 5.7 are shown in Table 5.8 for a sample size of 100 failures. Note that we can have more groups than failures. Some groups will have zero failures associated with them. We conclude that this method of grouping is very detrimental to the estimation of model parameters unless the number of groups is large (many times the number of failures). If, on the other hand, we group the failure time data based on an equal number of failures per group, the results shown in Table 5.15 are obtained. The improvement in the value of I_g is substantial. I_g indicates that there is still a 10 to 20 percent loss of information.

General conclusions should not be drawn from a limited study as this. However, it does appear that the basic execution time model is robust to grouping in general. Also, it appears that some care must be exercised when the logarithmic Poisson execution time model is used with grouped failure data. Specifically, the results shown in Tables 5.8 and 5.15 indicate that equal time groups should be avoided unless the number of failures per group is almost uniform.

TABLE 5.15
Values of I_g for equal number of failures per group for the logarithmic Poisson model

	Number of failures	
	100	50
Number of groups	I_g	I_g
5	0.395	1.2
10	1.115	0.854
15	0.833	0.794
20	0.894	0.821
50	0.84	0.761

CASE STUDY 5.2
EFFECT OF RANDOMIZING GROUPED DATA

In Case Study 5.1 we examined the effects of grouping failure time data. Here we will briefly look at the reverse process, that is, taking a set of grouped data and "converting" it into failure time data. We do this primarily because it may be convenient to implement software reliability estimation programs to accept just failure times as inputs.

Both simulated and actual failure data will be employed. The simulated data are the same as those from Case Study 5.1.[2] The actual failure data represent two projects, T38, given in Musa, Iannino, and Okumoto (1987), and T39, given in Table 5.16. For these projects, data were collected weekly. The number of failures occurring and the amount of execution time during each week are shown.

Grouped data can be converted into failure time data in several ways. Two of these are random and uniform assignments. The latter is the easiest to implement. Failure times are equally spaced in each group. The former is somewhat more complicated to implement but should be more realistic. In this method failure times are randomly assigned (according to a uniform distribution) in each group. The assumption used in random assignment is that the failure intensity varies slowly and can be considered constant for the duration of a group.[3]

As we did in Case Study 5.1, attention will be focused on the parameters $B\phi$ and $\lambda_0\theta$. In particular, we will consider the maximum likelihood estimate, the information content being of little use in this context. Results of the study are shown in Table 5.9 and 5.10 for simulated and actual data, respectively. The reader can see that for a reasonable number of groups the amount of error introduced by the random conversion can be neglected, in practice. The uniform conversion, while not necessarily bad, is never as good as the random conversion.

5.5 SUMMARY

Determination of the values of many parameters is straightforward. You must *predict* the values of the execution time component parameters from characteristics of the software product and the development process in the period before the pro-

---

[2]Groups for the simulated data for the basic execution time model were based on an equal amount of time per group. For the logarithmic Poisson execution time model, they were based on an equal number of failures per group.

[3]This assumption implies a homogeneous Poisson process where, conditioned on the number of failures experienced in a group, the times of the failures are independently and uniformly distributed over the period of the group [Cox and Lewis (1966)].

TABLE 5.16
Grouped failure data for system T39

Group no.	Group duration, CPU hr	No. of failures
1	62	5
2	63	25
3	66	10
4	24	7
5	8	4
6	206.5	4
7	60	0
8	65	2
9	59	0
10	163	1
11	62.5	0
12	60	6
13	61.5	0
14	66	5
15	64	0
16	109	5
17	186	1
18	51	0
19	180	2

gram can be executed. Afterwards, you can *estimate* them from failure data. Ordinarily, the estimation process should be automated. The means for determination of calendar time component parameters depends on the particular parameters, but it can involve data collection, use of historical data, and current project estimates.

PROBLEMS

5.1 Which of the following activities utilize limiting resources?
(*a*) Writing a user manual.
(*b*) Generating test cases based on test results.
(*c*) Filling out trouble reports.
(*d*) Attending a meeting of a trouble review board.
(*e*) Documenting a program correction.
5.2 What values will you get for total failures ν_0 and failure intensity decay parameter θ during the operational phase?
5.3 Can the software reliability estimation programs be used for hardware?
5.4 Can software reliability measurement be applied to a situation where a program is released to the field with some failures not yet addressed?
5.5 Can we apply a software reliability model when we run formal system tests at widely spaced intervals during the test period? Interval data are recorded for the formal tests

but not otherwise, except that number of failures and total execution time per day or week is noted.

5.6 Can software reliability models be applied to individual programmers who are testing subsystems?

5.7 Nonoperating time can affect hardware failures because aging can occur even without operation. Can this happen for software?

5.8 We log our failures in real times against a "clock" that keeps track of cumulative execution time. Since determining that a failure really occurred involves a delay, all the failures are logged at a time later than they actually occurred. Does this cause a problem in estimation during system test?

5.9 Do we count a fault found by a programmer on his or her own without testing?

5.10 We are examining our output data from testing by using a computerized analysis program. This makes location of failures much easier. Should the computer time used by this program be accounted for in any way?

5.11 We seem to be getting results with the basic execution time model that do not make sense. We removed some closely spaced failures from the failure interval data because we thought they were not true failures. Predictions of total failures expected increased. What is wrong?

5.12 What is the effect on the basic model parameter estimates of a failure that keeps occurring, can't be fixed, and is still counted?

5.13 How can corrected faults be proportional to identified failures? What you correct depends on what it is profitable to correct or what the customer pays for.

5.14 Can two or more resources be simultaneously limiting?

5.15 How can total failures of the basic execution time model be a finite value? If you run a program for an infinite time, won't you get an infinite number of failures?

5.16 The definition of the fault reduction factor B states that it relates *total* failures experienced to *net* faults corrected. Why is this distinction made?

5.17 Are any assumptions made about specialization of failure identification or failure correction personnel?

5.18 Are support staff (program librarians, etc.) counted in applying the theory?

5.19 Must all P_F failure correction personnel be retained on the project for the entire system test phase?

5.20 How do you calculate hours of availability for a computer?

5.21 Do the utilization factors ρ_C and ρ_F that are used hold for the entire system test phase?

5.22 How do you handle vacations and absences in computing calendar time durations?

5.23 If you obtain better data on your parameters during the test period, should you change them or will this adversely affect the results?

5.24 Is it necessary to establish the values of all the parameters when you are applying software reliability measurement during the period of field test?

5.25 Our test teams are required to do a substantial amount of test planning or replanning and test procedure debugging while testing is going on. Should these activities be taken into account in making calendar time predictions?

5.26 Would a program that is highly modular in terms of function affect the length of the failure queue that would be acceptable for each programmer?

5.27 We use different failure diagnosis tools during different phases of test. As a result, some new failures may be found that were missed during an earlier phase. How should this be handled?

5.28 In our project, failure identification and correction are done on different computers. What adjustments must be made in applying a software reliability model?

5.29 Why does the occurrence of a number of failures separated by short time intervals (compared to the intervals previously experienced) often lead to a *decrease* in the estimate of initial failure intensity? This seems counterintuitive.

5.30 Can the quality of the parameter predictions being made be checked by looking at a project history of such predictions?

5.31 We plot total (present plus the prediction of the additional amount required to meet the failure intensity objective) execution and calendar times against either present execution or calendar time. How should we interpret them?

5.32 During testing we record much data on tape and then examine these data interactively on a display afterwards. What is the significance of the examination time?

5.33 Every failure reported for our project goes to a problem review board before it is assigned to a programmer for correction. Sometimes the customer must approve before the failure is corrected. The process can add 1 to 4 days delay. Must predictions of additional calendar time required to meet the failure intensity objective be altered to account for this?

5.34 In our project, test cases are created by recording data in the field and then processing them. The rate at which these cases can be generated is limited, and this really paces our testing effort. Can this consideration be incorporated in the software reliability model?

5.35 How should regression testing be handled when doing software reliability modeling?

5.36 Is prediction of the initial failure intensity machine-dependent?

5.37 It appears that the accuracy of determining when a failure intensity objective will be reached will get worse for smaller objectives because the slope of failure intensity with respect to execution time is decreasing. Is this true?

5.38 A program with 50,000 source instructions and a source to object expansion ratio of 4 will be executed on a machine with an average instruction execution rate of 333,333 instructions/CPU sec. On similar projects, a fault exposure ratio of $K = 1.67 \times 10^{-7}$ has been experienced, along with a fault density of 6 faults per 1000 source instructions. The fault reduction factor $B = 1$. Estimate the initial failure intensity at the start of system test.

5.39 Our computer has a utilization of about 0.3. How should I set the value of the computer utilization factor?

5.40 It is difficult for us to obtain the cooperation necessary to collect resource expenditure data. We want to reduce data collection requirements to a basic minimum. What resource expenditure data are most important?

5.41 Our failure correction personnel and failure identification personnel use different computers. Does this mean that we may have four limiting resources?

5.42 All corrections made to our system must pass through a "software manufacturing" process. In this process, corrected source routines are recompiled and bound into a new system. Then the new system is formally tested by the test team. Is the software manufacturing process a limiting resource in the sense of affecting the calendar time component of the model?

5.43 Suppose that failures can be assigned to one of several people for correction rather than just one person. How do you account for this in the utilization factor for failure correction personnel?

5.44 During test we find a number of faults (and hence implied failures) by code reading.

How can we reflect these in our software reliability estimates?

5.45 How can the parameter θ_C, computer time used per unit execution time, be greater than 1?

5.46 We do program testing on one machine, correct faults on another, and verify that the faults have been removed on yet another. How do we apply the calendar time component of the model?

5.47 Do you really count *all* testing during system test in determining total execution time that has occurred?

SIX

PROJECT-SPECIFIC TECHNIQUES

In Chapter 5 we looked at the problem of parameter determination. In this chapter we will present ways of dealing with various special problems that have arisen from experience with a variety of projects. Interestingly enough, these problems generally do not result from advances in software engineering technology. Such advances may change values (for example, faults per delivered source instruction at the start of system test) but generally do not affect assumptions and basic concepts. In Chapter 7 we will see how to use all the techniques of Chapters 4 to 6 for specific applications.

6.1 UNOBSERVED FAILURES

A common problem that must be dealt with is the fact that some failures may not be observed. This occurs most frequently with less severe failures, and particularly failures that do not stop the execution of the program. Failures can be missed in hardware just as easily as software systems, provided the two are analogous in the strictness with which "failure" is defined. Even if the failures are observed, you often get incomplete reporting from the field. Sometimes this is just carelessness or lack of interest or motivation. At other times it may simply be due to the fact that field personnel are not as highly trained and sensitive to the importance of reporting failures as development personnel. The fact that some failures are not being observed or reported means that in general failure intensity is going to be underestimated. The saving grace is that usually the customers miss more failures than the system testers. In other words, any underestimating of failure intensity by the system test personnel is less than that the customers will underestimate. Thus, the customers will generally think the system is more reliable than the system testers do. This will be the case if the observation and reporting difference is greater than the change of environment in going from test to operation. Occasionally it may happen that things look worse in the field. If so, this may be due to rather poor system test planning. If system test doesn't represent the conditions that will be encountered in the field, then indeed you may see an increase in failure intensity when the program is released. This increase occurs when the effect of the change in environment is greater than the pseudo "improvement" you see because the customers are not observing some of the failures.

If you think it is desirable to adjust for unobserved and unreported failures, you can. However, it is a bit of a risky endeavor. You need good data on a similar project that indicate the proportion of failures that are missed. To find out how many failures are missed, you have to do a comprehensive analysis of the history of failure observations. You don't know how many have been missed until they are ultimately found. So it is best to do this on a project with a long operational history. You would look for "late" failures that "must" have occurred earlier and been missed. Earlier occurrence could be inferred if you know that the same input states were exercised earlier during the operational history.

Some projects use correction reports as well as trouble or failure reports. Correction reports close out failure reports for which repairs have been made and note the program changes. Other projects have reports of program changes available from automated configuration control systems. One might think that comparison of failure reports with correction reports could yield valuable clues about missing reports of failures. Unfortunately, they do not indicate the proportion of failures not observed. They only represent failures that have been observed and fixed, but not reported for some reason.

You should be careful to ascertain whether unobserved failures are significant. The fact that they are not observed *may* be a clue to a misunderstanding between developer and customer about what the system requirements really are. A large proportion of unobserved failures may indicate that inadequate attention has been given in system design to failure recording functions and procedures. This can particularly be a problem for unattended systems.

Special care must be exercised for failures identified by automated reporting systems. Since these systems must be programmed with respect to recognizing what behaviors constitute failures, there is a substantial risk that some failures will be missed. Frequently, the unexpected failures are the most significant ones; if they were known, they might have been eliminated in the design.

CASE STUDY 6.1
EFFECTS OF FAILURE OBSERVABILITY
ON FAILURE INTENSITY ESTIMATE

Let us consider how failure intensity estimates are affected when some failures are not observed. The basic and logarithmic Poisson execution time models will be used to investigate the effects at various times during testing.

The basic execution time model has been applied to an actual software project for which it is believed that some proportion (increasing with time) of failures were missed. Project personnel indicated that after a function was tested, less attention was paid to looking for failures associated with it, and therefore some failures may have gone unnoticed. Also a good portion of the latter data was collected by the end user of the product, who was known to have paid less attention to program behavior. Thus a higher proportion of failures probably was missed. The results for this project suggested that the model tended to underpredict the failure intensity.[1] In the following we present results that emanate from these observations.

Denote the probability that the ith failure goes unnoticed as $P(i)$. Many forms for $P(i)$ are possible but for simplicity we consider only the linear case (Figure 6.1), that is,

$$p(i) = p_1 + \frac{i}{a}(p_2 - p_1); \quad i < a \tag{6.1}$$

$$= p_2; \quad i \geq a \, .$$

At the start of system test the probability of not observing any particular failure will be p_1. As testing progresses this probability changes linearly to its final value of p_2. The rate of change is governed by the constant a. When p_2 is set equal to p_1, the proportion of missed failures is constant throughout the test phase.

BASIC EXECUTION TIME MODEL

The *expected* failure intensity at time t for the basic execution time model is given by

$$\lambda(t) = \nu_0 \phi B \exp(-\phi Bt) \, . \tag{6.2}$$

Simulations were conducted to see how closely the *estimated* failure intensity at time t follows the value given by Equation (6.2) when failures are missed according to Equation (6.1). The model parameters used in the following simulations were $\nu_0 = 250$ failures, $\phi = 0.005$/sec, and $B = 1$. One thousand different failure time sequences for this model were randomly generated. Then, failures were randomly removed with probability given by Equation (6.1). For each resulting failure time sequence, $\hat{\lambda}(t)$ was determined at various values of t and the ratio of $\hat{\lambda}(t)$ to $\lambda(t)$ was determined. Finally, the average value of this ratio was calculated using the results of all 1000 failure time sequences. Values of this ratio near 1 tell us that our estimation is about what is expected. Values less than 1 indicate an underestimation and values greater than 1, an overestimation. This entire process was repeated for different values of p_1 and p_2.

---

[1]This is entirely reasonable since the number of failures observed is less than normal. It appears that fewer failures are occurring in the same amount of time. Thus, the lower failure intensity.

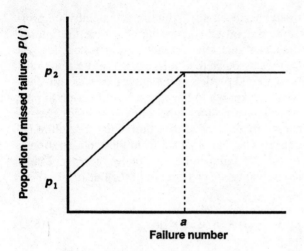

FIGURE 6.1
Probability that *i*th failure goes unnoticed.

Figure 6.2 shows how the ratio varies with t for some different values of (p_1, p_2). The results show that:

1. If $P(i)$ is constant $(p_1 = p_2)$, then estimates for failure intensity are low.[2]
2. If $P(i)$ increases with time, the estimate for failure intensity is low and becomes lower still as time passes.

---

[2]We would expect the value of the ratio to be about equal to $1 - p$, since this is the fraction of failures actually observed. The data do bear this out.

FIGURE 6.2
Effect of unobserved failures: estimated-actual failure intensity ratio for basic execution time model.

3. If $P(i)$ decreases with time the estimate for failure intensity is initially low but becomes better as time passes.

In summary, a simple correction [just divide by $(1 - p_1)$] to the estimated failure intensity can be applied if the proportion of missed failures does not change over time. When the proportion decreases over time, one of two things can be done. First, you can ignore the problem since the missed early failures do not significantly impact estimates made later. The second option is to divide the estimated failure intensity by the current probability of observing a failure. This option is only feasible if the mentioned probability can be estimated. When the proportion increases over time care must be exercised. Here the missed failures occur late during testing and they are the ones having the greatest impact on the estimated failure intensity.[3]

LOGARITHMIC POISSON EXECUTION TIME MODEL

The same simulations were conducted using a logarithmic Poisson execution time model with $\theta = 0.05$/failure and $\lambda_0 = 0.005$ failure/sec. Figure 6.3 shows how the ratio of $\hat{\lambda}(t)$ to $\lambda(t)$ varies with t for some different values of (p_1, p_2). The results show that the estimated failure intensity is low under a broad range of condi-

---

[3]In all this we are assuming that the missed failures do not constitute an implicit redefinition of what a failure really is.

FIGURE 6.3
Effect of unobserved failures: estimated-actual failure intensity ratio for logarithmic Poisson execution time model.

tions. For a constant $P(i)$, dividing the estimated failure intensity by $1 - p_1$ will result in values not far from those obtained when all failures are observed. The correction here is not as good as that for the basic model.

6.2 FAILURE TIME MEASUREMENTS

When making failure time measurements in execution time, there will sometimes be questions of interpretation to be resolved. The most basic principle is that the execution time is measured on the processor on which the program is running. This would mean, for example, that the time required to perform input-output functions on peripheral processors or controllers is not counted. Of course, if we are measuring the reliability of the peripheral processor software, then its run time *is* the quantity to measure. Care must be taken so that we only measure the execution of those functions that would be included in the deliverable product and normally operated by the customer. For example, the execution of utility programs that analyze or display data recorded from the output of the program for the purpose of failure identification should not be included in measuring the failure intervals.

Other considerations include approximations to execution time, failure time uncertainties, and handling of multiple installations of the same program.

6.2.1 Approximations to Execution Time

It certainly is best to collect failure data in terms of execution time if possible. However, there may be some situations where it is difficult to do this. Rather than give up, there are approximations that are possible. There are at least three different kinds of approximations that have been used: clock time, weighted clock time, and natural units.

If the average utilization of the system over a period comparable to a failure interval is almost constant, then clock time is a good approximation to execution time. What does this mean? Suppose failures are occurring hourly. If the average utilization over one hour is 0.60 and over another, 0.63, the approximation is good. If the average utilization is varying, then the weighted clock time approximation should be used.

For the weighted clock time approximation, you multiply short segments of clock time by utilization or some approximation to utilization. The products are then added. One example would be an interactive time sharing system where it is easy to get data on the number of users. You could approximate execution time by the product of clock time and fraction of maximum possible users.

Example 6.1. A time sharing system has a maximum feasible load of 40 users. This is defined for the particular system as the number that yields 0.8 utilization. Above this number, response time on this system becomes intolerable, although more users are physically possible. We sample the number of users at a randomly chosen instant within a 5-minute period. The 12 periods occurring in an hour are averaged to give users for that hour. The following table gives the figures. The fraction of maximum feasible users, multiplied by 0.8, yields an approximation to utilization.

Hour	Number of users	Approximation of utilization
8–9 A.M.	16	0.32
9–10 A.M.	36	0.72
10–11 A.M.	40	0.8
11–12 A.M.	36	0.72
12–1 P.M.	20	0.4
1–2 P.M.	36	0.72
2–3 P.M.	40	0.8
3–4 P.M.	40	0.8
4–5 P.M.	36	0.72
5–6 P.M.	24	0.48

If a failure occurs at 10 A.M. and another at 2 P.M., we may approximate the execution time interval by summing the utilizations in the intervening hours. This approach yields an interval of 2.64 CPU hr. ∎

The third kind of approximation is natural units. A natural unit would be some quantity that is easy to measure and that represents a constant average number of instructions executed. Some examples of natural units would be transactions, such as reservations in an airline or hotel reservation system, calls in a telephone switching system, or copies in a reproduction system.

Note that failure intensity values are now specified in terms of the new quantity. This may be an advantage if the quantity is a natural one for the application. However, adjustment of the failure intensity objective λ_F may be necessary. Also, two of the resource usage parameters may have to be adjusted. These are the computer time and the failure identification effort per unit execution time. Since these parameters are measured with respect to true execution time, they can be different when we are using approximations to it that differ by a proportionality factor.

Example 6.2. A microcomputer-controlled laser printer produces 1 copy/sec (3600 copies/hr). There is no convenient means for measuring the execution time of its software in the field. However, the number of copies produced is easily determined and recorded. We will determine failure events in terms of copies generated rather than time.

Let us consider the parameter adjustments required to model in this domain. We want the system to operate without failure for an extended working day of 10 hr. This particular system is utilized about half the time. Assume that the hardware is highly reliable and that the system reliability is determined by the software. We can establish a conveniently measured software failure intensity objective of 1 failure/18K copies. This would represent 1 failure/day. Note that we must measure computer time and failure identification effort required for system test in terms of number of copies and number of failures rather than execution time and number of failures. The per-copy component of computer time might be 0.001 CPU hr, and failure identification effort, 0.002 person hr. ■

Some special methods exist for approximating execution time in distributed systems. These were covered in Chapter 4.

6.2.2 Time Uncertainties

The time of a failure or start or end of a period of execution may be uncertain due to either limitations in data recording or in record keeping and reporting. To handle this situation, first determine the window during which the event must have occurred. Then choose the event time randomly (assuming a uniform distribution) within that window. The foregoing procedure will yield more accurate results than ignoring the failures and test periods that are not accurately recorded. The effect of the uncertainty can be determined by making estimates using the extreme values of the possible range of failure intervals.

A common application of the procedure is to situations where we only know the number of failures per day and the hours of run time for each day. The failures are assigned randomly within the window of the day's run time. This approach is readily generalized to the situation where m_W failures occur in a specified period of uncertainty t_W. All the failures are assigned randomly within this window. An alternative method is to divide the window into $m_W + 1$ segments of length $t_L = t_W/(m_W + 1)$ and assign the failures at t_L, $2t_L$, $3t_L$, and so on. However, this latter approach yields inferior results when model parameters are estimated, as shown in Case Study 5.2. If run time is not recorded, an estimate of average run time can be used, although this will cause a deterioration in accuracy and ability to predict. Note that data on a failures-per-day basis that are mixed with failure interval data can be handled with the preceding procedure.

Example 6.3. The following log of a day of testing was recorded. We have decided to use clock time as an approximation to execution time.

Event	Calendar time
Start test	8 A.M.
Failure 1	8:30 A.M.
Failure 2	9:30–10:20 A.M.
Failure 3	11 A.M.
Stop test for lunch	12 noon
Start test	1 P.M.
Failures 4, 5	1:00–4:20 P.M.
Stop test	5:00 P.M.

We convert the times of the events to minutes of clock time for convenience. We then select numbers from a random number table. We multiply these numbers by whatever constant is necessary to adjust their range of variation to the range of uncertainty of times. The failure times are thus established and the intervals calculated. The procedure is illustrated in the table below.

Event	Clock time (min)	Random number	Adjustment factor	Assigned clock time (min)	Clock time interval since last failure (min)
Start test	0			0	
Failure 1	30			30	30
Failure 2	90–140	67557	0.0005	63.8	33.8
Failure 3	180			180	116.2
Stop test	240			240	
Start test	240			240	
Failure 4	240–440	26446	0.002	292.9	112.9
Failure 5	240–440	97159	0.002	434.3	141.4
Stop test	480			480	

∎

Sometimes (although this is undesirable) the time reported for a failure is the time of identification rather than the time of occurrence. This adds to inaccuracy, but it may not be too serious if the mean execution time lag between failure occurrence and identification is relatively constant with time.

You must beware of the natural tendency of people to "save time" by logging closely occurring failures as happening at the same time. Doing this would result in an excessive number of zero failure intervals, which would yield an overly pessimistic estimate of potential failures in the system. If data have already been logged in this fashion, it is probably best to correct them as follows. Assume there are k identical times between the unequal times t_i and t_{i+k+1}. Pick k random time *points* (for example, from a random number table) in the range $[t_i, t_{i+k+1}]$ and order them as $t_{i+1}, t_{i+2}, \ldots, t_{i+k}$. The *intervals* that will replace the zero intervals will be found as

$$t'_{i+1} = t_{i+1} - t_i \, ,$$

$$t'_{i+2} = t_{i+2} - t_{i+1} \, ,$$

$$\vdots$$

$$t'_{i+k} = t_{i+k} - t_{i+k-1} \, ,$$

$$(6.3)$$

and t_{i+k+1} must be changed to $t_{i+k+1} - t_{i+k}$.

Time uncertainties can affect the accuracy of parameter estimates, as noted in the following case study.

CASE STUDY 6.2
EFFECT OF UNCERTAINTY WINDOW ON ESTIMATION

Failure time data are often rounded off to some degree. Just what effect this has on the maximum likelihood estimates [see Musa, Iannino, and Okumoto (1987)] of the model parameters for the basic and logarithmic Poisson execution time models will be briefly investigated. Actually only the parameter $B\phi$ for the basic model and $\lambda_0\theta$ for the logarithmic Poisson model need be considered. This is because maximum likelihood inference for all other parameters and derived quantities for both models is based on $B\phi$ and $\lambda_0\theta$, as noted in Musa, Iannino, and Okumoto (1987). We can let $B = 1$ for simplicity without loss of generality.

Suppose failure intervals that are recorded as t' actually lie in the interval $[\max(0,\ t' - \gamma/2),\ t' + \gamma/2]$, where γ is the uncertainty or precision of measurement. Consider an interval of testing lasting until t_e with m_e failures experienced. As the number of failures increases in this interval more precision in recording the time will be required. In fact, if the number increases sufficiently, it may be better to treat the data as grouped data (number of failures in a given time interval).

Define the relative accuracy of estimation as the ratio of $\hat{\phi}$ to ϕ, that is, the ratio of the estimated to true value. Also, let $\bar{t}'$ denote the average failure interval (AFI). Since we are considering a nonhomogeneous Poisson process, this quantity will increase with time.

Figure 6.4 shows the results of a simulation study based on the basic execution time model. Note that the relative accuracy is always less than 1.0. This means ϕ is underestimated. Consider a case where we are willing to accept at

FIGURE 6.4
Required time measurement precision for specified parameter estimation accuracy: basic execution time model.

most a 10 percent loss in relative accuracy. The precision required to achieve this goal can be determined from Figure 6.4. Here γ must be no larger than $\bar{i}'/1.28$ or $0.78\ \bar{i}'$. Since AFI increases as time goes by, the precision requirement becomes less strict. A little thought tells us that this is not entirely unexpected.

As a further illustration consider the case where $\nu_0 = 150$ failures and $\phi = 0.25 \times 10^{-4}/\text{sec}$. Then at $t_e = 40,000$ sec (11.1 hr), the expected number of failures would be $\mu(40,000) = 150 \{1 - \exp[-(0.25 \times 10^{-4})(40,000)]\} = 94.8$. This results in $\bar{i}' = 40,000/94.8 = 421.9$ sec. Therefore, each failure interval must be measured to within $\gamma = 0.78\ \bar{i}' = 329$ sec in order to not suffer more than 10 percent loss in accuracy in the estimation of ϕ. At $t_e = 80,000$ sec it is only necessary to measure to within $\gamma = 481$ sec. Note that our measurements can be less precise in this case.

Some projects have recorded time of failure to the nearest day. Is this sufficiently accurate to give satisfactory parameter estimates for the basic execution time model? Note from Figure 6.4 that accuracy is generally within 15 percent if AFI is greater than γ. That is, recording to the nearest day is probably satisfactory only if there is less than 1 failure per day on the average. This requirement becomes easier to satisfy as testing progresses.

Figure 6.5 shows similar results for the logarithmic Poisson model. Here the situation is more complicated, as the results depend on the value of $\lambda_0 \theta t_e$. Once again, assume we are willing to tolerate at most a 10 percent loss in accuracy. If the value of $\lambda_0 \theta t_e$ is 5, then γ must be no larger than 71 percent of the AFI. When $\lambda_0 \theta t_e$ increases to 10, then γ must be less than or equal to 50 percent of the AFI. As $\lambda_0 \theta t_e$ increases, the required percentage of the AFI is decreasing. However, the AFI itself is increasing. These two factors nearly cancel. This results in a roughly constant precision requirement. For example, let $\theta = 0.01/\text{failure}$ and

FIGURE 6.5
Required time measurement precision for specified parameter estimation accuracy: logarithmic Poisson execution time model.

$\lambda_0 \theta = 0.25 \times 10^{-3}/\text{sec}$. If $t_e = 20,000$ sec, the expected number of failures is $\mu(20,000) = (1/0.01) \ln [1 + (0.25 \times 10^{-3})(20,000)] = 179$. We have $\bar{\tau}' = 20,000/179 = 112$ sec. Thus, the required precision γ is $0.71\ \bar{\tau}' = 79.5$ sec. If $t_e = 80,000$ sec, then $\gamma = 87$ sec.

6.2.3 Multiple Installations

When there are multiple computers running the same program, you should interleave the failures from the different computers in the order in which they occurred. Then add the concurrently running execution times. This procedure is used because all you are really doing is exposing the same program to more testing. When a failure is found on one computer, all copies of the program on the other computers are normally corrected sooner or later. Consider the following example with CPU utilization of 1 for each of two systems. Both have the same average instruction execution rate (see Table 6.1). You will note that installation A starts executing at 8 A.M. We have a failure at 9 A.M. On installation B, we start at 8:30 and experience a failure at 9:30. We compute that failure 1 occurs after 90 CPU min, 60 CPU min of execution on installation A and 30 CPU min of execution on installation B. Failure number 2 occurs after 30 CPU min of execution on installation A and another 30 CPU min of execution on installation B. Thus failure interval 2 is 60 CPU min in length.

You might argue that times should be considered separately for each program and failure intervals computed for that program as a separate entity. Such an approach would indeed apply to hardware where wear is occurring and the different accumulated operation times for each system are significant. It *does not* apply to software! Remember that the program is only the logic and not the physical machine it is running on. The nature of that machine or its condition is *immate-*

TABLE 6.1
Example of interleaving failures from multiple installations (CPU utilization = 1)

Event	Calender time	Cumulative execution time (min)			Time between failures (min)
		Installation A	Installation B	All Installations	
Start of program execution on installation A	8:00 A.M.	0	0	0	0
Start of program execution on installation B	8:30 A.M.	30	0	30	0
Failure on installation A	9:00 A.M.	60	30	90	90
Failure on installation B	9:30 A.M.	90	60	150	60

rial. If the software copies are presented with the same operational profile, the runs for these copies may be different but the probability of a given run for any copy is identical. Hence whether execution time is experienced on one copy or many *does not matter*, and time periods may be grouped together.

In fact, there is another significant difference from the hardware situation. When a failure occurs and the fault that causes it is repaired, it is repaired for *all* copies at the same time. In actuality, there may be variations in repair time, but simultaneous repair is a good approximation. Thus the nature of the software changes with calendar time, and it is necessary to keep failure data synchronized between different copies with respect to calendar time. Hence the interleaving approach we have described.

The foregoing simple interleaving method assumes that all the computers have the same average instruction execution rate. If not, choose a "reference computer" and adjust all execution times and failure intensities to that machine. Let r_1 be the average instruction execution rate of computer 1 and r_2, that of computer 2. If computer 1 is chosen as the reference, then execution times on computer 2 are adjusted to the reference by multiplying them by r_2/r_1. Suppose machine 1 executes 1 million instructions/sec and machine 2 executes 2 million instructions/sec. Then execution time intervals on machine 2 would be multiplied by a factor of 2 when they were referred to machine 1. Obviously, that makes sense. Since machine 2 is twice as fast, intervals on machine 1 have to be twice as long to be equivalent in terms of instructions executed. It is really instructions executed that is related to the failure inducing stress placed on the software. However, it is more practical to work with execution time and adjust it when necessary. Note that the failure intensity objective should, of course, be specified in terms of the reference.

Example 6.4. A computer game is being tested on personal computers A and B. Machine A has an average instruction execution rate of 0.8 million instructions/sec; machine B, 1.6 million. Part of the test log for each machine is reproduced below. We want to refer all failure intervals to machine B and interleave both sets. We expect to end up with clock times in minutes.

Machine A		Machine B	
Event	Time	Event	Time
Start test A	8:00 A.M.	Start test B	9:20 A.M.
Failure A1	9:00 A.M.	Failure B1	9:50 A.M.
Failure A2	9:30 A.M.	Failure B2	10:00 A.M.
Failure A3	10:20 A.M.	Failure B3	10:50 A.M.
Stop test A	11:00 A.M.	Failure B4	12:00 noon
		Stop test B	12:30 P.M.

Time intervals on machine A must be referred to machine B by multiplying them by

$$\frac{r_A}{r_B} = \frac{0.8}{1.6} = 0.5 \ .$$

The process of interleaving and adjustment is illustrated below.

		Interleaved list				
		Clock time interval (min)				**Cumulative adjusted clock time — both machines (min)**
Event	**Time**	**Machine A**	**Machine B**	**Machine A adjusted to B**	**Both machines (adjusted)**	
Start test A	8:00 A.M.	—	—	—	—	0
Failure A1	9:00 A.M.	60	—	30	30	30
Start test B	9:20 A.M.	20	—	10	10	40
Failure A2	9:30 A.M.	10	10	5	15	55
Failure B1	9:50 A.M.	20	20	10	30	85
Failure B2	10:00 A.M.	10	10	5	15	100
Failure A3	10:20 A.M.	20	20	10	30	130
Failure B3	10:50 A.M.	30	30	15	45	175
Stop test A	11:00 A.M.	10	10	5	15	190
Failure B4	12:00 noon	—	60	—	60	250
Stop test B	12:30 P.M.	—	30	—	30	280 ∎

The resource usage parameters μ_C and θ_I depend on the average instruction execution rate of the computer to which they are referred. This is because the first deals with computer resource usage per failure and the second is a personnel resource usage per unit execution time. Thus, if measured on computer 2, they may be referred to machine 1 as follows: multiply μ_C by r_2/r_1 and divide θ_I by this ratio. In the example given, suppose the computer time μ_C required on machine 2 for failure identification and correction per failure is 1 hr. Then the parameter μ_C adjusted to machine 1 will be 2 hr. The necessary work per failure will take longer on the slower machine (essentially the same average number of runs must be made). If the failure identification effort per unit execution time is 4 person hr/CPU hr on machine 2, it will be 2 person hr/CPU hr on machine 1. The same amount of work must be done in both cases, but the execution time for machine 1 is twice as large. Hence, the effort per unit execution time is half as much. No adjustment for θ_C is necessary because a change in throughput affects computer time used and execution time equally. If failure correction or identification occurs on more than one machine, a reasonable approach may be to take a weighted average of each parameter in question. Each parameter would be measured on or referred to each machine in use, weighted by the appropriate resources (P_C or P_I) associated with that machine.

Example 6.5. In Example 6.4, resource usage parameter μ_C was measured for machine A at 1.2 hr/failure. Parameter θ_I was measured (also on machine A) at 20 person hr/CPU hr. The parameters must be adjusted to machine B. Denote the adjusted parameters with tildes. We have

$$\tilde{\mu}_C = \frac{r_A}{r_B} \mu_C = \frac{0.8}{1.6}(1.2) = 0.6 \text{ hr/failure}$$

and

$$\tilde{\theta}_I = \frac{r_B}{r_A} \theta_I = \frac{1.6}{0.8}(20) = 40 \text{ person hr/CPU hr}.$$ ∎

Large systems that are installed in many locations may have several versions or releases of the program in the field at one time. This can be the result of the need to spread the installation of a new release over a period of time. Other possibilities are differing needs of different locations as to the issue of new features versus reliability, or perhaps economic factors. Later releases usually have fixes for at least some of the failures experienced in the earlier releases, but they also typically have new features and performance improvements that introduce new faults. Sometimes, you may want to establish the failure intensity for each version. However, variation in failure intensity from release to release is often not great since the economic, marketing, customer need, and competition factors that caused the first version to be released at a certain reliability level may still be operative for the later versions. We are usually most interested in determining the status of the latest release. This can be done by using any of the techniques for evolving systems, as described in the next section. However, if the differences between versions are not great, it may be satisfactory and much simpler to pool all the data. This can be done immediately, or the failure intensities can be estimated for the separate versions and then an average taken.

Example 6.6. An electronic switching system is installed in 1000 central offices around the country. There are currently three different releases of software involved, as shown in the following table.

Release	Number of installations	Failure intensity (per K hr)
5	300	2.0
6	500	1.5
7	200	3.0

All failures are included in the failure intensity data, although only a very small proportion have a sufficiently severe impact to cause service interruption. You can find the overall failure intensity by taking an average of the separate versions, weighted by the proportion of installations of each. This is 1.95 failures/K hr. ∎

6.3   EVOLVING PROGRAMS

Reliability models assume that the program being executed is stable (not changing, except for those changes that result from failure correction). This is often not the case in reality. Programs can evolve due to either requirements changes or integration of parts during development. Requirements changes may occur to provide *enhancement* of the features of the system, in response to competition, changing customer needs, and other factors. They may be necessary for *adaptation* of the system to changing hardware and software. Frequently the latter changes occur because of the opportunity to reduce operating costs provided by technological progress. Finally, requirements may be changed to provide necessary or desirable system *performance improvement*. Such improvement might involve redesign for faster operation or program restructuring to improve maintainability (ease with which program can permit future evolution). Evolution also occurs naturally as part of the development process itself. It is quite common to test a system as it is integrated. Since evolution is essentially independent of the failure correction process, it must be dealt with separately.

There are two additional situations that are analogous to program evolution and can be handled in the same way:

1. A program is fully integrated but it is tested in a step-by-step fashion. One subsystem is turned on, then another, then another, and so on. Many systems undergo what is called "feature testing," where one feature after another is verified in sequence. If the features are highly correlated with modules that are disjoint, the effect is the same as if the program evolved sequentially.

2. A program is fully integrated and active but the observation of the subsystems for failures is handled in a step-by-step fashion. You start with a narrow focus of observation and then widen it subsystem by subsystem. This can happen when new failure diagnosis tools (usually diagnostic software) are added at intervals during test.

One clue to the presence of program evolution or an analogous situation may be provided by plotting total predicted execution time (from start of execution to attainment of failure intensity objective) against execution time. Assuming parameter estimation is of good quality, total execution time should be constant if the program is stable. A changing value suggests that it may not be.

There are three general approaches to handling evolution or its analogs:

1. View program change in terms of component configuration changes (that is, addition or removal of independent subsystems).

2. Ignore change, letting the model adapt its parameters to account for it.

3. Adjust times of failures to what they would have been if the complete final program had been present. Then process the failure times as you would for a stable program.

A summary of the approaches, the situations to which each is best suited, and the advantages and disadvantages of each is given in Table 6.2.

TABLE 6.2
Approaches to handling evolving systems

Approach	Best areas of application	Advantages	Disadvantages
Component configuration change	Small number of changes, each an independent subsystem	Reliability of each component and associated function known, making adjustments to different usage easier	Extra data collection Allocation of failures, execution time, resources, reliability objectives required Less accurate prediction
Ignoring change	Many small changes Different operational versions running simultaneously	Simple, minimum effort	Estimation and prediction errors
Failure time adjustment	Many changes of medium size	Good combination of reasonable accuracy and reasonable effort	Limited to one path of evolution Pure growth (or much extra work) required Final program size must be known (total and developed code)

6.3.1 Component Configuration Change

The component configuration changes approach generally works best when you have a small number of large changes, each resulting from the addition of an independent component. Each component should be substantial in size with relation to the overall program. If you have this situation, then you have one in which the system changes by virtue of adding subsystems. You estimate reliability of each component separately and then you combine the reliabilities to get overall system reliability, using the rules of Section 4.2. It will usually be best to use the same software reliability model for all software components. Execution times and failures must be assigned to each subsystem. Note that to assign execution times, you must know the average percentage of time each subsystem is executing.

The following quantities are determined separately for each subsystem:

1. model parameters,
2. initial failure intensity,
3. present failure intensity,
4. additional failures required to reach failure intensity objective,

5. additional execution time required to reach failure intensity objective, and

6. additional calendar time required to reach failure intensity objective.

The failure intensity objective of the system must be allocated among the subsystems by allocating reliability objectives. The determination of the additional calendar time required to reach the failure intensity objective will require an allocation of resources (failure identification and correction personnel and computer time) among subsystems. To determine overall system figures, the estimates of (4) and (5) are added, respectively. Quantities (2) and (3) are combined (also respectively) using standard combinatorial rules on their associated reliabilities. The rules applied depend on the structure that relates subsystem failures to overall system failure. The maximum of the subsystem values for quantity (6) is taken.

The approach can theoretically be extended to any number of subsystems. However, the increasing complexity of data collection and processing restricts the number. Also, the quality of statistical estimation may suffer at some point if the subsystems become too small to yield good samples of failures. Hence, this approach is best suited to the situation where a program grows in a small number of steps, each the addition of a large independent function. One example of this situation is that of an application program added to a special operating system. The two are designed to work together for a particular application. The operating system is developed before the application program.

The disadvantages of this approach are:

1. the extra data collection required because of the multiple components,

2. the need to allocate failures and execution time among the components,

3. less predictive validity (or later achievement of a specified degree of accuracy in predictive validity) due to smaller sample sizes, and

4. the extra effort required to allocate resources and reliability goals.

> **Example 6.7.** A word processing program is to be built from two major independent, equal size subsystems. Both must function for the system to operate. One is a special purpose operating system used for other products. The other is the application subsystem. When working together, each executes 50 percent of the time. We will apply the basic model to both subsystems. The special purpose operating subsystem is tested first by itself. It has an initial and present failure intensity of 1 failure/CPU hr. Total failures expected is 100. The application subsystem has an initial and present failure intensity of 10 failures/CPU hr. Total failures expected is 1000. The failure intensity objective for the overall system is 2 failures/100 CPU hr. We will simplify the example we are presenting by assuming that both subsystems will always be in the failure-correction-personnel-limited period. We have 25 debuggers. Average failure correction personnel effort per failure is 8 person hr. The workday is 8 hr. We want to find for the overall system:
>
> **1.** total failures,
> **2.** initial failure intensity,
> **3.** present failure intensity,
> **4.** additional failures required to reach failure intensity objective,

5. additional execution time required to reach failure intensity objective, and
6. additional calendar time required to reach failure intensity objective.

Total failures for the system is determined by adding those for the two subsystems to obtain 1100. The system initial and present failure intensities are identical here. They are obtained by adding the subsystem failure intensities, weighted by their utilizations, as per Equation (4.10). We have 5.5 failures/CPU hr.

Since the two subsystems have equal utilizations, they must run for equal amounts of additional execution time to reach their failure intensity objectives. Thus the choices of subsystem failure intensity objectives are constrained. Of course, together they must yield the system objective. We have

$$\lambda_F = 0.5\,\lambda_{F_1} + 0.5\,\lambda_{F_2} = 0.02\ ,\tag{6.4}$$

where λ_F is the system objective, and λ_{F_1} and λ_{F_2} are the subsystem objectives. Hence

$$\lambda_{F_1} = 0.04 - \lambda_{F_2}\ .\tag{6.5}$$

The additional execution time is obtained for the operating subsystem, using Equation (2.11), as

$$\Delta\tau = \frac{\nu_0}{\lambda_0}\,\ln\frac{\lambda_P}{\lambda_F}$$

$$= \frac{100}{1}\,\ln\frac{1}{\lambda_{F_1}}$$

$$= -\,100\,\ln\lambda_{F_1}\ .\tag{6.6}$$

For the application subsystem we have

$$\Delta\tau = \frac{1000}{10}\,\ln\frac{10}{\lambda_{F_2}}$$

$$= 100\,(\ln 10 - \ln \lambda_{F_2})$$

$$= 230 - 100\,\ln\lambda_{F_2}\ .\tag{6.7}$$

Since the execution times are equal we have

$$\ln\lambda_{F_1} = \ln\lambda_{F_2} - 2.30\ .\tag{6.8}$$

Now, substituting Equation (6.5) we obtain

$$\ln\,(0.04 - \lambda_{F_2}) = \ln\lambda_{F_2} - 2.30\ .\tag{6.9}$$

The solution is $\lambda_{F_2} = 0.036355$ failure/CPU hr. Thus $\lambda_{F_1} = 0.003645$ failure/CPU hr. The additional execution time, using Equation (6.6), is $\Delta\tau = 561.4$ CPU hr.

The number of additional failures to reach the failure intensity objective for the operating subsystem is, using Equation (2.9),

$$\Delta\mu = \frac{\nu_0}{\lambda_0}\,(\lambda_P - \lambda_{F_1})$$

$$= \frac{100}{1} \, (1 - 0.003645)$$

$$= 99.6 \text{ failures}. \tag{6.10}$$

For the application subsystem we have

$$\Delta\mu = \frac{1000}{10} \, (10 - 0.036355)$$

$$= 996 \text{ failures}. \tag{6.11}$$

The additional system failures and execution time required to reach the system failure intensity objective are obtained by adding the respective subsystem quantities. We obtain 1096 failures and 1122.8 CPU hr.

Consider the calendar time required for each subsystem. It may be seen from Equation (2.18) that the calendar time to execution time ratio is

$$\frac{dt}{d\tau} = \frac{\mu_F \lambda}{P_F \rho_F} = \frac{8}{P_F \rho_F} \lambda . \tag{6.12}$$

The subscript "F" denotes the failure correction personnel resource. If we integrate Equation (6.12), we obtain the calendar time required to meet the failure intensity objective. We have

$$t = \frac{8}{P_F \rho_F} \Delta\mu . \tag{6.13}$$

The calendar time required for each subsystem depends on the resources allocated to it. One tries to allocate resources for proper balance, so that the calendar times are approximately equal. Assume that two people are assigned to the operating subsystem and 23 to the application subsystem. From Figure 5.5 we estimate failure correction personnel utilizations for each of these subsystems. We have 0.55 and 0.365, respectively. From Equation (6.13), we obtain for the operating subsystem

$$t = \frac{8(100)}{2(0.55)} = 727 \text{ hr} = 91 \text{ days}. \tag{6.14}$$

We have, for the application subsystem

$$t = \frac{8(996)}{23(0.365)} = 949 \text{ hr} = 119 \text{ days}. \tag{6.15}$$

The calendar time required by the system will be the maximum of the subsystem times or 119 days. Note that a shift of one person either way between the subsystems would create a greater imbalance between subsystems and a longer total calendar time. ∎

6.3.2   Ignoring Change

The second approach of ignoring change is appropriate when the program is changing slowly and in a continuous fashion (or at least in relatively small steps). The continual reestimation of parameters, based on the latest data, will reflect the fact that they are changing due to program change. The parameters of some software reliability models may adapt more rapidly than others to change, although this is not known definitively at present. The estimates will be somewhat in error, since they are made by combining data from the execution of slightly different programs. Since recent data is weighted most heavily, the error will not be substantial unless the program is changing rapidly. The obvious advantage of this approach is that no extra data collection or other effort is required.

An extreme example of what happens when change is ignored is shown in Figure 6.6. Code changes were introduced in this system amounting to about 21 percent of total system size. The basic execution time model was applied. The plot shows the history of estimates of total failures and their 75 percent confidence interval as a function of calendar time. Note that the estimate of total failures increased by a factor of about 3. The actual total failures for the system increased immediately and discontinuously when the new code was added. However, there is a time lag in the estimates and possibly some tendency for them to overshoot. Note that the confidence interval increases in size during the period of greater uncertainty when the estimation algorithm recognizes it is dealing with data from a changed system. It then decreases, as the proportion of new data increases and the dimensions of the change become more evident. It will be seen that, except for the transition period, the estimation algorithm is quite robust with respect to even large program changes.

For a sudden and substantial change, you might consider discarding all the data on the old phase of the program. Estimates would be based on the new phase only. The disadvantage (a strong one) of this approach is the sometimes substantial period of time that can elapse before a large enough sample of data is in hand to make estimates of reasonable accuracy. The old data, when combined with the new, often yield a better estimate than no data at all. Whether you should discard old data depends on the size of the design change being made. Finally, the technique of failure time adjustment described in the next section may be superior to either using or not using old data, although it involves more effort.

The "ignore" approach is probably best if one is dealing with several different operational versions of a program that exist in the same time frame but on different computers. You could estimate reliability for each version separately. However, the effort required to do this is probably not justified if they do not differ from each other substantially and are all about equally debugged.

6.3.3 Failure Time Adjustment

The third approach is best when a program cannot be conveniently divided into separate independent subsystems. Also, the program should be changing rapidly enough to produce unacceptable errors in estimating model parameters. The errors are commonly exhibited as follows:

1. Present failure intensity tends to be underestimated in the early stages of a project, resulting in overly optimistic status evaluations. These are followed by long periods in which *apparent* progress is slight.
2. Completion date predictions are undefined or unstable.

FIGURE 6.6
Effect of substantial code changes.

The approach of adjusting failure times to what they would have been if the complete program had been present is fully developed theoretically in Musa, Iannino, and Okumoto (1987). The programs described in Section 5.3 can do the adjustment. Hence, the description of the approach here will be brief and nonmathematical. The method of failure time adjustment is dependent on being able to obtain a good estimate of the final size of the program.

There are three principal assumptions that are made in developing failure time adjustment:

1. **The program evolves sequentially.** This means that at any one time there is only one path of evolution of the program for which you are trying to estimate software reliability quantities. Sequential evolution is not a significant restriction. Several versions of a program may exist at one time in the field, each installed in a different set of sites. However, each version can be dealt with separately. In test, sequential evolution is characteristic of most projects, except possibly those with multiple test teams.

2. **There is pure growth.** The system changes by adding, not removing, code. Experience indicates that most design changes do not involve the removal of code. Those that do usually involve small reductions that can be neglected. It is possible to remove the restriction of pure growth in the case where there are substantial removals of code. You must carefully identify all failures that would not have occurred if the code had not been there and remove them from the data base. Thus, the cost of this greater generality is extra data analysis that is probably not worthwhile unless code removals are appreciable.

3. The number of faults introduced by program change is proportional to the developed code.

By *developed code*, we mean the sum of the new plus modified deliverable executable instructions.[4] In actuality, the number of faults is not totally dependent on size. If a better metric that relates to faults can be established, then we can substitute this improved metric into our procedure. An example might be a complexity metric. We use instructions because, with the present state of the art, it appears that this quantity does as good a job of predicting faults as anything available. Complexity metrics currently available do not add anything in terms of better prediction.

Let's look now at the effects of missing code and see what we do to compensate for them in failure time adjustment. The two effects we will describe counteract each other but do not necessarily exactly cancel. When the system is not yet at its final size, it executes faster and thus failures will be closer together in time. Adjustment spreads them apart again, as a function of the total object code ratio. The second effect that you observe is that with missing code, there are fewer faults. Hence failures tend to be farther apart and the failure intensity drops faster with execution time. To compensate for this effect with failure time adjustment, you reduce the failure spacing as a function of the developed source code ratio and the failure number. Depending on the relative sizes of the two effects, the spacing between two particular failures may either be increased or decreased by adjust-

---

[4]Code that is reused without change from a previous project or version is called *inherited code*.

ment. Although we have specified *object* code ratio and developed *source* code ratio, it is actually immaterial in each case whether you use object or source instructions since ratios are involved. Similarly, since *lines* of code generally have a high correlation with *instructions*, they may be used instead. They may be more readily available on some projects.

> **Example 6.8.** We are developing an application program for a personal computer whose final length will be 10,000 object instructions. At present, part of the program has been integrated and is being tested. This part has 5000 object instructions. Assume that this is a very simple program with no branches or loops. Faults have been introduced into the program every 100 instructions. The program executes at 1,000,000 instructions/sec. The program fails every time it encounters a fault. The final program will cycle at 100 repetitions/sec; the partial program, at 200. Thus the partial program has more opportunities to fail. However, the final program will have 100 faults; the partial program, 50. With fewer faults, the partial program will fail less often. Note that, without repair, both programs have a failure intensity of 10,000 failures/sec. The two effects we described have precisely canceled each other.
>
> Now look at the situation after 10 faults have been corrected in each case. The final program will have 90 faults and a failure intensity of 9000 failures/sec. The partial program will have 40 faults and a failure intensity of 8000 failures/sec. Note that with the partial program, repairs cause the failure intensity to decrease more rapidly than it would with the entire program present.
>
> Admittedly, this example is artificial. However, the oversimplification does not affect the principle. ∎

Failure time adjustment is dependent on being able to relate failure intensity to quantity of developed code or some other measurable characteristic(s) of the software. At present, this can be done only for the basic execution time model. In addition to failure times, you must supply information on the size of the program and the amount of developed code it contains at each failure. The adjustment calculation is generally too lengthy for manual computation, but it is straightforward in concept.

Failure time adjustment is done by stages. A *stage* is a period of execution during which the total code and the developed code remain constant. First you estimate the per-fault hazard rate ϕ based on stage 1 data. Then you adjust the stage 1 failure times, using that estimate, to the values they would have had if they had occurred with all the code present that is in stage 2. You estimate the per-fault hazard rate again. Then you adjust the failure times now associated with stage 2 (originally or by adjustment) to the values they would have had if they had occurred with all the code of stage 3 being present. This procedure continues until finally you adjust the failure times now associated with the next to last stage to the values they would have had if they had occurred in the last stage. Now you estimate total failures and initial failure intensity with all the code being present and all the failure times.

The formula for adjusting failure time t_i of stage k to stage l is derived in Musa, Iannino, and Okumoto (1987) as

$$\tilde{t}_i = -\frac{I_l}{\phi_k I_k} \ln\left\{1 - \frac{\Delta I_k}{\Delta I_l}\left[1 - \exp(-\phi_k t_i)\right]\right\}, \qquad (6.16)$$

when $\tilde{t}_i$ is the adjusted time. The quantities I_k and I_l are the numbers of object instructions in stages k and l, respectively. Similarly, ΔI_k and ΔI_l are the numbers of developed source instructions in stages k and l. The quantity ϕ_k is the per-fault hazard rate for stage k. Once the times have been adjusted to the last stage, normal estimation procedures can be applied. It should be noted, however, that the adjustment procedure is model-dependent. Hence, it is important to be consistent in the use of models for adjustment and for estimation.

For each stage we must measure the numbers of executable object and developed executable source instructions. However, measurement is often easiest in total source "lines" (comments, data statements, line continuations, etc., counted). Note that Equation (6.16) depends only on code ratios. As long as the ratio of executable object or source instructions to source lines is relatively constant throughout the program, lines can be used instead of instructions when necessary. Other quantities may also be used. The only characteristics that a substitute quantity must have are that:

1. It measures disjoint items.
2. Failures may be associated with the items.
3. Failures are distributed uniformly with respect to the items.

Some examples of alternative quantities are:

1. fraction of fields being processed in a file that is the exclusive output of a program, and
2. fraction of functions integrated.

It should be made clear that when a failure occurs, it must be associated with a unique stage, and that this association is fixed. Often a transition between stages does not coincide with a failure. Some execution time may have accumulated without a failure occurring. This accumulated execution time must be recorded and associated with the proper stage. After appropriate adjustment, it is added to the first failure time (which also has been properly adjusted) from the following stage.

You may ask how strongly the final adjusted failure times are affected by the number of stages. In fact, the number of stages is not important. It is the difference in the characteristics between the stages (I and ΔI) that determines the effect on the failure times. Ideally, a new stage is defined whenever I or ΔI change. However, ignoring small changes in I and ΔI and defining new stages only for the major changes will result in a smaller number of stages. This will simplify data collection requirements without materially degrading the quality of the adjustment.

It is assumed that the operational profile (possible input states for runs with their probabilities of being executed) is affected only by evolution because of the absence of code. That is, the selection of a run during a certain stage may not be possible because the required code has not yet been added (by plan). This can become a problem for systems in which the operational profile is highly nonuniform *and* the probabilities of occurrence of the most frequent input states are markedly different for different stages of integration. In that case, the adjustment procedure accounts for code being absent but does not completely compensate for the difference in operational profile. Note, however, that variation of the operational profile between stages of integration implies that these profiles do not represent the use of the program in the field. Either better test planning or compensation for the difference is required. Hence this "problem" is not really a problem related to the failure time adjustment.

The calendar time component of the model assumes that failures are randomly assigned among all the failure correction personnel for repair. Partial integration can conceivably upset the assignment, when the responsibility for the code being tested does not involve all of the members of the failure correction team. If each programmer doing failure correction "owns" a part of the integrated code, random assignment among all programmers will occur and partial integration will have little effect. If some programmers do not, the number of failure correction personnel should be appropriately reduced. The latter situation will yield satisfactory short-term predictions, but long-term predictions will have greater error since the number of personnel will not be constant.

To illustrate failure adjustment, consider the bank network of Case Study 1.1. Assume that the firm, during the first part of the test phase, is testing the system controller code necessary to perform all the interface functions implied by the system. It is also verifying the programs for deposits and withdrawals of cash by bank customers. Later during the test phase, the code necessary to allow transactions such as credit card payments and transfer of funds between accounts is integrated and tested along with the previous code. To adjust the failure data, the number of executable object and executable developed source instructions is measured before and after the latter code is integrated. For our example, assume that two-thirds of the code developed by the firm is tested initially in stage 1. Furthermore, all code is developed. No inherited code is used. This will lead to the adjusted failure interval data shown in Table 6.3. The adjusted times will then be used to obtain better estimates of the quantities shown in Figures 1.8 and 1.9.

6.4   CHANGES IN ENVIRONMENT

It has been noted that software reliability has been defined in terms of the environment in which a program executes. This refers to the operational profile or set of probabilities associated with the set of possible input states. Hence, if a program is executed in a different environment, the reliability can be expected to change. The determination of the changed reliability is perhaps best analyzed in terms of failure intensities. Let λ_1 be the failure intensity for the input states that the old

TABLE 6.3
Failure data for sequentially integrated system example

Failure number	Unadjusted failure time	Adjusted failure time
1	537	537
2	541	541
3	6461	6451
4	11623	11591
.	.	.
.	.	.
.	.	.

and new environments have in common. Let λ_2 be the failure intensity for the unique input states of the new environment. Let p_1 be the probability of being in an input state of the old environment; p_2, the new. Then the failure intensity λ in the new environment is

$$\lambda = p_1\lambda_1 + p_2\lambda_2 . \tag{6.17}$$

The foregoing is based on the assumption that the failures for any part of the input space for a stable program can be characterized by a homogeneous Poisson process. To determine p_2 and hence $p_1 = 1 - p_2$, you must know to what extent the environment has changed. For λ_1, you would use the present failure intensity for the old program. For λ_2, you would estimate the failure intensity for the new input states in the environment. In the absence of better information, it probably would be reasonable to use the initial failure intensity of the old program. It represents the failure intensity of input states that have not been executed before.

Example 6.9. A program has a failure intensity of 1 failure/hr when executing with the operational profile for which it was designed. When the program was originally tested, its initial failure intensity was 20 failures/hr. We expect that new conditions will occur for the program 1 percent of the time. We estimate the new failure intensity by assuming a failure intensity of 20 failures/hr for the new conditions. Using Equation (6.17) we have

$$\lambda = 0.99(1) + 0.01(20)$$

$$= 0.99 + 0.2$$

$$= 1.19 \text{ failure/hr} . \qquad \blacksquare$$

It would be theoretically possible to analyze two operational profiles on a microstructure level, looking at probabilities of occurrence and failure intensities for each input state. You could then compute the effect of a change in operational profile in a detailed fashion. However, this would require an enormous amount of data collection and computation. In practice, it would appear to offer little advantage over the vastly simpler and more economical approach just described.

Sometimes the input space expands at a rate that can be modeled. For example, after a new software product is released, users may try to apply the product in ways for which it was not designed. The rate at which the input space expands may be proportional to the execution time for the program, taken over all installations.

It is possible for the operational environment to be changing in such a way that the observed failure intensity remains approximately constant for a substantial period of time. This can occur during a system test period, for example, when a series of functions is being executed without repetition. This is sometimes called *feature test*, in contrast with the term *load test* that is used to describe testing for the normal operational environment that is expected for the program. If each function is associated with different code, then any correction that occurs after a failure does not affect succeeding runs. We thus pass from function to function and routine to routine, all having approximately the same fault density and hence the same failure intensity. The result is that we observe constant failure intensity for the period of the test. Frequently, this situation can be handled by using one of the techniques developed for evolving programs (see Section 6.3).

An example of a program that was executed in two different environments is given in Hamilton and Musa (1978). The program was an operating system that was installed on two essentially identical but physically separate computers. The two computers were kept in step with regard to software releases. The operating system on the first machine was being used primarily to provide batch service; on the second, time sharing service. The failure intensity at a common point in time was computed for the first use as 0.0201 failure/CPU hr, and the second use as 0.0163 failure/CPU hr. The foregoing represents a variation of about 19 percent.

There is a special change in environment that is of particular interest—the change from the test phase to the operational phase. The change results solely from the fact that input states are not generally repeated during the test phase.

We will define the *testing compression factor C* as the ratio of execution time required in the operational phase to execution time required in the test phase to cover the input space of the program. Let's first consider a simple example to clarify the concept, before making a more general formulation. Assume that a program has only two input states, A and B. Input state A occurs 90 percent of the time; B, 10 percent. All runs take 1 CPU hr. In operation, on the average, it will require 10 CPU hr to cover the input space, with A occurring nine times and B, one. In test, the coverage can be accomplished in 2 CPU hr. The testing compression factor would be 5 in this case.

A more general formulation of the testing compression factor is derived in Musa, Iannino, and Okumoto (1987) as

$$C = \frac{\sum_{k=1}^{Q_I} \dfrac{p_k}{p_{\min}} \tau_k}{\sum_{k=1}^{Q_I} \tau_k}. \tag{6.18}$$

Here Q_I is the total number of input states in the input space. The quantity p_k is the probability of occurrence of input state k. Note that $p_{\min}$ is the probability of occurrence of the input state that is least probable. Finally, τ_k is the run time for run type k. It is shown in Musa, Iannino, and Okumoto (1987) that this expression simplifies to

$$C = \frac{1}{Q_I \, p_{\min}} \qquad (6.19)$$

if all runs are of equal length. If the probability of occurrence of input state k is inversely proportional to its rank (that is, number) then Equation (6.19) becomes

$$C = \psi(Q_I + 1) - \psi(1) . \qquad (6.20)$$

The function ψ is the psi or digamma function [Davis (1962)]. A plot of C as a function of the number of input states Q_I for this situation is shown in Figure 6.7. It is interesting to note that C changes very slowly with Q_I. Hence the range of values of C to be expected is probably relatively small.

Equivalence partitioning increases the testing compression factor. This will be seen if you note that only one test need be run per input state *group* rather than input state. Thus the denominator in Equation (6.19) becomes smaller and the test compression factor larger.

The name *testing compression factor* comes from the fact that an amount of execution time in test can represent a larger amount of execution time in operation. This concept is analogous to that of stress testing for hardware. It offers promise in permitting the testing of high reliability systems in reasonable amounts of execution time, particularly if equivalence partitioning is employed. Note that equivalence partitioning must not be used to the point where the risk of missing failures increases substantially. The extra care required in test planning when equivalence partitioning is employed increases test planning costs substantially. However, the shorter test period required usually results in a net reduction in test costs.

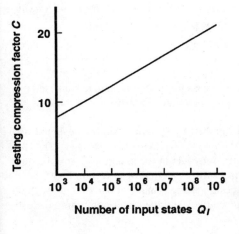

FIGURE 6.7
Testing compression factor versus number of input states for equal run lengths and occurrence probability inversely proportional to rank.

Execution times experienced in test should be multiplied by the testing compression factor. They can then be processed by software reliability estimation programs. Alternatively, the failure times obtained in test can be used to estimate test phase failure intensities, using the programs. These failure intensities should then be *divided* by the testing compression factor C to obtain the corresponding failure intensities to be expected in operation. The testing compression factor computed by formula may overestimate the actual testing compression factor achieved. In many test phases, some repetition of input states may occur, often deliberately due to regression testing. The computed testing compression factor should be divided by the average number of occurrences of each input state expected.

Sometimes testing is carried out at multiple sites, with one site maximizing test efficiency. The others conduct actual field tests in accordance with the operational profile expected in the field. When test data are combined from these sites, execution times from the "efficient" site should be multiplied by the testing compression factor for that site. Execution times from the other sites do not need adjustment, since these sites will have testing compression factors of 1.

6.5 OTHER CONSIDERATIONS

If testing starts before integration is complete, then there may be periods of inactivity in testing and debugging due to waits for programs not yet ready. These periods must be estimated separately and added to estimates of remaining t, or else t must not be viewed as "running" when they occur. Note that severe computer outages (one day or more) and delays due to requirements changes have not been included in the estimate of remaining test phase length. They must be added if expected.

6.6 SUMMARY

In this chapter we have absorbed a rich lore of experience gained from actual software projects. We have dealt with real world problems such as incomplete and inaccurate data collection, multiple installations, evolving programs, and changing environments. Reasonable solutions to these problems are available.

PROBLEMS

6.1 We plan to test our program first with a software environment simulator and later in the real environment. Would you expect present failure intensity to increase or decrease in making the transition?

6.2 Can software reliability measurement be applied to systems that are designed and tested "top down?"

6.3 Is there some way we can determine failure intervals in the situation where we only know that the failure occurred at some time during a period of uncertain length?

6.4 Does it make sense to handle substantial design changes made at one time by separating the pre- and post-change estimation procedures and then later combining the estimates in some way?

6.5 We are testing at multiple sites. Because of time lags in communicating and fixing problems, failures encountered at one site are often repeated at another. Does this cause any problem?

6.6 We are testing at two different sites, the development site and a field site. There is a time lag in releasing new versions of the program to the field site. Consequently, the field site is always testing an earlier release than the one we are testing at the development site. The later version does not have many new features but it does have fault corrections not included in the previous release. How can we handle this?

6.7 Can you account for a situation where the actual operating environment is much more demanding than the test environment?

6.8 How do we combine failure intervals from projects with several different versions of software simultaneously in test?

6.9 It is difficult for us to measure execution time associated with a tester running a particular test. Several tests are usually running simultaneously and they may all be serviced by some common processes. We *can* measure elapsed time and pinpoint the occurrence of failures with respect to it. We can also measure total execution time for the system at various elapsed times (for example, hourly). How can we convert elapsed time between failures into execution time? The number of users on the system varies, so utilization (the ratio of execution time to elapsed time) is not constant.

6.10 We are trying to determine the interval between failures for an interactive system with a varying number of users in which measuring execution time is difficult. Is there a better way of doing this than measuring clock time?

6.11 Suppose a known number of failures occur in a time window at unknown times. When you assign the failure times randomly within the window, why not assume a trend to the failure intervals?

SEVEN

APPLICATION PROCEDURES

A survey of typical uses of software reliability measurement was presented in Chapter 3. Now that we have armed the reader with a deeper understanding of the practical aspects of software reliability measurement in Chapters 4, 5, and 6, we will revisit the sphere of applications. We will describe the procedures to be employed and touch on some more advanced topics. We will not repeat the material presented in Chapter 3, so you may want to refer back to it. You will recall that Table 3.1 gives a summary of applications. Before we deal with the applications, however, we will examine three types of calculations that are common to many of the applications to gain some insight. These include the computation of:

1. system test duration,
2. system test resource requirements and cost, and
3. operational cost of failures.

Usually we have found it best to implement calculations in computer programs (Section 5.3). However, sometimes it is more convenient to perform short calculations manually, especially if one wants to gain some insight. A summary of the most useful formulas is provided for reference in Appendix B. We will group the applications to be discussed into several broad categories. These include system engineering, project management, management of operational phase, and evaluation of software engineering technologies.

7.1 BASIC DURATION AND COST CALCULATIONS

In computing costs, we will be dealing with only the reliability-dependent components, not total costs. This is satisfactory because other costs are readily calculated and added if total costs are needed. Many applications, however, are concerned mainly with finding the reliability that minimizes cost, and the foregoing components are totally satisfactory for this. When we say "reliability dependent" we refer to the differences in reliability obtained by varying the amount of testing. Reliability is affected by the support environment and methodologies used on the project. However, these factors are not easily varied while the project is underway.

The time required, resources needed, and costs associated with testing are mainly dependent on the initial reliability of the design and code and the reliability goal to be attained. Although program size influences the two foregoing quantities, it is far from the sole factor. Hence "person months per K lines of code" estimating is not generally appropriate, and a reliability-related approach must be taken.

Note that we can calculate system test duration and system test cost using the simulation program described in Chapter 5. This is the recommended procedure, but another approach is presented here to give the reader insight. Also, some may prefer quick hand calculations or may not have ready access to the program. The procedure is, for the most part, independent of the particular execution time component used. For illustration, we will use the basic model.

7.1.1 System Test Duration

To compute system test duration (excluding the test planning effort), we first determine the values of the execution time component parameters as described in Chapter 5.

The calendar time interval t consists of the sum of one to three periods. In each period, a different resource is *limiting*. This means that the resource produces the maximum ratio of calendar time to execution time for that period. That resource is indicated by the value of the index r: C is computer time, F is failure correction personnel, and I is failure identification personnel. We compute the duration of each period separately, based on its limiting resource. Then the durations are summed. We have

$$ t = \sum_r \frac{\Delta\chi_{rr}}{P_r \rho_r} . \tag{7.1} $$

The quantity $\Delta\chi_{rr}$ is the requirement for resource r during the period for which it is limiting. For example, it might be 100 person days. Note that it is generally not the same as the total resource requirement to meet the failure intensity objective $\Delta\chi_r$. Note that P_r is the quantity of resource r *available* (for example, 5 persons). The quantity ρ_r is the utilization factor for resource r. The resource utilization factor reflects the possibility that all of an available resource cannot be usefully employed.

Each resource requirement during its limiting *period* is given by

$$ \Delta\chi_{rr} = \theta_r \Delta\tau_r + \mu_r \, \Delta\mu_r . \tag{7.2} $$

Note that θ_r is the resource expenditure per unit execution time. The quantity μ_r is the resource expenditure per failure. The symbol $\Delta\tau_r$ represents the execution time interval for the *period*. The quantity $\Delta\mu_r$ is the number of failures experienced in the *period*.

To obtain the expected number of failures experienced in the period for the basic model, we use

$$\Delta\mu_r = \nu_0 \frac{\lambda_{r_1} - \lambda_{r_2}}{\lambda_0} \ . \tag{7.3}$$

The quantities λ_{r_1} and λ_{r_2} are the failure intensities at the boundaries of the limiting resource period. The execution time interval is determined from

$$\Delta\tau_r = \frac{\nu_0}{\lambda_0} \ln \frac{\lambda_{r_1}}{\lambda_{r_2}} \ . \tag{7.4}$$

The boundaries of the different resource-limited periods λ_{r_1} and λ_{r_2} are the present and objective failure intensities and the transition points [derived in Musa, Iannino, and Okumoto (1987)] λ_{rs} that lie within the range. We have for the potential transition points

$$\lambda_{rs} = \frac{P_s\rho_s\theta_r - P_r\rho_r\theta_s}{P_r\rho_r\mu_s - P_s\rho_s\mu_r} \ . \tag{7.5}$$

The subscripts (r, s) have the values (F, C), (F, I), and (I, C). You must determine which resource-limited periods actually occur from an examination of the boundaries and a determination of the maximum calendar time to execution time ratio for each period. To find the maximum calendar time to execution time ratio for each period we compute

$$\left.\frac{dt}{d\tau}\right]_{\max} = \max\left(\frac{\theta_r + \mu_r\lambda}{P_r\rho_r}\right) \ . \tag{7.6}$$

The quantity λ is any failure intensity in the range $[\lambda_{r_1}, \lambda_{r_2}]$.

Example 7.1. The resource usage parameters (with overhead included) for a software project to build an inventory control system are the following:

Resource	Resource usage	
	Per failure	Per CPU hr
Failure identification personnel (person hr)	3	5
Failure correction personnel (person hr)	8	0
Computer time (CPU hr)	1	1

The test team has 4 people and there are 12 debuggers. Everyone works a normal 8-hr day. The computer operates 16 hr/day, 5 days/week. Work hours and procedures are organized so that this time can be used. Thus $P_C = 2$. Computer utilization is 0.75. Failure correction personnel utilization is 0.333. Failure identification personnel utilization, as always, is 1. The initial and present failure intensity is 10 failures/CPU hr. The failure intensity objective is 0.1 failure/CPU hr. The number of total failures is 100. We want to determine the calendar time required to reach the objective, using the basic execution time model.

We must first establish the extent of each resource-limited period. We compute the potential transition point between the failure-correction-personnel-limited and failure-identification-personnel-limited periods as follows, using Equation (7.5):

$$\lambda_{FI} = \frac{P_I \rho_I \theta_F - P_F \rho_F \theta_I}{P_F \rho_F \mu_I - P_I \rho_I \mu_F}$$

$$= \frac{4(1)(0) - 12(0.333)(5)}{12(0.333)(3) - 4(1)(8)}$$

$$= \frac{-20}{12 - 32}$$

$$= 1 \text{ failure/CPU hr.}$$

The potential transition point between the failure-identification-personnel-limited and computer-time-limited periods is

$$\lambda_{IC} = \frac{P_C \rho_C \theta_I - P_I \rho_I \theta_C}{P_I \rho_I \mu_C - P_C \rho_C \mu_I}$$

$$= \frac{2(0.75)(5) - 4(1)(1)}{4(1)(1) - 2(0.75)(3)}$$

$$= \frac{7.5 - 4}{4 - 4.5}$$

$$= -7 \text{ failures/CPU hr.}$$

This potential transition point clearly falls outside the range of failure intensities (10 to 0.1 failures/CPU hr) we are concerned with. The potential transition point between the failure-correction-personnel-limited and computer-time-limited periods is

$$\lambda_{FC} = \frac{P_C \rho_C \theta_F - P_F \rho_F \theta_C}{P_F \rho_F \mu_C - P_C \rho_C \mu_F}$$

$$= \frac{2(0.75)(0) - 12(0.333)(1)}{12(0.333)(1) - 2(0.75)(8)}$$

$$= \frac{-4}{4 - 12}$$

$$= 0.5 \text{ failure/CPU hr.}$$

There are three potential resource-limited periods: 10 to 1, 1 to 0.5, and 0.5 to 0.1 failures/CPU hr. We must evaluate the derivative of calendar time with respect to execution time for each resource at some point in each of these periods, using Equation (7.6). At $\lambda = 10$ failures/CPU hr we have

$$\left.\frac{dt}{d\tau}\right]_I = \frac{\theta_I + \mu_I\lambda}{P_I\rho_I} = \frac{5 + 3(10)}{4(1)} = \frac{35}{4} = 8.75 \,,$$

$$\left.\frac{dt}{d\tau}\right]_F = \frac{\theta_F + \mu_F\lambda}{P_F\rho_F} = \frac{0 + 8(10)}{12(0.333)} = \frac{80}{4} = 20 \,, \text{ and}$$

$$\left.\frac{dt}{d\tau}\right]_C = \frac{\theta_C + \mu_C\lambda}{P_C\rho_C} = \frac{1 + 1(10)}{2(0.75)} = \frac{11}{1.5} = 7.33 \,.$$

The period from 10 to 1 failures/CPU hr is failure-correction-personnel-limited. At $\lambda = 0.8$ failure/CPU hr we have

$$\left.\frac{dt}{d\tau}\right]_I = \frac{5 + 3(0.8)}{4(1)} = \frac{7.4}{4} = 1.85 \,,$$

$$\left.\frac{dt}{d\tau}\right]_F = \frac{0 + 8(0.8)}{12(0.333)} = \frac{6.4}{4} = 1.6 \,, \text{ and}$$

$$\left.\frac{dt}{d\tau}\right]_C = \frac{1 + 1(0.8)}{2(0.75)} = \frac{1.8}{1.5} = 1.2 \,.$$

The period from 1 to 0.5 failures/CPU hr is failure-identification-personnel-limited. At $\lambda = 0.1$ failure/CPU hr we have

$$\left.\frac{dt}{d\tau}\right]_I = \frac{5 + 3(0.1)}{4(1)} = \frac{5.3}{4} = 1.325 \,,$$

$$\left.\frac{dt}{d\tau}\right]_F = \frac{0 + 8(0.1)}{12(0.333)} = \frac{0.8}{4} = 0.2 \,, \text{ and}$$

$$\left.\frac{dt}{d\tau}\right]_C = \frac{1 + 1(0.1)}{2(0.75)} = \frac{1.1}{1.5} = 0.733 \,.$$

The potential transition point at $\lambda_{FC} = 0.5$ failure/sec is not real, since failure identification personnel are still limiting at 0.1 failure/sec. You might also have concluded this from the fact that failure identification personnel were limiting just above 0.5 failure/sec. Consequently, a transition *from* a failure-correction-personnel-limited period could not have occurred. Then, the period from 1 to 0.1 failure/CPU hr is failure-identification-personnel-limited.

Next, we will calculate the expected number of failures experienced and execution time elapsed for each period, using Equations (7.3) and (7.4). For the failure-correction-personnel-limited period we have

$$\Delta\mu_F = \nu_0 \frac{\lambda_{F_1} - \lambda_{F_2}}{\lambda_0} = 100 \; \frac{10 - 1}{10} = 90 \text{ failures}$$

and

$$\Delta\tau_F = \frac{\nu_0}{\lambda_0} \ln \frac{\lambda_{F_1}}{\lambda_{F_2}} = \frac{100}{10} \ln \frac{10}{1} = 23.0 \text{ CPU hr.}$$

For the failure-identification-personnel-limited period we have

$$\Delta\mu_I = \nu_0 \frac{\lambda_{I_1} - \lambda_{I_2}}{\lambda_0} = 100 \; \frac{1 - 0.1}{10} = 9 \text{ failures}$$

and

$$\Delta\tau_I = \frac{\nu_0}{\lambda_0} \ln \frac{\lambda_{I_1}}{\lambda_{I_2}} = \frac{100}{10} \ln \frac{1}{0.1} = 23.0 \text{ CPU hr.}$$

The failure correction effort required during the failure-correction-personnel-limited period is, from Equation (7.2)

$$\Delta\chi_{FF} = \theta_F \Delta\tau_F + \mu_F \Delta\mu_F$$

$$= 0(23.0) + 8(90)$$

$$= 720 \text{ person hr.}$$

The failure identification effort during the failure-identification-personnel-limited period is

$$\Delta\chi_{II} = \theta_I \Delta\tau_I + \mu_I \Delta\mu_I$$

$$= 5(23) + 3(9)$$

$$= 142 \text{ person hr.}$$

The calendar time expended during the failure-correction-personnel-limited period is, from Equation (7.1),

$$t_F = \frac{\Delta\chi_{FF}}{P_F \rho_F} = \frac{720}{12(0.333)} = \frac{720}{4} = 180 \text{ hr.}$$

The calendar time expended during the failure-identification-personnel-limited period is

$$t_I = \frac{\Delta\chi_{II}}{P_I \rho_I} = \frac{142}{4(1)} = 35.5 \text{ hr.}$$

Thus the total calendar time is

$$t = t_F + t_I = 180 + 35.5 = 215.5 \text{ hr.}$$

Dividing by the 8-hr day, we obtain 27 days.   ∎

7.1.2 System Test Resource Requirements and Cost

The starting point for computing resource requirements and cost is also the determination of the values of the execution time component parameters. Then find the expected number of failures

$$\mu = \nu_0 \left[1 - \frac{\lambda_F}{\lambda_0} \right] \tag{7.7}$$

that must be experienced and the associated execution time

$$\tau = \frac{\nu_0}{\lambda_0} \ln \left[\frac{\lambda_0}{\lambda_F} \right] \tag{7.8}$$

to decrease the failure intensity from λ_0 to the failure intensity objective λ_F. Normalized values of these quantities are plotted in Figures 7.1 and 7.2 as a function of the failure intensity ratio λ_0/λ_F. In Figure 7.1, the fraction μ/ν_0 of total failures that must be experienced to reach the failure intensity objective is plotted. Note that as the failure intensity ratio approaches infinity, the fraction of total failures that must be experienced approaches 1. In Figure 7.2, we plot a normalized execution time increment $B\phi\rho$, where B is the fault reduction factor and ϕ, the per fault hazard rate. As the failure intensity ratio approaches infinity, the normalized (and hence actual) execution time increment approaches infinity. Each of the three *total* resource expenditures χ_r is given by

$$\chi_r = \theta_r \tau + \mu_r \mu , \tag{7.9}$$

where r has the values C, F, and I. As the failure intensity ratio approaches infinity, the failure identification and computer resource expenditures approach infinity logarithmically. The general shape of the curves is shown in Figure 7.3. The failure correction resource expenditure approaches the product of total failures and failure correction effort per failure. The general shape of the curve is the same as that shown in Figure 7.1. To get overall cost, multiply each χ_r by its cost rate and

FIGURE 7.1
Variation of fraction of total failures to be experienced with failure intensity ratio—basic execution time model.

FIGURE 7.2
Variation of normalized execution time increment with failure intensity ratio—basic execution time model.

total the results. Note that cost approaches infinity as the failure intensity ratio approaches infinity. The general shape of the cost curve is shown in Figure 7.3. For large failure intensity ratios, the cost curve approaches a logarithmic shape. Suppose you decrease the failure intensity objective or increase the failure intensity ratio by a factor of 2. Then the cost of achieving the more stringent goal is less than twice as much. This might seem counterintuitive. However, with the basic model, the removal of "later" faults in a system reduces failure intensity by a larger factor than removal of "early" faults. The reduction factor is $\omega/(\omega-1)$, where ω is the number of faults remaining. Thus, although the execution time between failures and consequent costs are increasing rapidly, the foregoing countervailing factor makes the relationship between cost and failure intensity sublinear.

The foregoing approach implicitly assumes that idle time for all resources during the project can be profitably employed in other activities and should not be charged as a cost. If this is not true for any resource, the cost for that resource should be determined as follows. Multiply t from Equation (7.1) by the total number of personnel (or dedicated computers) and the resource rate.

Example 7.2. We will calculate the resource requirements and cost of system test for the inventory control software project of Example 7.1. The personnel cost (including loading or overhead) is $75/hr. The computer cost is $500/CPU hr. We will first use Equation (7.7) to compute the expected number of failures that must be experienced to reach the failure intensity objective. We have

$$\Delta\mu = \nu_0 \left(1 - \frac{\lambda_F}{\lambda_0} \right)$$

FIGURE 7.3
General form of failure identification effort, computer time, and cost curves with failure intensity ratio—basic execution time model.

$$= 100 \left[1 - \frac{0.1}{10} \right]$$

$$= 99 \text{ failures.}$$

The associated execution time, using Equation (7.8), is

$$\Delta\tau = \frac{\nu_0}{\lambda_0} \ln \left[\frac{\lambda_0}{\lambda_F} \right]$$

$$= \frac{100}{10} \ln \left[\frac{10}{0.1} \right]$$

$$= 10 \ln 100$$

$$= 46.0 \text{ CPU hr.}$$

The failure identification personnel effort is, from Equation (7.9),

$$\chi_I = \theta_I \tau + \mu_I \mu$$

$$= 5(46.0) + 3(99)$$

$$= 527 \text{ person hr.}$$

We have, for the failure correction personnel effort

$$\chi_F = \theta_F \tau + \mu_F \mu$$

$$= 0(46.0) + 8(99)$$

$$= 792 \text{ person hr.}$$

The computer time is

$$\chi_C = \theta_C \tau + \mu_C \mu$$

$$= 1(46.0) + 1(99)$$

$$= 145 \text{ CPU hr.}$$

The total personnel effort is 1319 hr. Multiplying by the cost rate of \$75/hr, we obtain a personnel cost for system test of \$98,925. The computer cost, using a rate of \$500/CPU hr, is \$72,500. Thus total system test cost is \$171,425.

Note from Example 7.1 that the failure correction effort during the failure-correction-personnel-limited period was 720 person hr. Subtracting this figure from the total effort of 792 person hr, you will see that 72 person hr were expended during the failure-identification-personnel-limited period. Similarly, the failure identification effort during the failure-identification-personnel-limited period was 142 person hr. Subtracting this from the total effort of 527 person hr, you will see that 385 person hr were used during the failure-correction-personnel-limited period. ∎

7.1.3   Operational Cost of Failures

The first step in computing reliability-dependent cost for the operational period is to establish the cost of each failure. You should consider factors such as the cost of disrupted service on operations, the cost of restoring the system to operation, the impact of lost customers, and the cost of possible product liability actions. Restoration involves such activities as:

1. making a service call,
2. terminating an unsatisfactorily operating program in an orderly fashion,
3. reconstructing relevant data bases,
4. reloading and restarting the program, and
5. documenting the circumstances of failure.

Usually the underlying fault is not repaired in the field but is corrected in the next release of the software. However, field repairs may be undertaken for critical failures or critical systems. In that case, the costs of fault detection and correction at the central site *and* repair distribution and installation must be added to operational period costs. We generally assume a cost per failure that is independent of failure intensity. This appears to be generally valid, but the cost can increase nonlinearly when failure intensities are large. A greater than linear increase can arise from increased costs of restoration when closely spaced failures interact with each other. An even more likely source of nonlinearity is the impact of lost customers. Customer defections may increase markedly after some level of tolerance is exceeded.

The expected life of the release of the system must be estimated, and the number of systems installed must be determined. The product of the two foregoing factors gives total operational hours expected for all installed systems for this release. If we multiply operational hours by failure intensity objective and cost per failure, we obtain an expression for total operational cost of failures for the release. Implicit in the calculation is the assumption that failure intensity per CPU hour is constant over the life of the release. In general, this is true because usually there are no substantial changes (enhancements or repairs) to a program between releases. Sometimes reported failures per calendar period (day, week, etc.) vary with time, but this is due to variations in operating time and number of installations.

We have focused on software failure intensity and software-failure-caused costs. However, in many cases we will want to take a broader view. We will determine computer *system* failure intensity and account for costs resulting from all aspects of system failure.

> **Example 7.3.** Consider a securities portfolio tracking and evaluation program that is installed at 1000 locations. It is considered to have a useful life of 2 years. It operates 250 days/year. On the average, we can expect 2 CPU hr of execution time per

day. The total execution time of each program copy is thus 1000 hr. The total operational hours over all copies is 1,000,000. Suppose the failure intensity objective is 2 failures/1000 hr. Then we can expect 2000 failures. If the cost of a failure averages $1000, then the total operational cost of failure for this system is $2,000,000. ∎

7.2 SYSTEM ENGINEERING

You may be concerned about the accuracy with which parameters on a particular project can be estimated. If this is a problem, you should note that inaccuracies usually affect absolute rather than relative values. Many and perhaps most system engineering decisions are concerned with relative values of alternatives. In any case, we can and should perform calculations with different values of a parameter to determine the sensitivity of a decision to parameter inaccuracy. As experience is gained and more data is available, it should be possible to determine parameters more accurately and hence improve the *absolute* accuracy with which costs, schedules, and other quantities can be estimated.

7.2.1 Reliability Specification

Specification of reliability to a designer involves the determination of a system reliability objective, which we will consider shortly. It also involves "allocation" of the reliability to the system components, if the designer is responsible for just a component. Good allocation depends primarily on gaining a good technical understanding of the relative difficulties of achieving different levels of reliability for the components in question. "Difficulty" should be considered particularly in economic and schedule terms. Example 7.7 provides a simple illustration of the allocation process. An example of a specification placed on a designer would be "Software subsystem X must have a reliability of 0.99 for a 10-hr period."

7.2.2 Failure Restoration Resource Requirements and Costs

Predictions of failure restoration resource requirements and costs are closely related. Both depend on determination of the failure intensity that will be experienced in the operational phase. The following examples should be illustrative.

> **Example 7.4.** A software-based system that operates 40 hr/week was released with a failure intensity of 0.025 failure/hr. The average time (including travel) required for a repair person to restore the system after a failure is 4 hr. How many systems can one repair person maintain?
>
> Note that the expected number of failures in one week will be one, requiring 4 hr for restoration. Thus one repair person can theoretically handle 10 systems. In actuality, each repair person should be assigned fewer systems, perhaps seven. This would allow for variations in the occurrence of failures that could result in a backlog of failures awaiting restoration. Such a backlog might be unacceptable from a system availability viewpoint. Apply queueing theory to find the utilization factor for repair

personnel that is acceptable. An alternative strategy would be to operate at a higher utilization factor and handle backlogs with overtime.   ■

Example 7.5. Assume in Example 7.4 that the loaded salary of the repair person is $25/hr. Since 4 hr/week of restoration work are required on a system, the monthly cost for this effort is $433, based on $4^{1}/_{3}$ weeks/month. However, if a lighter load is assigned to each repair person to ensure rapid response and good system availability, the cost would be $619/month.   ■

7.2.3 Reliability-Schedules-Resources-Cost Trade-offs

The investigation of trade-offs among reliability, schedules, resources, and cost involves the following general procedure. You choose several values of each parameter that is to be varied. Apply either execution time model to compute the effects of parameter variations. Examine the results and iterate this procedure as required. Usually you choose the parameter values to include the extreme values that are reasonably possible, so that the influence of the parameters can be quickly determined. Reliability and failure intensity vary with the average instruction execution rate of the machine on which a program is running. Hence you may consider function and performance as additional factors in making a trade-off. For example, assume that a retail store online transaction processing program A, developed for machine A, has half the failure intensity of program B, developed for machine B. But suppose that program B runs five times as fast. The failure intensity with respect to transactions is $2^{1}/_{2}$ times better for program B.

It is possible to develop an initial project schedule for the system test period *before testing begins* by use of the equations given in Section 7.1.1. Alternatively, one may use the simulation program (Chapter 5), which implements these equations. We can predict the number of failures that must be experienced (and the associated execution time required) to attain the failure intensity objective. Predictions of system test cost may be made, using the equations of Section 7.1.2 (or again, the simulation program). The accuracy of the foregoing *pretest* predictions depends on how well the parameters can be predicted. At present, limited data from a few projects are available to answer this question. Much more data are required. However, pretest predictions may be of substantial value if looked at *relative* to one another. Examining the changes induced by varying different parameters may be helpful in deciding on project trade-offs.

Since the execution time component parameters may be continually refined by *reestimation* during test, it is easy to continually reestimate derived quantities (with confidence intervals). Recall that the derived quantities include:

1. the present failure intensity,
2. the additional number of failures that must be experienced in order to reach the project failure intensity objective, and
3. the associated additional execution and calendar times and completion date.

We can also calculate resource requirements and costs, giving us the capability to relook at reliability-schedule-resource-cost trade-offs at any time during test. Programs for making these calculations were discussed in Chapter 5.

7.2.4 Setting a Failure Intensity Objective

The first question one must ask in setting a failure intensity objective is, "*Who* is the customer?" The second is, "What does the customer want?" And third, "Which objective is best for you, in the broadest sense, in your particular competitive environment?" Consider a delivered product with a rapid rate of technological obsolescence. The approach taken may be different from that for a stable product delivered internally within a company for use in providing external service. For example, when computing costs in a cost-based approach to setting the objective, it is necessary to know "costs to whom?"

There are at least three principal methods used in establishing the failure intensity objective for a system:

1. system balance,
2. release date, and
3. life cycle cost optimization.

The first approach, system balance, is primarily used in allocating reliabilities among components of a system. It is particularly applicable to systems in which the development is especially challenging. This could be because the system uses state-of-the-art technology or because the reliability requirements are severe ones. Hence we often use it for military systems. The basic principle to be followed is to *balance* the difficulty of development work on different components. The components that have the most severe functional requirements or are most advanced technologically are assigned less stringent reliability requirements. In the case of software, functions never implemented before or based on untried algorithms might fall in this category. Components that are relatively standard and that are used in common practice are assigned more stringent reliability requirements. For software, this might include previously tested routines that will be reused. This approach generally leads to the least costly development effort in the minimum time.

The second approach, release date, is used when product release date is particularly critical. Schedule criticality can result from military requirements or market window necessities. Alternatively, the product may be a component of a larger system with severe delivery date requirements. This approach involves keeping the release date fixed. The failure intensity objective is either established by the resources and funds available, or is traded off against these quantities.

In the release date approach, it is desirable to have some sense of how failure intensity trades off with release date. First, we determine how failure intensity trades off with execution time. We then convert to dates. The failure intensity at the start of system test may be assumed to have been established by the nature of the project and the programming environment. We obtain the relationship between the ratio of failure intensity change in system test λ_0/λ_F and execution time τ for the basic execution time model from Equation (2.11) as

$$\tau = \frac{\nu_0}{\lambda_0} \ln \frac{\lambda_0}{\lambda_F} . \tag{7.10}$$

For the logarithmic Poisson execution time model, it is obtained from Equation (2.12) as

$$\tau = \frac{1}{\theta\lambda_0} \left[\frac{\lambda_0}{\lambda_F} - 1 \right] . \tag{7.11}$$

Since the quantities ν_0, λ_0, and θ are fixed in any given case, the comparative variations of execution time τ with failure intensity ratio λ_0/λ_F will be as shown in Figure 7.4. Note that the increase in execution time with larger ratios of failure intensity is greater for the logarithmic Poisson model (linear rather than logarithmic).

Example 7.6. Use the failure data for system T1 [provided in Table 12.1 of Musa, Iannino, and Okumoto (1987)] to estimate parameters for both the basic and logarithmic Poisson models. The following results are obtained, if the testing compression factor $C = 1$ (in other examples using system T1 in the book, it is 15.1).

Basic	Logarithmic Poisson
$\lambda_0 = 17.8$ failures/CPU hr $\nu_0 = 142$ failures	$\lambda_0 = 39.9$ failures/CPU hr $\theta = 0.0236$/failure

By using Equations (7.10) and (7.11) we can determine the length of the system test period for various failure intensity improvement factors.

	Execution time (CPU hr)	
Improvement factor	Basic	Logarithmic Poisson
10	18.4	9.56
100	36.7	105.1
1000	55.1	1060.9
10,000	73.5	10,619

∎

The relationship of calendar time to execution time will vary with the values of the calendar time component parameters. However, the general shape will be as shown in Figure 2.21. If we "combine" this figure with Figure 7.4, we obtain the general shape of the relationship of calendar time with failure intensity ratio, shown in Figure 7.5. The relationship can be used to determine the failure intensity ratio and hence the objective, given the release date and the resources available.

FIGURE 7.4
Comparative variation of execution time with failure intensity ratio—basic and logarithmic Poisson execution time models.

The third approach, life cycle cost optimization, applies particularly to the software component of a system, although it can readily be adapted to the overall system as well. The basis for optimization is the assumption that reliability improvement is obtained by more extensive testing, which of course affects costs and schedules. Costs and schedules for other phases are assumed to be constant. This assumption is reasonable. Reliability improvement techniques such as structured programming and design reviews are commonly implemented on a "yes-no" basis dependent on their cost effectiveness. You do not ordinarily trade off the degree to which structured programming is employed with reliability. The part of development cost due to testing decreases with higher failure intensity objectives, while operational cost increases (Figure 7.6). Thus total cost has a minimum.

To find this minimum, you must first compute the system test cost. This can be done manually (Section 7.1.2) or by using a simulation program (Chapter 5). Sometimes, you may wish to add an "opportunity cost" to system test cost [Mittermeir (1982)]. This is the cost of profits lost or expenses incurred because the release date of the program must be delayed for additional testing. Then the operational cost can be computed as noted in Section 7.1.3. We can now add system test cost and operational cost of failures to obtain the *reliability-dependent component* of total system life cycle costs. Note that there will also be development and operational costs that are independent of reliability but that add to total system life cycle costs. Suppose that the reliability-related component of total system life cycle costs can be expressed analytically as a function of failure intensity objec-

FIGURE 7.5
Variation of calendar time with failure intensity ratio—basic and logarithmic Poisson execution time models.

FIGURE 7.6
Failure intensity objective λ_F Life cycle cost optimization.

tive λ_F. Then we can use calculus to find the value of λ_F that minimizes the expression. Otherwise, a search process is used to find the value.

7.2.5 Reliability Allocation

Reliability allocation deals with the setting of reliability goals for individual components such that a specified system reliability goal is met *and* the component goals are "well balanced" among themselves. Well balanced usually refers to approximate equality of development time, difficulty, or risk or to the minimization of overall system development cost. The first step in the allocation process is to describe the system configuration, as discussed in Chapter 4. Next, trial component reliability allocations are selected, using best engineering judgment. Compute system reliability for this set of component reliabilities. Compare the result against the goal. Adjust component reliabilities to move system reliability toward the goal, and component reliabilities toward better balance. Repeat the process until the desired goal and good balance are achieved.

Example 7.7. A space vehicle will use three identical onboard computers, each with an independently designed and developed program that performs the identical function. The overall reliability goal for this vehicle is 0.999 for a 100-hr mission. Development costs are estimated as follows for different alternatives.

Program		Computer	
Reliability (100 hr)	Cost	Reliability (100 hr)	Cost
0.91	$ 3M	0.91	$ 300K
0.92	$ 3.25M	0.93	$ 400K
0.93	$ 3.5M	0.95	$ 500K
0.94	$ 3.75M	0.96	$ 600K
0.95	$ 4M	0.97	$ 800K
0.97	$ 4.5M	0.98	$ 1.5M
0.99	$ 5M	0.99	$ 5M

The computers operate simultaneously. Outputs are subjected to a sanity check. If any output passes, the system is considered operational. The sanity checking routine is considered to have a reliability of 1. Note that if a computer fails, the sanity checker cannot run and the output from that machine is considered to have failed. How should we allocate reliability goals to the computer and the program to minimize total development cost?

This is a concurrently functioning system with the event diagram of Figure 7.7. R_C denotes the reliability of the computer; R_P, the program. Let R_{sys} be the overall system reliability. Applying the rules for AND and OR event logic, we have

$$R_{sys} = 1 - (1 - R_C R_P)^3 .$$

For $R_{sys} = 0.999$, we have $R_C R_P = 0.9$.

Try $R_C = 0.95$ and $R_p = 0.95$. This will give the requisite system reliability. Note that cost of achieving this hardware reliability is relatively low and the total cost is \$4.5M.

Try a more difficult goal for the hardware: $R_C = 0.96$. Note that $R_P = 0.94$ will provide the proper overall reliability. Now the total cost is \$4.35M.

It is apparent we are headed in the right direction. A trial of $R_C = 0.97$ and $R_P = 0.93$ yields the proper overall reliability and a cost of \$4.3M.

A trial of $R_C = 0.98$ and $R_P = 0.92$ indicates we have gone too far. Improving the hardware this much is getting costly. The overall cost is now up to \$4.75M.

Thus we choose $R_C = 0.97$ and $R_P = 0.93$. ∎

7.2.6 System Simulation

A system simulator can be used to predict reliability of a software system before it is constructed. You must be able, from the system design, to determine the segments of the system and the transition probabilities between them. Also, we must know the size of the segments (executable source instructions) and the fault rate. Some estimate of the proportion of time for which the execution of a fault leads to a failure is required. You can now establish for each segment the probability it will fail when executed.

FIGURE 7.7
Event diagram for reliability allocation.

A Monte Carlo simulation is now conducted. For each run, use a random number generator to determine which transitions between branches are made and whether a failure occurs in a branch. Record all failures with their times. A large number of runs are made. Use the set of failure intervals to estimate model parameters, present failure intensity, and software reliability. Obviously, the determination of the last two quantities is based on the assumption of a particular model.

7.3 PROJECT MANAGEMENT

First, we should note that many of the studies done in the system engineering phase are often repeated during development. Conditions change, and project management needs guidance to adapt.

At present, software reliability measurement has been applied during development primarily to the *system* test phase of projects. However, we can also apply it to subsystem testing. The subsystem should have a size of approximately 5000 source instructions or greater. It may prove possible to extend use of the theory to unit testing by grouping of units. When systems are small, estimates are likely to have wide confidence intervals for a large part of the test period and hence be of limited value. Also, if the number of people involved is small, performance (in terms of resources required for debugging) may depart substantially from the average, yielding inaccurate calendar time predictions. We can handle this by replacing average resource requirement values for debugging by individualized values obtained through measurement or estimation.

Estimates of test period duration may be combined with estimates of the length of system requirements analysis, design, and program unit coding phases to produce overall project estimates. An approach to elapsed time estimation that can be applied to either individual phases of a project or the entire project has been developed by Putnam (1976). It is based on a Rayleigh personnel profile. Substitution of an execution time model for the Rayleigh model in the test phases should yield better results. More information (for example, the failure intensity objective, initial failure intensity, and total expected failures) is taken into account.

The present failure intensity will normally exhibit steady (ignoring statistical fluctuations) improvement with time during testing. A sharp rise in failure intensity usually indicates new faults introduced by code modification or exposed by extension of testing into new environments. The latter case may indicate inadequate test planning. An unusually slow decrease in failure intensity usually indicates that a substantial number of faults remain. Another possibility is that we are introducing or exposing new faults at roughly the same rate that faults are being corrected.

One question that occasionally occurs when an unreliable release is encountered in a multirelease project is, "Should we regress to a previous version from the present one?" This question can be answered by tracking present failure intensity for each version. Suppose that the new version is not meeting the failure intensity objective and the old one is. If the difference between the failure intensities is substantial, it will probably be worth the effort to regress.

The tracking of the failure intensities of different subsystems of an overall system is sometimes useful. You might want to determine the relative priorities to be given to the subsystems with respect to failure correction. The relative criticalities of the functions implemented by the subsystems may affect the decision. Also, knowledge of how system failure is related to failures of the individual subsystems can be important.

Another application of software reliability modeling relates to the use of overtime. Consider how use of *selective* overtime for those debuggers who have a failure backlog affects the calendar time required for the testing effort. Let α be the overtime fraction (ratio of overtime to standard time for each work day). Now the effective *available* personnel are increased by the factor $(1 + \alpha)$ and hence the calendar time for the failure-correction-personnel-limited segment of the test phase is reduced by that factor.

It is shown in Musa, Iannino, and Okumoto (1987) that the probability for each debugger that there are one or more failures awaiting correction or being corrected is ρ_F. Only those debuggers who have failures to work on will be assigned overtime. Hence the *actual* fraction of overtime work is $\alpha\rho_F$ for the failure-correction-personnel-limited segment. For example, suppose $\rho_F = 0.2$ and $\alpha = 0.2$. Assume that the entire test phase is failure-correction-personnel-limited. Then calendar time is reduced by a factor of $1 + \alpha = 1 + 0.2 = 1.2$. The actual overtime fraction is $\alpha\rho_F = 0.2 (0.2) = 0.04$. With 50 percent premium pay, this represents a 2 percent increase in cost. The premium pay is the only extra cost. No extra work is required. It is merely shifted in time. The value of *selective* overtime is clearly shown. Note the importance, however, of applying overtime only for the limiting resource. There will be no beneficial effect if applied to a nonlimiting resource.

There is a graphical method for determining when (in execution time) a failure intensity objective will be reached for the basic execution time model [Okumoto (1985)]. This approach may be useful for quick and dirty calculations. Taking the logarithm of both sides of Equation (2.7) we obtain

$$\ln \lambda = \ln \lambda_0 - \frac{\lambda_0}{\nu_0} \tau . \qquad (7.12)$$

If we plot the model on semilogarithmic paper, it becomes a straight line. It has now become an easy matter to project the model to where it intersects the failure intensity objective, and read off the execution time.

A control chart is a useful tool for management to monitor, control, and predict the quality (or the failure intensity) of a software system being tested. The control chart is constructed based on confidence limits for the future failure intensity. If the future failure intensity data conform to a pattern of random variation within the control limits, the process will be judged as being in control. Departures from the pattern are investigated and assignable causes tracked down.

Example 7.8. To illustrate the method, we use the first 100 failures of System T1 [see Table 12.1 of Musa, Iannino, and Okumoto (1987)]. Failure intensities are computed for 20 data points, with each data point based on 5 failures. Each failure intensity is computed from times of failures spaced 4 failures apart. We determined the 95 percent confidence limits for various values of failure intensity. Figure 7.8 shows the observed failure intensity along with the confidence limits. The failure intensity data beyond 100 failures are plotted on the control chart developed based on the first 100 failures. As can be seen from Figure 7.8, these new failure intensity data points continue to fall within the limits on the chart. Therefore, with 95 percent confidence the failure intensity process may be judged to be in a state of statistical control. The method for constructing confidence limits for future failure intensity is described in detail in Musa, Iannino, and Okumoto (1987). ∎

7.4 MANAGEMENT OF OPERATIONAL PHASE

7.4.1 Reliability Demonstration Testing

The situation frequently arises where it is desirable or necessary to prove that a given level of reliability has been achieved. This situation occurs particularly when software is being developed by a subcontractor. You may be involved in such a demonstration either as a party letting the contract or as a subcontractor.

The purpose of a reliability demonstration is to determine if the failure intensity objective is met with high confidence or not. In conducting a demonstration, you assume that the proper operational profile has been executed. It must represent actual operation. You also assume that there will not be any repair of the software. You are testing the product as it has been delivered to you or as you are delivering it. Our reliability demonstration approach is based on sequential sampling theory. Sequential sampling theory provides an efficient approach to testing a hypothesis by taking just enough data and no more. The data points are added one by one and you stop as soon as you can reach a decision.

We have constructed a chart (Figure 7.9) which tests whether or not the failure intensity objective you have established is met within a factor of 2 (discrimination ratio). There is a 10 percent risk of falsely saying that the objective is not met when it *is*. Similarly, there is a 10 percent risk of falsely saying that the objective is met when it is *not*. We have chosen for you what we feel to be a reasonable discrimination ratio and reasonable risk levels to simplify the approach. If different discrimination ratios or risk levels are desired, a different chart must be constructed.

Let's go through the steps for conducting a reliability demonstration. First, you have to establish what the failure intensity objective is that you are testing. We now run the test and record the time of the next failure that is experienced. The failure time is then normalized by multiplying it by the failure intensity objective. The normalized failure time is then located on the reliability demonstration chart. If it falls in the "accept" region, then the failure intensity objective is considered met with high confidence. If it falls in the "reject" region, there is little possibility of meeting the objective. It is not worth testing further. If it falls in the "continue"

FIGURE 7.8
Observed failure intensity data along with the control chart constructed from the first 100 failure intervals of the data set T1.

region, the result is uncertain. You should continue to test. It is legitimate to keep testing as long as you are in the "continue" region. However, in some practical cases "reject" is assumed after a specified period of normalized time if "accept" has not occurred.

Example 7.9. A personal computer manufacturer wishes to know if the software house furnishing the operating system for a new machine has met the failure intensity objective of 0.1 failure/CPU hr. A series of tests are applied and failure data are recorded.

   The first failure occurs at 8 CPU hr or 0.8 normalized time units. This falls in the "continue" region of Figure 7.9. The second failure occurs at 19 CPU hr or 1.9 normalized time units. Again, we are in the "continue" region. The third failure occurs at 60 CPU hr or 6.0 normalized time units. Now, we clearly fall in the "accept" region. We can stop testing and assume with high confidence that the failure intensity objective must be within a factor of 2 of the specification. ∎

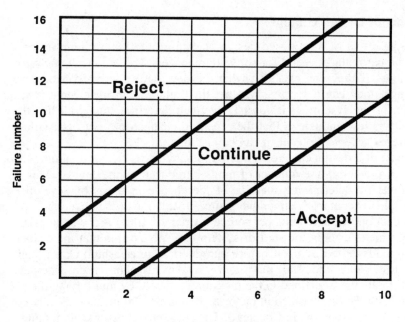

FIGURE 7.9
Reliability demonstration chart.

The construction of a different chart is not difficult [Grant and Leavenworth (1980)]. Let γ be the discrimination ratio. The quantity α is the risk (probability) of falsely saying that the objective is not met when it *is*. The quantity β is the risk of falsely saying that the objective is met when it is *not*. Define

$$A = \ln \frac{\beta}{1 - \alpha} \tag{7.13}$$

and

$$B = \ln \frac{1 - \beta}{\alpha} . \tag{7.14}$$

Then the boundary between the "reject" and "continue" regions of the chart is given by

$$\frac{A - n \ln \gamma}{1 - \gamma} , \tag{7.15}$$

where n is the failure number. The boundary between the "continue" and "accept" regions is given by

$$\frac{B - n \ln \gamma}{1 - \gamma} . \tag{7.16}$$

7.4.2   Impact of Design Change

Determining the effect of a proposed design change on the failure intensity of a program can be particularly useful for software managers who are managing operational programs. If they can establish what the new failure intensity would be after the change, they can determine whether this failure intensity meets the service objective for the system. If it doesn't, they can defer the change. When the failure intensity is low enough so that the proposed change does not push failure intensity above an acceptable level, it can be installed.

The impact of a design change on a program may be predicted, assuming the basic model, by predicting the number of faults introduced by the change. This is most easily done by determining the size of the change in terms of developed (new or modified) executable deliverable source instructions (or lines). Then we apply known data on average faults per source instruction (line) at the appropriate point in time. This is usually the start of system test. We assume that the change has been thoroughly tested by itself before introduction, in a fashion akin to unit or subsystem test. Hence the "start of system test" data are appropriate. Compute the number of faults that remained in the program at release by multiplying the remaining failures by the fault reduction factor B. Remaining failures are usually estimated by one of the programs in Chapter 5. The basic model assumes that failure intensity is proportional to the faults present. Hence we may predict the failure intensity λ_A just after the design change as

$$\frac{\lambda_A}{\lambda_B} = \frac{\omega_A}{\omega_B}. \tag{7.17}$$

Note that λ_B is the failure intensity just before the design change. The quantities ω_B and ω_A are the expected faults remaining just before and after the change, respectively.

The impact of the design change on resource expenditures, cost, and schedules may be determined by computing these quantities for both λ_B and λ_A. We can do this for either a fixed objective or a fixed schedule. The former case is appropriate when product quality level is paramount. The latter is better when meeting a deadline or getting a product to market rapidly is most important.

In the foregoing calculation, we implicitly ignored, for simplicity, any effect the change might have on failure intensity by lengthening the program and hence reducing its execution frequency. Usually the effect is negligible.

We utilized the assumption that the failure intensity is proportional to the faults present. Note that we are implicitly assuming that the code of the design change will be executed with the same frequency as that of the existing program, on the average. We could have a special situation, however. For example, suppose that the design change is in a routine that is executed very frequently. Then the ratio of failure intensities after to before the change should be multiplied by the ratio of average execution frequency of the change to average execution frequency of the existing program. Ordinarily the foregoing situation will occur only for a small and hence localized design change.

Example 7.10. The latest run of the software reliability estimation program on a word processing program indicates 500 total failures expected. It shows 485 already experienced. The basic model is being applied. The fault reduction factor is 1. The same program indicates a present failure intensity of 0.06 failure/CPU hr. If a change of 2000 developed source instructions is introduced, what will be the effect on failure intensity? Assume that inherent faults per source instruction have been measured at 0.005.

There are 15 remaining faults. The change will introduce 10 new faults. The failure intensity after the change λ_A will be, using Equation (7.3):

$$\lambda_A = \frac{\omega_A}{\omega_B} \lambda_B = \frac{15 + 10}{15} (0.06) = 0.10 \text{ failure/CPU hr}.$$

∎

7.4.3 Measuring Ultrahigh Reliability

There is great interest in measuring reliability at ultrahigh levels. The measurement is important for systems where failure is of a life critical nature. Examples of such systems include nuclear power reactors, aircraft control and air traffic systems, and space vehicle control. The following evaluation was performed for a component of one of these systems.

CASE STUDY 7.1
NUCLEAR POWER AGENCY

A nuclear power agency uses a computer-based monitoring system for its reactors. The operating system (which we denote "P38") for the computer is employed for this and other applications in an estimated 5000 installations throughout the world. It is desired to evaluate the reliability of the system. Failure data collected on a per-month basis are shown in Table 7.1. A total of 17 failures have occurred in 43 calendar months of operation. Each system runs 24 hr/day. Computer utilization is constant. Coupled with the fact that 5000 systems are in operation, this translates into 1.57×10^8 hr of operation.

Failure time data are required as input for the estimation program. The raw data were converted into this format by randomly selecting the failure times in each appropriate month. The resulting failure times are listed in Table 7.2. Note also that the total time of operation is greater than the time of the last failure. This denotes failure-free time, that is, 3906 years of failure-free execution has accumulated since the last failure. Note also that the data in this table and the following results pertain to a *single copy* of the software system.

Two sets of results are presented. The first consists of estimates of the lower confidence limit of the expected number of total failures (Table 7.3) using the basic execution time model. For example, we are 95 percent certain that at least 20 failures (3 more in addition to the 17 that have already been experienced) will

TABLE 7.1
**Monthly failure data
for system P38**

Month[1]	Number of failures
8/79–9/79	0
10/79	1
5/80	1
7/80	2
11/80	2
2/81	1
3/81	1
6/81	1
8/81	1
9/81	1
10/81	1
12/81	2
1/82	1
3/82	1
5/82	1
6/82–2/83	0

[1]Missing months had no failures.

TABLE 7.2
**Converted failure time data for
system P38**

Failure number	Failure time (yr)	Months from start of operation
1	932	3
2	4035	10
3	4696	12
4	4893	12
5	6369	16
6	6524	16
7	7882	19
8	8170	20
9	9339	23
10	10400	25
11	10542	26
12	11036	27
13	11696	29
14	11905	29
15	12266	30
16	12954	32
17	14000	34

Note: Total time of operation is 17,906 yr.

TABLE 7.3
Lower confidence limit on
the expected total failures

Confidence level	Confidence limit
95%	20
90%	21
75%	25
50%	33

occur at some time. Estimates of the upper confidence limit are not reliable due to the small sample size.

The second set of results (Table 7.4) concerns the failure intensity of the software system. The results show that the most likely value for the failure intensity is 0.867 failure/1000 yr using the basic model. It is 0.895 failure/1000 yr using the logarithmic Poisson model. Results for both models are compatible until we reach the higher confidence limits (that is, 90 and 95 percent). Larger failure intensities are predicted by the logarithmic Poisson model.

7.4.4   Controlling Level of Preventive Maintenance

Many organizations generate fixes for software in the field in response to failure reports and then ship these fixes to the various installations. Responses are not made to all failures, nor are fixes necessarily sent to all sites. Local managers frequently exercise considerable discretion over whether the fixes are installed or not. How should we select which repairs should be implemented?

Software reliability concepts provide some guidance. Each fault has associated with it a set of failures that it can cause. Each failure is the result of a particular run being made. The sum of the probabilities of occurrence of these different runs represents the contribution that the fault makes to the overall failure in-

TABLE 7.4
Confidence intervals for present failure intensity

Confidence level	Failure intensity (failures/1000 yr)	
	Basic model	**Logarithmic Poisson model**
Most likely value	0.867	0.895
50%	0.638–1.143	0.689–1.197
75%	0.506–1.372	0.579–1.494
90%	0.394–1.633	0.492–1.908
95%	0.333–1.810	0.445–2.24

tensity. Thus the failure intensity contribution of the fault depends on the operational profile.

The failure intensity contribution has an effect on the operation of the program, with each failure resulting in some financial cost. The preparation, dissemination, and installation of fixes have definite financial costs also. In addition, there is some risk that the installation of a repair to a fault may introduce other faults as well. A reasonable approach to deciding which faults one should concentrate on would be to conduct a brief analysis of the foregoing cost impacts.

Adams (1984) notes that usually a system has a relatively small number of faults that have large contributions to failure intensity. These are usually found early in the use of the system. One should vigorously pursue development and installation of fixes for these faults. It may, however, be wise for a local site manager *not* to install fixes on a preventive basis for all faults that have been found. The better strategy may be to observe which failures occur frequently for your own operational profile (your local profile may differ from the system average global one). You can then install corrections for just those faults that are causing those failures.

7.5 EVALUATION OF SOFTWARE ENGINEERING TECHNOLOGIES

Evaluation of a new software engineering technology requires that you first establish a technology base (that is, the "old" technology) or a "control" technology. We will then compare the new technology with it. The technique to be evaluated must be carefully described and defined. What appears to be a single technique may actually turn out to be a complex of related techniques. It is proper to evaluate such a complex. However, there is more risk of difficulty in this evaluation. All members of the complex may not be applied with equal vigor in all circumstances. A suitable experiment to compare the new technique with its control is then devised. The statistical theory of experimental design may be helpful in guiding the experimenter toward efficient investigation. Efficiency is often very important in view of the large cost of many software engineering experiments.

We have two common alternatives to use in making comparisons, a fixed schedule and a fixed objective approach. In the fixed schedule approach, one measures failure intensity for both the experimental and the control method after equal amounts of test. We judge any improvement in failure intensity against the cost of applying the technique. This method is best when the release data are constrained (as they might be, for example, by marketing considerations). In the fixed objective approach, you test in both cases until the same failure intensity is reached and then compute the saving in cost involved, if any. The saving is the reduction in test costs due to a shorter test period, with the cost of applying the technique subtracted.

A common result of new software engineering technologies applied during phases before test, if they are effective, is to reduce the number of inherent faults. Assume the basic model. A 10 percent reduction (for example) in inherent faults will reduce ν_0, the total number of failures in infinite time, by 10 percent, per Equation (5.1). It will also decrease λ_0, the initial failure intensity at the start of test, by 10 percent, per Equation (5.2). The failure intensity curve is described by

$$\lambda = \lambda_0 \exp\left(-\frac{\lambda_0 \tau}{\nu_0}\right), \tag{7.18}$$

where τ is execution time. Thus the principal overall effect is to lower the curve, the amount being 10 percent at $\tau = 0$.

Now, reaching a given failure intensity objective λ_F from the initial failure intensity λ_0 requires that $\Delta\mu$ failures be experienced and $\Delta\tau$ of execution time expended. We have

$$\Delta\mu = \nu_0 \left(1 - \frac{\lambda_F}{\lambda_0}\right) \tag{7.19}$$

and

$$\Delta\tau = \frac{\nu_0}{\lambda_0} \ln\left(\frac{\lambda_0}{\lambda_F}\right). \tag{7.20}$$

Both $\Delta\mu$ and $\Delta\tau$ will be reduced by the new technology in this example, but by less than 10 percent. Let $\lambda_F = 0.01 \ \lambda_0$. Then $\Delta\mu$ will be reduced by almost 10 percent and $\Delta\tau$ by slightly over 2 percent. The net effect on the duration and cost of the test period will depend on various resource and cost parameters, but will probably fall somewhere between 2 and 10 percent. A slightly different view is that with a fixed failure intensity objective, a successful software engineering technology reduces the failure intensity ratio that must be attained over the test period. Thus duration and cost of test can be reduced as shown in Figures 7.2 and 7.3.

Sometimes the new technology may affect the size of the program as well as the number of faults it contains. For example, writing a program in structured form may result in a somewhat longer program. Here the linear execution frequency (average instruction execution rate divided by size) will be reduced. The analysis of the effect of the new technology will be slightly more complicated, since it affects two parameters.

7.6 DOCUMENTATION DEBUGGING AND OTHER APPLICATIONS

It appears that we can generally apply software reliability concepts, methodologies, and tools to products of certain systematic creative processes and to the processes themselves. This becomes apparent when you realize that software development is one of a number of such creative processes. These processes are characterized by an initial implementation followed by a period of "failure" detection through "test" and fault correction. Hardware design is one example of such a potential application. Another is writing.

Note that a draft of a paper, article, or document receives its "system test" through reading by reviewers. We do the reading against the "system requirements" of conveying information to meet particular needs. Needs might be diagnosing a software failure or determining how to add a change. The test "runs" represent attempts to attain information to meet these needs. The "operational profile" represents the range and relative frequencies of these needs. It is reasonable to assume that any particular run occurs randomly with a probability expressed by the operational profile. A "failure" is any situation in which the reading of the text does not convey the information required to meet the need. The fault is the particular deficiency in the text that is responsible for the failure. The failure intensity will decrease with time as the document is "repaired." Software reliability models can be applied to this situation. We can establish an objective for the document such as "0.95 'reliability' in obtaining the required information for various needs per hour of reading." The foregoing may be a useful approach to the evaluation of user manuals and program documentation. It might also conceivably be applied to the evaluation of requirements or design specifications.

7.7   SUMMARY

A wide range of applications in four major areas has been presented. You need to keep these possibilities in mind, along with the data and effort required to implement them, as you analyze a project's needs. This will permit the establishment of a sound basis for the implementation of software reliability measurement and prediction on a project.

PROBLEMS

7.1 The Soft Landing software service company has won a service contract to provide recovery service for a patient control and billing system. The service is provided to doctors in a region who own personal computers. It has a failure intensity of 1 failure/100 CPU hr. The average system runs 10 CPU hr/week and there are 600 doctors to be serviced. The average service person can make 2 service calls daily, including travel and allowing for enough spare personnel to prevent excessive service backlogs from building up.

How many service personnel do we need? Assuming a cost of $200/call, what annual contract fee must we charge each doctor to achieve 20 percent profit on sales?

7.2 A software project manager desires to evaluate the cost effectiveness of design reviews on a project. The program has 50,000 source instructions. Previous experience indicates 8 faults/1000 instructions and an initial failure intensity of 10 failures/CPU hr when design reviews are not conducted. These data were collected for a similar program of the same size on a machine of the same speed at the start of system test. It is found that design reviews reduce the fault figure to 6.

Assume that the fault reduction factor $B = 1$. For simplicity, assume that the entire system test period is failure-correction-personnel-limited and that all resources are profitably employed (none are idle at any time). Loaded salary is $50/hr and computer (CPU) time is \$1000/CPU hr. The system at delivery must have a failure intensity of 1 failure/10 CPU hr.

Data taken in similar environments indicate that 6 person hr are required for failure correction per failure. This effort is independent of amount of execution time. We require 5 person hr of system test team effort and 2 CPU hr of chargeable computer time per hr of execution time. Also, we need 3 person hr of system test team effort and 0.5 CPU hr of computer time per failure.

The design reviews require 3 meetings, each attended by 10 people and lasting 6 hr. Follow-up activities require 200 person hr of time.

Does the design review pay off? If so, what is the saving?

7.3 A program has an initial failure intensity of 10 failures/CPU hr. We want to test and debug this program until a failure intensity of 1 failure/10 CPU hr is achieved. Assume the following resource usage parameters.

Resource usage	Per hr	Per failure
Failure identification effort	3 person hr	2 person hr
Failure correction effort	0	6 person hr
Computer time	1.5 CPU hr	1 CPU hr

(a) What resources must be expended to achieve the reliability improvement required? Use the logarithmic Poisson execution time model. Assume a failure intensity decay parameter of 0.05.

(b) If the failure intensity objective is cut in half, are the resources required doubled?

7.4 A company is planning an online order processing system. It will process orders received and generate bills. It breaks down the work involved into tasks, writes work orders on those tasks, and orders materials. We wish to establish the failure intensity objective for the system that will minimize total system cost over an estimated lifetime of 2 years. Faults are not to be corrected in the field for this system. They will be fixed at the next release. Assume for simplicity that the hardware components of the system are much more reliable than the software and hence may be neglected in this analysis. Also, for simplicity, assume that the entire system test period is failure-correction-personnel-limited. All resources are profitably employed. None are idle at any time. The system is expected to operate 250 days/yr, 8 CPU hr/day. The average total cost impact of a failure (in terms of reduced efficiency, extra supervisory time and other work required to "straighten out the mess," etc.) is \$10,000. The cost of the requirements, design, code, and unit test phases is independent of the failure intensity achieved.

The software consists of 100,000 source (400,000 object) instructions. Programmer loaded salary is \$50/hr and computer (CPU) time is \$1000/CPU hr. There are 25 program designers available for debugging. Testing is to be paced so that no debugger has more than 2 failures awaiting correction, with 90 percent probability. Average instruction execution rate is one million object instructions per CPU second. On similar projects, a value of fault exposure ratio $K = 2.222 \times 10^{-7}$ has been experienced. We can estimate the average fault density at 5 faults/1000 source instructions. Assume that the fault reduction factor $B = 1$. Data taken in similar environments indicate that 5 person hr are required for failure correction per failure. This effort is independent of amount of execution time. Similarly, 4 person hr of system test team effort and 1 CPU hr of chargeable computer time are required per hr of execution time. We need 2 person hr of system test team effort and 1/2 CPU hr of computer time per failure.

What is the failure intensity objective that minimizes total life cycle cost? What is the minimum cost of system test and operational failures? What is the length of the system test period (in calendar time) for the minimum failure intensity objective? What is the reliability of the optimum system for 1 day of operation?

7.5 The following problem will use the basic execution time model. We are conducting a system analysis for the proposed software system COMPROD to determine the range of cost choices available as a function of failure intensity objective. We wish to investigate costs for failure intensity objectives ranging from 1 to 5 failures per 100 CPU hr. The following system test costs (with ranges of variation) have been determined.

Failure intensity objective (per 100 CPU hr)	System test cost (K $)	Range of system test cost (K $)
1	1585	1230–1840
2	1490	1160–1710
3	1440	1100–1650
4	1400	1070–1600
5	1360	1040–1560

Compute the overall component of system cost that is dependent on reliability (failure intensity objective). Assume that the system will operate for 4 years, 250 days/yr, 10 CPU hr/day. There will be 5 installations of the system. The total cost impact of a failure is estimated to be $100. What is the optimum value for the failure intensity objective? What range of values does this objective take on as a result of inaccuracies in the knowledge of total failures and initial failure intensity?

7.6 A program has a failure intensity objective of 0.1 failure/CPU hr. It is run for 50 CPU hr with no failures occurring. How confident are we that it has met its objective?

7.7 A change to 2000 source instructions is being made in a program of 100,000 source instructions. The fault density of the base program at the start of system test was 5 faults/1000 source instructions. Assume that the fault reduction factor $B = 1$. The initial failure intensity of the base program was 2 failures/CPU hr. It was released with a failure intensity of 6 failures/100 CPU hr. Fixes of faults are not made during the operational phase. What is the expected impact on failure intensity of the operational program?

7.8 Can we use a software reliability model to help establish the priority with which different subsystems should be tested?

7.9 Assume that we can make overtime available to failure identification personnel (as a percentage of regular work time) to be used whenever it will expedite the work in progress. How much can be profitably used?

7.10 What is the impact of inefficient programs on failure intensity? Couldn't an inefficient program give a spuriously low failure intensity?

7.11 Should we try to balance failure intensities between different components of a system so that they are *equal*?

7.12 What are the effects of better testing on the variation of failure intensity with execution time?

7.13 How would you determine the effect of built-in tests (audits) on software reliability?

7.14 How can you rapidly (without substantial calculations) make predictions of the execution time required to reach various failure intensity objectives?

EIGHT

IMPLEMENTATION PLANNING

In Chapter 3 we discussed overall planning on how to apply software reliability measures to your project. We would now like to continue this effort to the detailed planning stage. There are some general detailed planning steps that you should consider. You may wish to augment these steps with steps that are specific to your project as well.

You should realize that one always encounters resistance when introducing new ideas in an institution or project. Some of this is desirable. It serves to protect the organization against uncritically considered ideas and hasty decisions. It prevents disruption of processes that are functioning well. Some of the resistance is undesirable but natural. Change disturbs people, forcing them to learn new knowledge and skills, adapt, and invest extra efforts. Hence you can expect some hostility. You may feel it is unjustified. However, if you can see things from the viewpoint of the people affected, you will usually be more effective. It is important to try to understand the existing system before introducing change. Then you will retain its good features. Also, you are giving the project members the implicit message that you are interested in their problems and respect the competence they have exhibited in solving them in the past.

One thing that you must consider is the definition of failure for your project. Do you want explicit definition through requirements documents or do you want to consider any program behavior that may be unsatisfactory to customers as a failure? You should also think about whether you wish to classify failures by severity. If so, how many classes do you want to have and how will you establish them?

After this, you need to determine whether your system will be operating in different modes. Then you need to think about your system, and determine what its configuration is and how you will be breaking it down into components. If you expect the system to evolve, then you need to determine how this is going to take place. What, if anything, should you do about taking the evolution into account?

You must choose which model or models you will apply. You need to plan how you will go about determining parameters for the model. How will you select a failure intensity objective? How will you establish the parameters for resource usage? You should anticipate any special problems regarding resource quantities or utilizations that may require some special adjustments to the parameters.

You have established many of the basics of your detailed plan. Consideration now has to be given to the process of data collection. To what extent will you collect data? Will you be collecting data during both test and operation? Will you be collecting data during subsystem test as well as system test? What types of data do you need to collect? Will you be collecting failure data? Resource usage data? What general project information will you need? Think about any special considerations. Will you be able to measure execution time or must you make an approximation to it? Are there multiple installations? If so, will there be different computers with different average instruction execution rates? How are you going to motivate and train your data takers? What recording procedures will you use? How will you be going about the process of data scrubbing? How will you feed back results to members of the project, particularly the data takers and managers? Do you plan to conduct a prototype experiment? How are you going to go about this?

Finally, you need to think about the tools that you will need, such as programs for conveniently handling calculations. Some useful programs are suggested in Chapter 5. Which of these will you need? Where will you obtain them? Or will you develop them? What has to be done to install and use them? What machine and operating system will you be running them on? Are there any changes that need to be made to adapt these programs to that machine?

8.1 DATA COLLECTION

Careful planning and organization are necessary if one is to collect data of high quality. You need to identify a project contact who is interested in the data collection effort and will take charge of it.

It may seem obvious to tell you that you need to spend some time thinking about what data you are going to collect. Unfortunately, this step is frequently ignored, with undesirable results. You should have a clear purpose in mind for each piece of data and a clear understanding of how the data will be processed to achieve that purpose. Establishing this linkage will expose weaknesses in your plans that need correction (or perhaps it will show that a certain objective isn't feasible) and avoid wasted effort. Is the data item that you plan to collect worth the cost of collecting it? Many people seem to take the approach that if the data might be of any potential value whatsoever, they should be collected. The problem with this approach is that it places such a burden on the data collectors that they soon become weary and disillusioned. Then you get a real deterioration in all the data that you are trying to collect, including the important data. Also, there is a definite cost in collecting data and the more data you collect the greater the cost.

You can impose a substantial overhead on a project, which will then discourage project managers and members in the future from cooperation with you.

Look carefully at possible alternatives for each piece of data that you are thinking of collecting. One might be the possibility of approximating data. Approximate data, if satisfactory in quality, may be easier, less expensive, and less burdensome to collect than precise data. Another alternative you should consider is collecting the data at a lower frequency. You may not really need the amount of data that you are planning to take. Finally, look hard for multipurpose data. Perhaps by slightly changing some of your requirements, a data item that you collect can serve several purposes. Maybe it doesn't serve all of them perfectly, but it is good enough, and it reduces the collection burdens considerably.

Probably the most important issue, however, is how to obtain the cooperation of personnel on the project in collecting the data. One approach to this problem is to obtain the support of the manager of the data takers and have that manager order them to do the things that you require. "Management by machismo" may secure for you a blizzard of paper, but these data will generally be provided grudgingly and without much consideration or thought. Consequently, they will usually be of questionable quality.

We believe that the following approach is generally more fruitful:

1. Obtain the motivated participation of the data takers.
2. Make the collection mechanism as easy as possible.
3. Collect and scrub the data in real time.
4. Provide feedback of results obtained from the data on a regular and timely basis.

8.1.1 Motivating Data Takers

The first question that needs to be tackled is how one can motivate the data takers. Analyze why you are collecting the data, and how your goals can be related to those of the data takers. It is usually most effective to appeal to the strongest motivations of the data takers. In order, these are typically: direct personal benefit, project benefit, and benefit to the profession. Thus, if you can show any direct personal benefit from collecting the data, do so. For example, you may be giving the people involved in the data collection effort some feedback on the software product they have produced. This can be particularly helpful if it is from a different perspective than the usual feedback they receive. People are usually very interested in getting feedback on their performance, as long as it is done in a nonjudgmental way. The feedback helps them to improve and grow in their profession. The second best approach is to show that the data collection effort will be of direct project benefit. Most people realize that if they cooperate in something that benefits the project they are working on, their colleagues and their management will notice this, and it will be to their credit. Third, many professionals are truly interested in advancing the state of their field. If you can show that what you are doing will help achieve this, they are often willing to go to a certain amount of trouble to help you. However, you really have to be honest with them in showing what you are trying to accomplish. If they think that the data are of poor quality for the objective or that the research effort is meaningless, you will not appeal to them.

Enlist the participation of the data takers in planning how the data collection effort will be applied to their project. The sense of participation engendered will usually materially improve the degree of cooperation attained. Furthermore, letting the data takers plan the details of the effort will actually result in concrete benefits. They will usually know many details about the project that would elude you. We have found it helpful to explicitly ask the data takers to give us the benefit of their experience. We have tried several formats in working with data collection personnel on a project. They are usually the members of the test and development teams and are professional software engineers. The approach of coming in with a totally organized plan and informing people how to carry it out does not seem to work. On the other hand, the approach of sitting down and saying we have a problem and how are we going to solve it generally does not work too well either. Most of the people involved are not willing to devote a large amount of time to solving your problem. The approach that seems to work best is to start with a first draft of a data collection plan. Provide it to the data collection personnel to read if they desire. Then call a meeting and present its main features. Ask the participants to identify problems and to suggest improvements. Generally you will then have a small number of problems to deal with. You elicit the participation of the attendees at the meeting in solving the problems. Hopefully you go away from the meeting with a set of suggested changes to your plan. Sometimes you may have some action items that have to be resolved, and perhaps another meeting may be required before things stabilize. Finally, you modify and issue the plan. Generally, we have found that the group in any given meeting should not be larger than 15 or so. It is difficult to have a participative session with a larger group.

Once the plan has been established, it must be disseminated. Data takers should be given a clear technical understanding of the purpose of the data collection, if it isn't already obvious to them from the planning session. This is important. They must be able to make intelligent decisions when confronted with the many special problems that can occur in trying to reduce reality to a box on a form. We have found that an oral presentation is usually best for this purpose rather than written material. A meeting affords attendees the opportunity to ask questions and test their understanding of the material presented. The written material may be useful as an adjunct for later reference, however.

It is, of course, highly desirable to convince project management as well as the data takers of the value of the collection effort. However, convincing the data takers is probably most important, provided project management at least acquiesces in what you are doing. Attention to detail is more important than organization or coordination in this activity.

8.1.2   Making Data Collection Easy

Data collection is at best an annoying and burdensome chore that often gets in the way of one's primary work. Hence, every effort must be bent toward reducing this chore as much as possible. Can you reduce the number of people involved in collecting a particular data item? For example, one person might be able to estimate a quantity with satisfactory accuracy. It may be unnecessary to collect data individually from five people and average them.

Try to integrate your data collection activities with other data collection activities and with the primary work that is proceeding in parallel. Combine forms whenever feasible. Automate the collection (that is, make human intervention unnecessary) if possible, building appropriate tools into the software development environment. The advantages of automated data collection are the reduced burden and greater accuracy. The principal disadvantage is that this mode is generally unsatisfactory when interpretation is needed in establishing the data values. Sometimes online data collection, perhaps in a conversational mode with a menu or "fill in the blanks" template that is presented to the person entering the data, is appropriate. This is particularly true when the activity for which you are collecting data is also being operated online. Many people prefer talking to writing. Consider the possibility of telephone reporting of your data if it is feasible. Probably the best thing here is to have someone that will record the data live, so he or she can straighten out any difficulties. The second best alternative would be to have a recording device to which the data taker can dictate. If you are using forms, invest some effort in designing them for ease of use and ease of computer entry. The form should provide enough space to record the information required and should elicit the information in the natural order in which the person would provide it. A simple matter such as providing someone to collect the forms and answer questions about filling them out may make a big difference.

It is important to make a trial run of your data collection procedures. No amount of planning can predict all the snags you will encounter, since many of these will result from human misunderstanding, misinterpretation, or miscommunication. Definitions of data items to be collected may not be clear, important data may be missed, collection systems may malfunction, computer programs may not work in all situations, and special unanticipated cases may arise. It is desirable to have a meeting of the participants in the trial to critique it and uncover and solve the problems. One possible time for the trial run is during subsystem test prior to system test, perhaps for one subsystem.

8.1.3   Collecting and Scrubbing Data in Real Time

It becomes more and more difficult to correct data as they age, since people's memories fade rapidly. Consequently, the project must collect data promptly as events occur and it needs to have a knowledgeable person reviewing all data as they are collected. You must be careful about how much of this function is delegated to a clerk. Even if the clerk is well trained, there should never be complete delegation. There will always be important nonroutine aspects of the data whose significance can be appreciated only by persons with a software engineering background. Pursue missing reports and missing data promptly. This will increase the quality of the data indirectly as well as directly. The data takers will know that someone is interested, that their input is being used, and that it is easier to submit data correctly in the first place than to subject themselves to pestering. Question the data actively. Apply the data promptly for your purposes (for example, generate reports), and see if the results appear correct. Involve project personnel in looking at the reports for reasonableness. Identify data collection problems.

There are three problems that commonly occur with failure reports. First, trouble or maintenance reports do not always imply program failures. They may be used to request new features. The user may be dissatisfied with some program characteristic and report it as a failure. They may represent failures, but they are failures in documentation rather than failures of the program. For example, the user manual is not clear on something. Therefore, what someone thinks is a program failure really is not. A second consideration is that the time that is recorded on a trouble report may not be the actual time that a failure really occurred. There have been some instances where the date that is recorded happens to be the date at which the person recording the trouble wrote it down or even perhaps the date at which the trouble report was received by the data collection group. Finally, data takers sometimes record multiple failures that occurred close together as happening at the same time. This can result in multiple zero failure intervals. A failure intensity that was steadily decreasing suddenly exhibits a discontinuous jump to infinity. Multiple zero failure intervals can substantially distort the estimation of model parameters.

If it appears that there is widespread misunderstanding of the meaning of certain items or if serious data collection problems exist, hold an additional meeting with your data takers to clear up these difficulties. Request their participation and the benefit of their experience in resolving these problems. However, we have found it usually not wise to hold general meetings to discuss localized problems. It is better to discuss them only with the people involved. Otherwise, people who are collecting data correctly will resent the implied criticism and the waste of their time.

8.1.4　Results Feedback

It is strongly recommended that you provide feedback of derived results to participants on a regular and timely basis. You should particularly make sure that the promised benefits from the data collection effort are not missing due to poor follow-through. Certainly, you cannot always guarantee that the expected benefits from the data collection effort will materialize. However, do not guarantee that the results will not be useful by neglecting to provide timely reports or any reports at all, providing inaccurate reports, or supplying reports that do not present material well. Scrutinize the reports to be sure that they are well organized, incorporate useful material, and are in a format that is easily grasped. Present material in graphical form (color is nice) whenever appropriate and possible. Ask your data takers and project managers what they think of the reports. If they are using them, how are they using them, and for what purpose? Do they appear valid? Is the format convenient and readable? Modify them if they can be improved to better satisfy the needs of the project. In addition to other benefits, this approach helps maintain the sense of participation and motivation of the data takers.

Interpret the meaning and describe the possible uses of the reports to the managers involved. If they use them and find them helpful, their backing will make the data collection effort easier. Further, you will show them that the resources and money devoted to data collection are paying dividends.

Personally analyze the format of the reports and what they are used for. Your extra experience may suggest improvements and uses not seen by the users. Users often do not see future possibilities in a report, even when they understand present needs. They may not appreciate that the possibility exists for changing their method of operating and doing things they never thought of before.

8.1.5 Record Keeping

Records should be kept in such a fashion that information is not lost when project personnel are transferred. They should be readily interpretable so that the information is available for use on similar projects in the future. One convenient way of recording failure times is to note them on the trouble reports or failure reports that many projects use for all formal testing and that are commonly used in the field during operation. It may be possible to automatically record time at regular intervals during test along with the output quantities one is monitoring for the purpose of locating failures. Then time of failure can be established precisely.

Another approach is to take run-time data in a log. A log can also be used for recording (possibly interactively) any occurrence that might be a failure. An example of a form used to log testing activities and failures is provided in Figure 8.1. The event code differentiates failures from beginning and end of test and changes in program size. The system code permits events to be separated by component or system. One purpose of separation is to permit adjustment of execution times for software components running on machines of different average instruction execution rates. The window is used to bound events whose precise time is uncertain. A time can then be selected randomly within those bounds. The information on instructions and developed instructions is used for failure time adjustment.

Observation of failures may occur at the time of program operation or when analyzing program output afterwards. Therefore, it has proved best to allow 1 or 2 days to elapse after a test run before using the failure interval data. Then false failures can be weeded out and the results thoroughly analyzed to minimize missed failures. Experience indicates that after analysis one is more likely to miss failures than to report false ones. Faults found by a programmer without test (by code reading or other means) during the test period should not be counted as failures. They

FAILURE DATA COLLECTION FORM

(Left justify)								(Right justify)											(Left justify)
Event Code	System Code	Date				Event Time or Window Start Time					Window End Time			Instructions	Developed Instructions	Comments
		Mo	Day	Yr		Hr	Min	Sec			Hr	Min	Sec			
1-8	9-16	17-18	19-20	21-22		23-24	25-26	27-28			29-30	31-32	33-34	41-48	49-56	57-80

Event Code: Presence of number indicates a failure event; B, begin test; E, end test; G, program growth. If event is known only within a window, window start and end times are filled in.

FIGURE 8.1
Sample testing activity and failure log.

221

are not "failures" by definition. When the development environment is such that test is accompanied by extensive code reading, the value of the fault reduction factor may be affected.

8.2   USE OF CONSULTANTS

We have mentioned the use of consultants in Chapter 3 to assist in implementing software reliability measurement in an organization. Consultants frequently play an important role in technology transfer. This includes both professional external consultants and individuals inside an organization, who by virtue of their technical leadership and initiative have a seminal impact throughout the organization. In order for consulting to be effective, consultant and consultee must each understand both roles. Sometimes one person may take on both roles during a project. For example, you might engage a consultant to advise in applying software reliability measurement to a project. You might then take on the role of consultant yourself in trying to disseminate the consultant's ideas to your project team.

8.2.1   Consultee

Engaging a consultant, of course, involves the expenditure of resources by the consultee. Frequently, compensation and expenses of the consultant are outweighed by the cost of effort expended by other project personnel. A substantial investment of effort by project personnel is usually desirable, so that they can learn from the consultant and apply this knowledge in the future. The potential benefits from effective consulting generally dwarf the resources expended. For all the foregoing reasons, we will concentrate on maximizing the effectiveness rather than minimizing the costs of the consultant. In fact, the cost-cutting strategy usually backfires. A generous attitude toward the consultant will often result in extra efforts and benefits for the project.

The consultee should place great importance on the process of selecting the consultant. The extra cost of a consultant of superior quality is negligible with respect to the likely greater benefits. It is important for you to realize that you are not just "buying" expertise from the consultant but trying to apply expertise effectively in the solution of project problems. Therefore, you must be open and honest in providing the consultant with information. It is desirable to truly incorporate the consultant as a part of your team. Invest some effort in determining the needs and problems of your project and conveying them to the consultant. Provide any technical background information that may be relevant to the problem, and give the consultant some guidance about which information is likely to be most important. If you provide a set of reports and memoranda, a rank ordering of the value of this material is useful.

One area of information that is frequently overlooked, but that is vital, is that of organizational power structure and politics. The consultant may develop good ideas, but it is likely that they will wither on the vine without this knowledge. You need to help the consultant help you by identifying the key people on the project with respect to the particular area being addressed. These may be people with power in either the formal structure (for example, managers) or the informal structure (for example, people generally recognized as technical innovators, initiators, or mentors among their peers).

It usually pays to devote some effort to determining and understanding the motivations of the consultant. It is often possible to relate these motivations to the goals of the project. Then you multiply both the effectiveness of the consultant to the project and the achievement of the consultant's goals. There are many consultants "with a mission" who are more interested in spreading a set of ideas than in their compensation. An organization can profit by helping. Positive feedback, when appropriate, to the consultant, to your management and project, and to potential "customers" of the consultant can be especially productive.

Finally, feedback of all kinds is important. The consultant usually has only a short time to learn the needs of the project and the appropriate background, develop appropriate recommendations, and help implement them. Hence, a high level of interaction is essential. It is particularly important for the consultant to be able to report problems that are interfering with the ability to work. A consultant needs to be told when he or she is on the wrong track. Honesty with tact on both sides will usually be most effective.

8.2.2 Consultant

The role of the consultant is demanding, in that he or she must work rapidly and efficiently to be effective. The first order of business is to define project needs and problems. Next, the consultant must identify information sources and evaluate their relative importance. Third, the consultant develops plans about what should be done.

At this point, it is necessary to gain an understanding of the formal and informal power structures of the organization and the organizational politics. The key people should be identified. It is desirable to concentrate one's efforts on them and to gain an understanding of their attitudes and motivations. The plans of what should be done are considered in the light of the reality of the organization. They should then be modified into a set of objectives that have a realistic chance of success. An approach that has frequently worked has been to search for project objectives that are also likely to satisfy the objectives of the individual key players. The consultant must then seek strategies that will sell them on this synergy. In the case of software reliability measurement where new concepts must be disseminated, the consultant should look for high visibility activities that will make as many project personnel aware of the concepts as possible. He or she should also look for "multiplier" activities that enlist other people in the cause and spawn other activities.

Once a plan of action has been developed, project members must be sold on the plan. Here, the help and ideas of the key people that have been cultivated can be vital. It usually helps if the consultant has developed a thorough understanding of the needs of the project and its environment *and* exhibits this understanding with high visibility. It is desirable to fit new approaches into the existing ones. Use of terminology, concepts, and approaches already familiar to project members and in use on the project is helpful. The consultant should be generous with praise and credit for good aspects of the project and good performance of its members. The praise should be provided directly to the people involved, to their managers, and to people on other projects with whom he or she may come in contact. Positive feedback is important not only as a strategy for getting ideas accepted, but also as a way of making sure that the project team understands which things are being done right and should not be changed. Negative aspects must be dealt with honestly, privately, and with tact, but not avoided. The consultant must maintain project confidentiality when he or she deals with several projects. However, when the consultant has obtained the necessary permission, he or she is in an excellent position to spread good ideas. Ensuring that the idea originators get proper credit will strengthen relationships.

8.3   SUMMARY

In this chapter you have learned how to plan and implement software reliability measurement and prediction for your project. Particular attention was paid to the collection of data and to how to work with a consultant in this field.

REVIEW OF SOFTWARE AND SOFTWARE DEVELOPMENT FOR HARDWARE ENGINEERS

This review will first cover computer hardware and architecture. It will then discuss the languages used for controlling computers and the system software that provides an improved human interface. Finally, the process of software development is outlined.

A.1 COMPUTER BASICS

A computer in the most general sense is a logical device whose operation is directed by a sequence of instructions called a program. Creating this sequence is the job of the programmer. Although many people think of computers as machines that do general purpose processing, the broad definition we have given is necessary because there are many special purpose processors as well. Virtually all computers work with binary numbers or *bits*. The basic hardware of the computer consists of logic circuitry that performs various Boolean operations on these bits such as "AND" and "OR."

The *instructions* that constitute a program are strings of bits that follow a definite format. Certain bits represent the operation or function to be performed and others represent the addresses in memory of one or more operands. The instructions combine operands in various ways and store the results in memory at specified addresses. Memory to store intermediate results is an important part of a computer, in view of the fact that the operations that can be performed are relatively simple ones. Almost all useful functions, when implemented on computers, require a series of machine instructions with intermediate storage of the results to perform their tasks. Although instructions can perform operations at the bit level, in general they operate on larger entities. These include the *byte*, which consists of 8 bits, or the *word*, which can range between 8 and 64 bits. Word lengths of 16 and 32 bits are the most common.

Machine instructions are not necessarily the lowest level of programmable logical functions in the computer. In many computers, the instructions activate various logical functions in the machine through *microcode*. That is, the instructions are interpreted in terms of lower level logical primitives. Microcode permits the instruction repertoire of a computer to be changed either to add improvements or to tailor it to some special application.

Memory is frequently organized in a hierarchical fashion based on the time required to access it. For example, a machine may have a high-speed small semiconductor memory called a *cache*, which contains currently active or about-to-be-active instructions. The main memory will be a slower semiconductor memory or core memory, also directly accessible or addressable by the computer's processor. The machine will also have *secondary storage*, connected to the computer by a high-speed data channel. The secondary storage itself may be hierarchical. The most active files or data sets will reside on disk and the less active files on some sort of *mass storage system*.

The conventional computer, before the widespread application of integrated circuits, consisted of a processor, a main memory, secondary storage, and various peripheral devices. With the advent of inexpensive chips and computer-aided design of these chips, computer architecture began to diversify in many ways. For example, processing may be performed by several processors in a multiprocessor configuration. Peripherals, especially input-output devices, may, in effect, be specialized computers on their own. Many small computers may be connected together to form a *distributed processing system*. In a distributed system it is common for different functions or roles to be assigned to each computer or to groups of computers. Specialized machines may be provided for managing a data base. There are array or vector processors that process arrays (structured collections) or vectors of data with multiple processing elements. Computers may be configured into *networks* that, in effect, are loosely coupled distributed processing systems.

The process of programming first involves an analysis of the functions one wishes to perform. These are generally broken down into smaller and smaller subfunctions (the "top-down" approach) until one arrives at a level where the subfunctions are already implemented. This level may be at the level of machine instructions. It may also be at the level of previously programmed or *reusable* subfunctions. Obviously, the latter situation is preferable from the viewpoint of programming productivity. Consequently, it is often desirable when designing to develop general purpose subroutines. These can then be reused for many other situations.

Once the program has been prepared, it must be verified. Experience has shown that the complexity of even the simplest program is such that you can't be sure it will "work" in all circumstances without verification. By "work" we mean "perform the functions for which it was designed." Verification can involve checking of the program itself. However, it *always* involves testing the program by executing it for the functions it is required to perform. Checking of the program itself can be performed by several means. The program may be inspected by the programmer or a colleague for common flaws. You may step through the program as if simulating its execution for different cases. You might even attempt a correctness proof, which is a formal mathematical demonstration that the program functions to meet the requirements. Such a proof is generally quite difficult and may not be practical or economic.

A.2 COMPUTER LANGUAGES

As noted previously, the basic instructions in a computer consist of strings of bits. These are referred to as *machine language*. Machine language is difficult and tedious for the programmer to deal with. Therefore, *assembly languages* were developed early in the history of computers to provide a better human interface. An assembly language assigns more readily understood codes to operations instead of a string of bits. These are command names or their abbreviations such as "ADD" or "MUL." It also permits the programmer to assign names to locations in memory. Thus, assembly language is easier for programmers to understand and work with. An *assembler* (a computer program itself) translates the operation and operand symbols into the strings of bits of machine language that are needed to actually operate the computer. The assembly language program is called the *source program*. The binary program output by the assembler is called the object program. An assembler may generate an *object program* for the machine on which it is running or for a different target machine, in which case it is called a *cross assembler*.

Although assembly language was a substantial improvement over machine language, it was still far from being natural in terms of being suited to the way in which people usually think. The second step in improving the human interface was the introduction of *high-level languages*. These are languages that express operations in a form akin to formulas or equations. This is contrasted with assembly language, which is a series of single operations performed on one or more operands. High-level languages are translated into machine language by *compilers*. The process is called compilation. There are also programs called *interpreters* that accept statements written in high-level languages and translate them in real time to machine language statements that are immediately executed. Interpreters are useful for programs that are dynamic (that is, changing rapidly), such as sets of commands for a user who is interacting with a computer in real time. Interpretation, of course, is much slower than execution because of all the extra translation required. Hence, if a program is relatively stable, it is more efficient to compile it and then execute, rather than interpret it every time it is needed.

FORTRAN was the first of the high-level languages. It is still in wide use on many machines, although it lacks many of the features of the more modern languages. COBOL is commonly used in the business field. ALGOL is popular in Europe. BASIC and to some extent PASCAL are frequently used on personal computers. PL/1 is a powerful but correspondingly difficult to learn language that has many adherents. C is popular among scientific and university users. It is widely used in telecommunications applications. A new language, Ada, has been developed and is intended as a standard in the United States Department of Defense. In addition to the general high-level languages just mentioned, there are many specialized application languages. These have been developed for particular fields, such as APT for programming of machine tools and GPSS for simulation.

Current languages are but another step on the road toward a better interface between computer and human. The explosion of personal computers has resulted in new ways of commanding a computer. These include selecting operations from menus that are displayed on a screen. You may use graphic symbols that are highly evocative. For example, pointing to a picture of a file will store data. Pointing to a waste basket symbol will destroy the data. Investigators in artificial intelligence are carrying this movement toward more natural means of expression to machines even further.

A.3 SYSTEMS SOFTWARE

We have been talking about the bare hardware computer. In reality, users of computers interact with an extended machine, which consists of hardware plus systems software, that eases the job of working with the computer.

The most basic piece of systems software is the *operating system*. The operating system administers all the resources of the computer including the processor or processors, memory, secondary storage, and peripherals. It allocates these to users as they require them. One of its most basic functions is to load programs into the machine for execution. In larger machines it is common to use *multiprogramming*. That is, the programs of many users are loaded into the machine at the same time. Each is located in a different partition of the main memory and all share the processor. When a machine operates in the *batch processing* mode, each program in turn is commonly given control of the processor until it must wait for an input/output operation to be completed. The other common mode of operation is the *time-sharing* mode. In this mode, each program is allowed to run only for a limited slice of time, commonly much less than 1 second. This type of operation is necessary when users are working in an interactive mode. Response times to commands of users working interactively must be in the region of fractions of a second to be satisfactory.

Some operating systems implement a method of addressing storage called *virtual storage*. The amount of main memory that is available to a program at any given time is limited. It is generally less than the total size of the program and its data. The virtual storage concept allows the programmer to assign memory locations as if a very large memory were available for use. The virtual storage operating system then handles the paging of parts of the program and its data from secondary storage to main storage and back as the program parts and data are required for execution.

There are many other functions of operating systems including:

1. file management (management of secondary storage),
2. assigning and controlling priorities to different system users,
3. protecting user files so that only those persons designated by the user can read the files or write to them (this is a *computer security* function),
4. control of who has access to the machine by use of passwords and other security measures,
5. accounting and charging for usage, and
6. recording performance characteristics of the machine and its systems software so that it can be tuned for more efficient operation.

Compilers, assemblers, and interpreters are generally considered as systems software.

Data base management systems provide facilities for organizing data items (as contrasted with files) in a structured fashion into data bases. They furnish facilities for accessing the data items in various convenient ways, such as searching for data items with a field (part of a data item) having a specified "value." A "value" can be a number, a name such as "Zook," or a logical variable like "TRUE" or "FALSE." Graphics system software provides facilities for constructing common graphical figures (for example, curves or bar plots) and specifying their attributes (line texture and thickness, color, etc.). Diagnostic and debugging tools create environments in which a program can be executed in a controlled fashion and data needed for diagnosis of problems can be specified and recorded.

A.4 THE SOFTWARE DEVELOPMENT PROCESS

The development of software as a usable, marketable, profitable product (*software engineering*) is a considerably more complex undertaking than the development of a program that works. Several books have been devoted to this topic [Shooman (1983), Pressman (1982), and Myers (1976)]. It includes development of documentation, training, and other necessary support facilities. Ordinarily the program must be capable of evolving easily to meet changing user needs.

Frequently, the users of the software product are unsophisticated when it comes to computers. Thus the user-machine interface, or the way in which the user tells the machine what to do, must be carefully designed. It must be simple to learn. It must be easy to remember. It must work in a way that minimizes the risk of introducing wrong commands. When the program doesn't work properly, possibly due to user error, it must be easy to diagnose what went wrong. Finally, the program must not depend on the intelligent intervention of the user to help it over situations that may not have been considered beforehand. If a program is just written for yourself, it is often no great tragedy if you have not considered all the cases that can occur. You can simply handle the resulting problem in real time. But this is not true of software developed for a general user.

Most software products are too large and complicated to be produced by an individual. They involve a team of software engineers, sometimes one of substantial size. Thus software development frequently involves all the problems that can arise in "designing by committee." These problems are usually more severe than those involved in simply working together as a team to perform some task. To all the issues of group dynamics are added the communication difficulties of trying to think and create together. The foregoing considerations have been emphasized because a little programming is truly a dangerous thing. It is traditional for the programmer who takes on the responsibilities of the software engineer to find this out the hard way.

A.4.1   Design and Coding

As previously noted, software is built in a process of sequential steps that in general proceed from the top down, that is, from a few high-level concepts to many lower-level concepts. The lower-level concepts can either be instructions or standard software packages that are selected for use in this application. Although the software development process is sequential, it is also iterative. The process of filling in more detail often results in problems that make it necessary to modify some of the higher-order concepts. Also, although both hardware and software can evolve with time to meet changing customer needs or exploit new technology, software can do so somewhat more easily. While the hardware is often standard, software is readily tailored to a customer's needs, and it can be continually retailored as the customer's needs evolve. These evolutionary and adaptable aspects of software complicate the process of its development. They add to the iterative nature and thus the high degree of interactivity in the development process. Evolution tends to erode the integrity of the original software design. Continuing reintegration of high-level concepts and system testing is thus needed for software to a much greater extent than it is for hardware.

A software project starts either as the result of a customer requesting a product or marketing or technical personnel seeing an opportunity to develop a product that can be profitable. This product may be solely a software one but it is often a hardware-software system. In the "product opportunity" case, the concept of the product is developed, marketing analyses are done, and costs and potential profitability are investigated. Prospective customers may be consulted directly. The result of this is a system concept. The system concept, which can also emanate from a specific customer request, is further detailed by examining the functions the system must perform and the needs it must meet. The result is a requirements definition. The requirements definition for a large system may be hundreds of pages in size.

There is a great danger at this point that the requirements definition may not represent what the customer really wants. This can occur because the requirements definition is usually generated by the developer. It is easy for this to diverge from the customer's needs. This is particularly true because the requirements definition is often lengthy and technical in nature. The user frequently does not have the time or the background to understand it fully. Therefore, it is often desirable to express the requirements in a way the user can grasp. It is important that they be expressed in terms of the functions the user wants to accomplish. One way of doing this is to prepare a draft of the user manual that will ultimately be used for the operational program. An even better but more expensive way to communicate with the user is to prepare a *rapid prototype*. This is a model or "draft version" of the system that clearly exhibits the user interface and principal user functions. If the user then exercises the prototype in the same way as the final system would be employed in operation, valuable feedback can be generated for the developer.

The project now enters the design phase. Depending on the size of the project, you proceed through a hierarchy of designs until the system has been divided into detailed functions that can be assigned to individual software developers. Thus, the overall system may be divided into subsystems with the interfaces between subsystems being defined, subsystems divided into components, and so forth. Various design methodologies have been proposed to make this process more efficient and less prone to error. Many projects conduct *design inspections* in which the design is carefully examined by various people from different viewpoints.

Each of the programmers assigned to a detailed function then carries out the process of detailed design. This involves dividing the assigned function into modules and establishing the interfaces. The structure and format of the data are defined. The subfunctions in each module are outlined. Again, various design methodologies have been developed to help this process. Design languages have been developed for specifying designs. Some design languages have associated tools that check the design for completeness, consistency, and other important attributes.

When the detailed design is complete, the programmer proceeds to code the various modules, compile or assemble them, and test each of them as a unit. *Editors* are used to create and modify the code. Compilers or assemblers find many of the syntactic faults. *Syntactic faults* are violations of the syntactic structure of the language being used. A recent development is the syntax-driven editor, which guides the programmer in the construction of syntactically valid statements in the language being written. With this tool, programs do not have syntactic faults that must be corrected after compilation. Semantic faults cannot be automatically diagnosed. They must be found either through careful inspection of the code (by the original programmer or others) or through testing. *Semantic faults* are mistakes in meaning, such that the computer is not instructed correctly about one's desired action.

To conduct a unit test, the programmer must develop various *test drivers* to exercise each of the modules. Also, each programmer will utilize diagnostic or debugging tools, which represent another component of systems software. These tools build scaffolding around the executing program. They make it possible to, in effect, insert temporary changes into the program that make it stop at various points and print out the values of important variables. By wisely choosing the *breakpoints* and the variables to be printed, the programmer can verify correct operation of the program or isolate problems. Rapid isolation is a key to efficient debugging.

It is frequently common in the unit test stage to keep track of the *coverage* of the program. By "coverage" we mean the percentage of instructions (or better, branches or paths) that have been executed in the testing so far. Complete coverage is not usually attained, but coverage is a useful index of the thoroughness of testing. Note that complete coverage is a necessary *but not sufficient* condition for finding all the faults.

Editors and diagnostic and debugging tools form the programming environment. It is highly desirable that all parts of the programming environment be designed to function together, using commands and programmer interfaces that are consistent with each other.

A.4.2 Test

Once the modules have been developed and tested to a programmer's satisfaction, they are generally turned over to another individual or group that integrates them to form larger entities. Integration generally proceeds in a hierarchical fashion through component integration, subsystem integration, and finally, system integration. For a smaller system, system integration alone may occur. When you reach the level of system integration, the entire system is generally operated as a unit. Software is tested against inputs that represent what the program will encounter in actual operation. As you move from unit test to system test, there will be a transition from structural to functional testing. *Structural testing*, sometimes called "white box" testing, uses knowledge of the program structure to plan efficient tests. Test planning for structural testing requires the involvement of the programmer. *Functional testing*, often called "black box" or system testing, requires only knowledge of the system requirements. A user or system engineer can do the test planning for functional testing. In fact, it is probably best that one of them and not the programmer do it. Careful functional test planning is necessary to ensure that the operational environment is represented correctly, so that the testing of a program does truly represent its eventual use. Functional testing is sometimes divided into feature testing and load testing. *Feature testing* involves the testing of each program feature or function in sequence with as little repetition as possible. *Load testing* tries to represent the operational environment as accurately as possible with regard to relative frequencies of demand for various functions.

Also, the testing must be reasonably comprehensive. In theory, the program should be tested for every possible input state or set of input variables that can occur. In practice, this is impossible because the number of different input states is astronomical. Equivalence partitioning can be used to reduce this number. An *equivalence partition* or *equivalence class* is a set of similar input states that are believed to have the same failure behavior. Thus it is necessary to run only one input state to establish whether a fault is associated with the partition. The determination of equivalence classes is both an art and a gamble. You try to group functionally similar input states together, or states that appear likely to exercise the same program paths. But there is no guarantee that you have done this correctly! It is probably wise to occasionally execute more than one input state from an equivalence partition. Also, you must recognize that some inevitable uncertainty must remain about the thoroughness of the testing.

Some special techniques may be employed for the verification of critical systems such as nuclear power plants, defense systems, and air traffic control systems. Critical outcomes that must be avoided are enumerated (for example, reactor meltdown). A thorough analysis of all the sets of conditions that can lead to these outcomes, called a *fault tree analysis*, is made. Appropriate defensive actions are taken in the program to prevent these conditions from occurring [Leveson (1986)].

When system testing is complete, the system is generally delivered to the customer. The customer may require verification testing before accepting the product. Verification testing is generally either performed by the customer with the developer's help or by the developer under the customer's direction. Once a program has been accepted, it is said to be in the operational phase. In this phase, the software generally continues to evolve, as customers find through use of the system that certain improvements are necessary or desired. At the same time, there are generally some residual faults in the software that are causing it to fail in various ways. The customer will request that these be corrected. The principal activity after delivery is often referred to as one of *program maintenance*. But this term is somewhat misleading to people familiar with the concept of hardware maintenance. The maintenance of software does not involve a replacement of parts that wear out or the preventive replacement of parts that are likely to fail. Rather, it includes the improvement of both the reliability and the features of the software. Often it is required by functions that change as a customer's needs change. Also, changes may be necessary to handle changes in the hardware or software environments in which a program operates. And thus, it would probably be better if we used the term *software evolution*.

A.5 SUMMARY

Computing systems may be viewed as a functional hierarchy of logic and memory. The "lower" levels are simple in function and implemented in hardware. The intermediate levels may involve software, firmware (programs permanently recorded in memory that can't be changed), or complex hardware. The higher levels are sophisticated in function and generally implemented in software. The quality of the human interface generally improves as you approach the higher levels.

The software development process is complex, iterative, evolutionary, and fraught with potential for the introduction of faults. Developing software as a product is orders of magnitude more difficult than developing it as a personal tool. It is common for people who have learned to program to be deceived into thinking that they therefore know how to develop software products. As in any other branch of engineering, much training and experience are necessary to become a proficient and professional software engineer.

SUMMARY OF FORMULAS FOR APPLICATION

B.1 FAILURE INTENSITY-RELIABILITY (FOR CONSTANT FAILURE INTENSITY)

$$R(\tau) = \exp(-\lambda\tau)$$

$R(\tau)$ = reliability
λ = failure intensity
τ = execution time

B.2 BASIC EXECUTION TIME MODEL

B.2.1 Execution Time Component

Failures experienced (expected)

$$\mu(\tau) = \nu_0 \left[1 - \exp\left(-\frac{\lambda_0}{\nu_0}\tau \right) \right]$$

Present failure intensity

$$\lambda(\tau) = \lambda_0 \exp\left(-\frac{\lambda_0}{\nu_0}\tau \right) \qquad \lambda(\mu) = \lambda_0 \left[1 - \frac{\mu}{\nu_0} \right]$$

Reliability

$$R(\tau' \mid \tau) = \exp\left\{ -\left[\nu_0 \exp\left(-\frac{\lambda_0}{\nu_0}\tau \right) \right] \left[1 - \exp\left(-\frac{\lambda_0}{\nu_0}\tau' \right) \right] \right\}$$

Additional failures to failure intensity objective

$$\Delta\mu = \frac{\nu_0}{\lambda_0}\left(\lambda_P - \lambda_F \right)$$

Additional execution time to failure intensity objective

$$\Delta\tau = \frac{\nu_0}{\lambda_0}\ \ln\left(\frac{\lambda_P}{\lambda_F} \right)$$

Relationship between parameters

$$\frac{\lambda_0}{\nu_0} = B\phi$$

B = fault reduction factor
μ = failures experienced (expected)
$\Delta\mu$ = additional failures (expected)
τ = execution time
τ' = execution time measured from the present
$\Delta\tau$ = additional execution time
λ_0 = initial failure intensity
λ_P = present failure intensity
λ_F = failure intensity objective
ν_0 = total failures (expected)
ϕ = per-fault hazard rate (constant)

B.2.2   Calendar Time Component

$$\frac{dt_r}{d\tau} = \frac{1}{P_r\rho_r}\left[\theta_r + \mu_r\,\lambda_0\exp\left(-\frac{\lambda_0}{\nu_0}\tau \right) \right]$$

t = calendar time
τ = execution time
r = index of limiting resource (C = computer time, F = failure correction personnel, I = failure identification personnel)
P_r = resource quantity
ρ_r = resource utilization

θ_r = execution time coefficient of resource usage
μ_r = failure coefficient of resource usage
λ_0 = initial failure intensity
ν_0 = total failures (expected)

B.2.3   Parameter Prediction

Inherent faults

$$\omega_0 = \omega_I \, \Delta I$$

Total failures

$$\nu_0 = \frac{\omega_0}{B}$$

Linear execution frequency

$$f = \frac{r}{I}$$

Initial failure intensity

$$\lambda_0 = fK\omega_0$$

ω_0 = inherent faults
ω_I = inherent faults per developed source instruction
ΔI = developed executable source instructions
ν_0 = total failures
B = fault reduction factor
f = linear execution frequency
r = instruction execution rate
I = executable object instructions
λ_0 = initial failure intensity
K = fault exposure ratio

B.3   LOGARITHMIC POISSON EXECUTION TIME MODEL

B.3.1   Execution Time Component

Failures experienced (expected)

$$\mu(\tau) = \frac{1}{\theta} \ln (\lambda_0 \, \theta\tau + 1)$$

Present failure intensity

$$\lambda(\tau) = \frac{\lambda_0}{\lambda_0 \, \theta \, \tau + 1} \qquad\qquad \lambda(\mu) = \lambda_0 \exp\left(-\, \theta\mu\right)$$

Reliability

$$R(\tau'|\, \tau) = \left[\frac{\lambda_0\theta\tau + 1}{\lambda_0\theta(\tau' + \tau) + 1}\right]^{1/\theta}$$

Mean time to failure

$$\Theta(\tau) = \frac{\theta}{1 - \theta}\,(\lambda_0\theta\tau + 1)^{1-\frac{1}{\theta}} \qquad (\theta < 1)$$

Additional failures to failure intensity objective

$$\Delta\mu = \frac{1}{\theta}\,\ln\left[\frac{\lambda_P}{\lambda_F}\right]$$

Additional execution time to failure intensity objective

$$\Delta\tau = \frac{1}{\theta}\left[\frac{1}{\lambda_F} - \frac{1}{\lambda_P}\right]$$

μ = failures experienced (expected)
$\Delta\mu$ = additional failures (expected)
τ = execution time
τ' = execution time measured from the present
$\Delta\tau$ = additional execution time
λ_0 = initial failure intensity
λ_P = present failure intensity
λ_F = failure intensity objective
θ = failure intensity decay parameter
Θ = mean time to failure

B.3.2 Calendar Time Component

$$\frac{dt_r}{d\tau} = \frac{1}{P_r\rho_r}\left[\theta_r + \mu_r\,\frac{\lambda_0}{\lambda_0\,\theta\,\tau + 1}\right]$$

t = calendar time

τ = execution time

r = index of limiting resource (C = computer time, F = failure correction personnel, I = failure identification personnel)

P_r = resource quantity

ρ_r = resource utilization

θ_r = execution time coefficient of resource usage

μ_r = failure coefficient of resource usage

λ_0 = initial failure intensity

θ = failure intensity decay parameter

B.4   RESOURCE REQUIREMENTS

$$\Delta \chi_r = \theta_r \, \Delta\tau + \mu_r \, \Delta\mu$$

$\Delta\chi_r$ = resource quantity

θ_r = execution time coefficient of resource usage

μ_r = failure coefficient of resource usage

$\Delta\tau$ = additional execution time

$\Delta\mu$ = additional failures

GLOSSARY OF TERMS

We have tried to make this glossary of terms reflect present standard usage. In most cases it is in conformance with *The IEEE Standard Glossary of Software Engineering Terminology* [IEEE (1983)], which is also an ANSI (United States) standard. Consequently, the terminology used in describing historic works in the field may not always be the same as that used in the works themselves.

availability: expected fraction of time during which system or component is functioning acceptably

calendar time: chronological time, including time during which a computer may not be running

clock time: elapsed time from start to end of program execution, including wait time, on a running computer

common-cause failures: failures arising from the same cause and hence unlikely to be independent of each other

computer utilization: fraction of clock time the processor is executing

concurrent: consisting of components that function at the same time

confidence bound: one limit of a confidence interval

confidence interval: range of values within which a parameter is expected to lie with a certain confidence

coverage: sum of probabilities of occurrence of input states tested

deterministic: possessing the property of having only one value at a given time *deterministic testing*: testing in which all selection of runs has been planned and prescribed in advance

developed code: new or modified deliverable executable instructions

environment: operational profile

equivalence partition: set of input states that appear likely to be similar in that a given fault will result in a failure no matter which input state is activated

evolving program: program that is changing for reasons other than correction of failures

execution time: CPU time or time spent by processor in executing a program

expected value: mean of a random variable

failure: see "software failure"

failure intensity: failures per unit time, the derivative with respect to time of the mean value function of failures

failure interval: time between failures

failure severity: classification of a failure by its operational impact

failure time: accumulated elapsed time at which a failure occurs

fault: defective, missing, or extra instruction or set of related instructions that is the cause of one or more actual or potential failure types

fault exposure ratio: proportionality factor that relates failure intensity with the rate at which faults would be encountered if the program were executed linearly

fault reduction factor: net reduction in faults per failure experienced

fault-tolerant: incorporating design features to protect against effects of defects

grouped data: failure data in the form of number of failures in some interval

hazard rate: probability density (per unit time) of failure given that failure has not occurred up to the present

inference: the process of making a model specific, based on data that have been collected

inherent fault: fault associated with original software product (whether new or modified) at completion of coding

inherited code: deliverable executable instructions that are reused from a previous application (this code is usually well debugged)

input space: the set of all possible input states for a program

input state: set of input variables for a particular run

input variable: any data item that exists external to a run and is used by the run

least squares fit: a method of fitting a curve to data in which the parameters of the curve are determined so as to minimize the sum of squares of deviation of the curve from the data *limiting resource*: the resource that controls the relationship between execution time and calendar time

maximum likelihood estimation: a form of parameter estimation in which those parameters are selected that maximize the possibility that the data that have been observed could have occurred

mean: the average value of a random variable, where the values that a random variable can have are weighted by the associated probabilities

mean time to failure (MTTF): expected value of the failure interval

mean time to repair (MTTR): expected value of the time required to restore to normal operation

mean value function: function that expresses the average value of the number of events experienced by a random process at each point in time

nonhomogeneous: possessing characteristics that vary with time

operational mode: one possible operational profile (among two or more) in which program can operate; mode is usually a function of installation or time

operational profile: the set of all possible input states (input space) with their associated probabilities of occurrence

output state: set of output variables for a particular run

output variable: any data item that exists external to a run and is set by the run

parameter: a quantity that, when specified, gives specific form to the general form of a model

parameter estimation: the process of establishing parameter values for a model, based on data

parameter prediction: determination of parameter values from characteristics of the software product and the development process

planned parameter: calendar time component parameter relating to resource quantities available and their utilizations, readily determinable from project person responsible

Poisson: a particular probability distribution and random process

predictable parameter: parameter whose value can be determined from properties of the software product and development process

prediction of parameter values: see "parameter prediction"

prescribed work period: the amount of time (usually specified in hours) per calendar time unit (usually per week) the average project member can work upon request

probability: the fraction of occasions on which a specified value or set of values of a quantity occurs, out of all possible values for that quantity

probability distribution: the set of probabilities corresponding to the values that a random variable can take on *program*: a set of complete instructions (operators with operands specified) that executes within a single computer and relates to the accomplishment of some major function

random: possessing the property of having more than one value at one time, each occurring with some probability

random process: a set of random variables arranged by some other variable (usually time)

random testing: testing where selection of input states is random with selection probabilities equivalent to operational profile probabilities

random variable: a variable that possesses the property of randomness (see "random")

regression test: a test case or run that repeats an input state that was previously executed

resource usage parameter: calendar time component parameter that describes resources required for functions such as failure identification and correction

robust system: system that handles unexpected input states in a way that minimizes performance degradation, data corruption, and undesirable output states

run: a subdivision of the execution of a program, usually based on the accomplishment of a user-oriented function (during test, often called a "test case")

sampling with replacement: selecting from a population, with the states that are selected being returned for the possibility of being selected again

sampling without replacement: selecting from a population, with the states that are selected being eliminated from the possibility of being selected again

sequential: consisting of components that function one after another

software failure: departure of program operation from requirements

software reliability: probability of failure-free operation of a program for a specified time in a specified environment

software reliability model: general form for characterizing software reliability or a related quantity as a function of failures experienced or time

stable program: program in which code is unchanging, with program neither evolving nor being repaired

stage: period of execution during which total code and developed code remain constant

statistically significant: sufficiently different to be attributable to cause, not random fluctuation

testing compression factor: ratio of execution time required in operational phase to execution time required in test phase to cover the input space of the program

total failures: number of failures that will occur in infinite execution time

utilization: proportion of time a resource is used

GLOSSARY OF NOTATION

A uniform set of symbols has been adopted in this book for clarity and consistency. They may differ from the symbols used in the original works. The symbols listed here are those used frequently throughout the book. Any departures from the definitions noted here are special exceptions necessary for clarity that are defined when they occur.

Variables denoting time can be modified by adding the subscript "i" or any integer to indicate the ith failure or the failure number denoted by the integer. In addition, a prime (') indicates a difference (for example, inter-failure time in the case of τ').

Other general conventions which are used are: the caret (ˆ) denotes estimate and the tilde (˜) denotes an adjusted, transformed, or predicted value.

When looking up a symbol with a numeric subscript, note that the subscript will often be indicated in the glossary with a generic symbol such as i or k. Similarly, if the subscript is C, F, or I, look for the generic subscript r.

B	Fault reduction factor (average ratio of rate of reduction of faults to rate of failure occurrence)
C	Computer time when used as a subscript; otherwise, testing compression factor
$E[X]$	Expectation of X or mean of random variable X

f	Linear execution frequency r/I; failure probability density function $dF(t)/dt$
F	Failure-correction personnel
i	Index indicating sequential number of a failure event, $i = 1, 2, \ldots$
I	Failure-identification personnel when used as a subscript; number of deliverable executable object instructions in the program when used with failure time adjustment
I_k	Number of deliverable executable object instructions for stage k
I_S	Number of inherent source instructions
j	Alternate for i
k	Generic index for use with other than failure times (for example, component or stage number)
K	Fault exposure ratio
l	Alternate for k
m_Q	Bound on number of failures allowed to queue up for correction by any debugger
p_k	Probability of occurrence of input state k
p_{kl}	Transition probability (from component k to component l)
$p_{\min}$	Probability of occurrence of rarest input state
P_{m_Q}	Probability that no debugger has m_Q or more failures to work on at any given time
P_r	Available quantity of resource r where $r = C, F, I$
q_{kl}	Probability of failure occurring during transition from component k to l
Q_I	Total number of input states
Q_P	Total number of components
Q_X	Code expansion ratio or ratio of object to source instructions
r	Resource when used as a subscript; otherwise, average instruction execution rate
R	Reliability or probability of failure-free operation
R_k	Reliability of component k
t	Cumulative calendar or generic time
t_e	A specific deterministic time denoting the end of failure data
t_i	Time of ith failure
t'	Calendar or generic time since last failure (realization when this time is a random variable)
$\bar{t}'$	Average failure interval or t/m
t'_i	Failure interval following $(i - 1)$th failure
$\hat{t}_i$	Adjusted failure time
ΔI	Number of deliverable developed executable source instructions

ΔI_k	Number of deliverable developed executable source instructions for stage k
$\Delta\mu$	Increment of expected failures (especially, number associated with reaching failure intensity objective)
$\Delta\tau$	Increment of execution time (especially, amount associated with reaching failure intensity objective)
$\Delta\chi_r$	Increment of resource r where $r = C, F, I$
$\Delta\mu_r$	Expected number of failures during resource r period
$\Delta\tau_r$	Execution time interval for the resource r period
$\Delta\chi_{rr}$	Usage of resource r during its limiting period
θ	Failure intensity decay parameter of logarithmic Poisson execution time model
θ_r	Execution time coefficient of resource usage where $r = C, F, I$
Θ	Mean time to failure (MTTF)
λ_k	Component failure intensity
λ_{rs}	Potential transition point between different resource-limited periods
λ_t	Failure intensity in clock time
λ_τ	Failure intensity in execution time
λ_F	Failure intensity objective
λ_P	Present failure intensity λ_0
λ_0	Initial failure intensity
$\lambda(t)$	Failure intensity function $d\mu/dt$
μ_{kl}	Mean duration spent in component k before going to component l
μ_r	Failure coefficient of resource usage where $r = C, F, I$
$\mu(t)$	Expected number of failures experienced by time t or $E[M(t)]$
ν_0	Expected failures experienced in infinite time
ρ_k	Probability of control residing in component k
ρ_r	Utilization of resource r during its limiting period where $r = C, F, I$
ρ_C	Average utilization of computer
τ	Cumulative execution time (realization when execution time is a random variable)
τ_k	The execution time for a run corresponding to input state k
ϕ	Model parameter representing constant per-fault hazard rate
ϕ_k	Per-fault hazard rate for stage k
χ_r	Requirement for resource r where $r = C, F, I$
ψ	Psi (digamma) function
ω_I	Inherent fault density (with respect to source instructions)
ω_0	Number of inherent faults

PROBLEM SOLUTIONS

CHAPTER 1

1.1 First, the term "software reliability" is in general use, like it or not. However, we have deliberately decided to promote the usage further to emphasize compatibility of software and hardware reliability calculations and their joint use in computing system reliability. It is true that software doesn't wear out. "Software reliability" is really a measure of confidence in the design. Design confidence could be estimated for hardware systems. It usually isn't, because wear-out phenomena tend to swamp out design defects for most hardware systems.

1.2 First, a random model of behavior is just like any other model, an *approximation* to reality. The question is not whether the model is perfect but whether it is better than other (for example, deterministic) models. Hardware failures are not purely random. They do have deterministic causes that could be found given enough time and technology. We view hardware failures as random because it is easy to do so and this model is sufficient for making the predictions we find necessary.

There are a large number of ways in which *humans* fail and introduce faults into software. It is easiest (and satisfactory for prediction purposes) to model this behavior as a random process. Furthermore, the *use* of software systems (and hence the determination of which faults will cause failures) often is best modeled by a random process. You might even say that a deterministic view of software failure makes no sense. If you could inexpensively predict the failures that would be encountered in a particular usage, why wouldn't you correct the underlying faults?

1.3 Manipulation of the failure intensity estimate is possible. You must know at least one input state that fails and one that succeeds. You then select them in the proportions you desire. However, we aren't really interested in behavior of the program for an artificial set of tests. We are concerned with the typical environment of inputs (usually randomly sequenced) that will normally be encountered. Manipulation of tests for hardware is possible and just as unreasonable as for software. For example, you can obtain a very large failure intensity for most automobile tires by running them over a set of spikes.

1.4 Suppose people do learn the weaknesses of a system and avoid them rather than request the software designer to correct them. This acceptance is equivalent to a redefinition of the system requirements. Incidentally, there is no reason why usage of the remaining functions should not be regarded as a random process.

1.5 That depends. One essential is that the level of coverage be much closer to 1 than the reliability being measured. The other is that the probabilities of selection in test be the same as in operation (or the differences be known so you can compensate for them). If these conditions are satisfied, repeated runs do no harm except that the efficiency of testing is degraded.

1.6 Yes and no. A change in the environment is likely to result in more failures if the program has not been tested in the changed environment. However, failures can also occur in a familiar environment. It should be pointed out that hardware failures are also likely to increase when the environment changes. The increase may be less noticeable because of the failures that are constantly occurring due to wear-out.

1.7 In general, yes, but the answer is more complicated than that. When we speak of hardware reliability, we usually mean *physical* reliability or the probability that a system will survive physical failure mechanisms. Software reliability refers to design reliability or the probability that the system is free from behavior that departs from the system requirements. Both types of reliability are dependent on the usage of the system. However, systems are often built so that they are physically tolerant to a wide range of uses. Hence physical reliability may not be as susceptible to changes in usage as design reliability is.

The reliability of a hardware system is really dependent on both physical reliability and design reliability, although only the former is usually considered. The reliability of a software system is dependent only on design reliability.

1.8 Often, where recovery consists of a system reload plus perhaps a data base recovery, the time for the reload (and recovery, where applicable) is the MTTR. This is analogous to a hardware system where units are replaced by spares and later repaired. The actual software debugging and correction time doesn't normally apply, because the system would not be shut down while this activity was in process.

1.9 It means that enough runs must be made such that the sum of the probabilities associated with those runs in the operational phase approaches 1.

1.10 Yes. Your method is approximately equivalent to the assumption. The random selection of input states during test is usually done with the probability of selection of a particular input state proportional to the probability of selection it is expected to experience in use. Random selection will then result in an ordering of tests that is approximately the same as the order of their probability of occurrence.

CHAPTER 2

2.1 *Objective of 10 failures/CPU hr.* For the basic execution time model:

$$\Delta\mu = \frac{\nu_0}{\lambda_0}(\lambda_P - \lambda_F) = \frac{120}{20}(20 - 10) = 60 \text{ failures},$$

$$\Delta\tau = \frac{\nu_0}{\lambda_0}\ln\frac{\lambda_P}{\lambda_F} = \frac{120}{20}\ln\frac{20}{10} = 6\ln 2 = 6(0.693) = 4.16 \text{ CPU hr.}$$

For the logarithmic Poisson execution time model:

$$\Delta\mu = \frac{1}{\theta} \ln \frac{\lambda_P}{\lambda_F} = \frac{1}{0.025} \ln \frac{50}{10} = 40 \ln 5 = 40(1.609) = 64 \text{ failures},$$

$$\Delta\tau = \frac{1}{\theta} \left[\frac{1}{\lambda_F} - \frac{1}{\lambda_P} \right] = \frac{1}{0.025} \left[\frac{1}{10} - \frac{1}{50} \right]$$

$$= 40 \, (0.1 - 0.02) = 3.2 \text{ CPU hr.}$$

Note that the additional failures required are approximately the same but the additional execution time is somewhat less for the logarithmic Poisson execution time model.

Objective of 1 failure/CPU hr. For the basic execution time model:

$$\Delta\mu = \frac{\nu_0}{\lambda_0} (\lambda_P - \lambda_F) = \frac{120}{20} (20 - 1) = 114 \text{ failures},$$

$$\Delta\tau = \frac{\nu_0}{\lambda_0} \ln \frac{\lambda_P}{\lambda_F} = \frac{120}{20} \ln \frac{20}{1} = 6 \ln 20 = 6(3.00) = 18 \text{ CPU hr.}$$

For the logarithmic Poisson execution time model:

$$\Delta\mu = \frac{1}{\theta} \ln \frac{\lambda_P}{\lambda_F} = \frac{1}{0.025} \ln \frac{50}{1} = 40 \ln \frac{50}{1} = 40 \, (3.91) = 156 \text{ failures},$$

$$\Delta\tau = \frac{1}{\theta} \left[\frac{1}{\lambda_F} - \frac{1}{\lambda_P} \right] = \frac{1}{0.025} \left[\frac{1}{1} - \frac{1}{50} \right]$$

$$= 40(1 - 0.02) = 39.2 \text{ CPU hr.}$$

Note that as failure intensity objectives get smaller, the additional failures and execution time required to reach them become substantially larger for the logarithmic Poisson than the basic execution time model.

2.2 Usually most but not all failures result in the correction of the faults that caused them. We actually estimate failures rather than faults required to reach the failure intensity objective. The terminology "failures that must be experienced" is intuitively awkward but necessary for strict accuracy.

2.3 Convert the reliability level to a failure intensity objective. Then find the additional failures from Equation (2.9) or (2.10), depending on model used, or by running a software reliability estimation program.

2.4 Not necessarily. It approaches $\theta_r/P_r\rho_r$, which can be greater or less than 1.

2.5 You are missing one very important concept. The spacing between faults in "instruction space" is not the same as the spacing between failures in "execution space." The reasons for this are twofold:

1. Except in very trivial cases, code is not "straight line" but has many loops and branches.

2. Even if code were "straight line," the state of the machine will most likely not be constant and hence the fault associated with an instruction may or may not be exposed at one particular execution of the instruction.

Experience to date has shown that intervals between failures typically represent cycling through the program a large number of times. The picture you paint depends on all the faults being uncovered in one cycle through the program, which just doesn't happen in practice. With multiple cycles, the fault density *is* reduced when the first fault is corrected. *On the average* the failure intensity will decrease. Thus the failure intensity *does* change as testing progresses.

CHAPTER 4

4.1 The event diagram for the configuration is shown in Figure E.1. Note that the position of the mainframe operating system is in *series* with all the other components. It is *not* in each of the two parallel branches representing the mainframe hardware reliability. This is because the two programs are identical copies of each other. A failure occurring in one copy would have occurred in the other copy as well. Since these two software components are not independent of each other in regard to failure behavior, redundancy does not improve reliability. Let R_x be the required reliability for the mainframe operating system. Applying combinatorial rules for concurrently functioning components, we obtain:

$$0.90 = 0.99 \ (0.95) \ [1 - (1 - 0.98)^2]R_x,$$

$$0.90 = 0.9401 \ R_x,$$

and therefore

$$R_x = 0.9573.$$

4.2 The application programs are not considered (in effect, they can be viewed as having a reliability of 1). The calendar time failure intensities for the operating and time sharing systems will be 0.01 and 0.005 failure/hr, respectively. These numbers do not change if one processor should fail. The prime shift reliabilities are found to be 0.905 and 0.951, respectively. The combined reliability of the two processors is found as 0.9999. Combining all the "series" elements, we find an overall system prime shift reliability of 0.856.

4.3 Suppose you expect that the compiler will be reliable by the time you finally recompile the program before delivery to the customer. Then do not count failures due to bad compilation when making estimates of program failure intensity or reliability. If it will probably still be unreliable, you may wish to make your estimates twice, with the compiler-caused failures *included* in one estimate and *excluded* in the other. You

FIGURE E.1
Event diagram.

will then have a range of failure intensities or reliabilities with the extreme values representing a reliable compiler and an unreliable one.

4.4 You can continue testing or restart. It doesn't matter. If degraded data cause another failure, then the second event is really part of the first failure and shouldn't be counted again. However, if the system is required to recover from the first failure by cleaning up the data, the second failure is counted because it represents a failure of the *recovery mechanism*.

4.5 No, as far as we can determine. On the projects that have been observed to date, no correlation has been seen between complexity or subtlety of fault and phase of the test period.

4.6 Usually not. But suppose you are estimating failure intensity based on all failures, and deriving failure intensities for different failure severity classes from it by use of average proportions of severities. Then you may be temporarily overestimating the severe failure intensity just after the severe failures have been removed. However, the estimate will be correct in the long run. We should remark that your experience is *not* typical. Most projects do not have any correlation between severity and point in the test phase.

4.7 Yes, to some extent, *for that particular interval*. Reloads generally occur either just after a failure (to clean up the system) or randomly with respect to failures (routine periodic reloads). For any sample of failures of reasonable size, the effects tend to average out, so the estimation of failure intensities is reasonable. In any case, we never try to predict *individual* failure intervals. Note that if the frequency of reload is changed substantially on a long-term basis, this could conceivably result in a different failure intensity.

4.8 Yes, but this usually occurs less than 5 percent of the time. If in doubt, be consistent. Classify the failure as nonsoftware if it doesn't reappear on a rerun with all software and with known nonsoftware inputs exactly the same.

4.9 A system or component is *fault tolerant* if it operates satisfactorily in the presence of faults [defects that would cause failures (that is, unsatisfactory operation) if not counteracted]. "Hardware" and "software" fault tolerance refer to the source of the faults. Software components may be hardware-fault-tolerant or software-fault-tolerant or both. Hardware components are often hardware-fault-tolerant but usually not software-fault-tolerant. Software is said to be *robust* if it responds to nonfunctional inputs in a way that minimizes performance degradation.

4.10 Not directly, since test driver failures are not considered to be failures of the system being tested. Occasionally, test driver failures are so substantial that they result in a distortion of the operational profile being executed. Then the reliability measured for the system being tested may be in error.

4.11 No. We have repeated failures, just as if the software were executed on the same machine for the same input states. Whether the repetitions should be counted depends on circumstances and the objectives you have in collecting your data. This has been covered elsewhere.

4.12 Since the software components are not being repaired, the relationship between reliability R_k and failure intensity λ_k for component k is found from Equation (2.13) to be

$$R_k = \exp(-\lambda_k t) .$$

Note that time has been expressed generically. Using Equation (4.1) we have the overall system reliability

$$R = \prod_{k=1}^{Q_P} \exp(-\lambda_k t) = \exp\left(-t \sum_{k=1}^{Q_P} \lambda_k\right),$$

where Q_P is the number of components. But this is of the form

$$R = \exp(-\lambda t),$$

where λ is the system failure intensity. Hence

$$\lambda = \sum_{k=1}^{Q_P} \lambda_k.$$

4.13 Yes, as long as it is a requirement for that software component. Note that in this case the fault may be complex and distributed throughout the software component, since it relates to insufficient speed of execution.

4.14 If the only system requirement is to process work, the answer is "no." Failures relate only to external behavior of the system, not internal malfunctions.

4.15 No. You can interpret "requirements" as "user needs." Then if program operation departs from user needs, a failure is recorded. This interpretation may be the most useful and practical one from the customer's viewpoint. However, it does pose some legal and contractual problems. Most contractors will probably insist that the customer assume the responsibility for requirements faults and will not agree to counting their operational effects as failures.

4.16 In general, don't count them in test but do in the operational phase.

4.17 These failures should not be counted nor should execution time spent in unit test. Unit test involves testing only a small part of the software. Here you would have a retrogression, since a substantial part of the system would already have been in test. Suppose that the ratio of faults corrected in unit test to failures experienced in system test is relatively constant. Then you could adjust for the extra faults being corrected from unit test by increasing the fault reduction factor B.

CHAPTER 5

5.1 (b), (c), and (e). Note that testing in which the planning of tests depends on the results of previous tests can be inefficient. This approach typically lengthens the critical path of the schedule. It can also result in underutilization of the test team and even the debuggers. In addition, the resultant tests that are run may differ substantially in operational profile from those that would be encountered in operation, since test results are controlling.

5.2 Infinity and 0, respectively.

5.3 Yes. You will probably get the same results as for software in the operational phase.

5.4 Yes. You can predict the failure intensity to be expected by backing up in the test phase by the number of failures outstanding. Estimation of parameters and calculation of various quantities of interest are performed at this point.

5.5 Yes. You could rederive the maximum likelihood estimation formulas to account for missing or unknown data and change the supporting computation programs accordingly, but that would not be worthwhile. Picking failure times randomly within the period to which they are limited (for example, day or week) will give better results than assuming that the data are completely missing.

5.6 Yes, nothing prevents it. In practice, however, if the subsystems are *too* small, estimates made may have wide confidence intervals for a large part of the test period. Hence they may be of limited value. If calendar time predictions are to be accurate, you may wish to use resource parameter values that are either measured or adjusted to apply to the particular individuals involved.

5.7 No.

5.8 It could. It is best to subtract the delay from all the failure times before processing them.

5.9 No. There may be faults found and fixed indirectly as the result of correcting failures found during test. We may subtract the average number of such faults from the number of new faults spawned. The net remainder is used in computing the fault reduction factor *B*.

5.10 This computer time should not affect execution time intervals between failures, since these relate to the execution of the program that is to be delivered *only*. However, the analysis program could expend a limiting resource. If so, it must be accounted for by the calendar time component of the model.

5.11 Nothing, except your conception of what should happen. The prediction of total failures is dependent on the trend in failure intervals, not the total number. If the failures removed were near the start of test, you could have a failure interval trend that increases more slowly, yielding an increase in the total failures predicted.

5.12 The estimated total failures will be infinite. Note that the fault reduction factor *B* will be 0, so that the actual number of faults can be finite.

5.13 If the user determines that some failures are not to be corrected (either by direct order or by what is paid for), the specification has been effectively changed. The system behavior in question is no longer unacceptable. Thus the failure has been redefined out of existence. Once this category of failures has been removed from consideration the number of faults that can be corrected does relate to the number of failures identified.

5.14 Only the computer time and failure identification personnel resources can be simultaneously limiting. The following relationships between parameters must occur for this to happen:

$$\frac{\mu_C}{\mu_I} = \frac{\theta_C}{\theta_I} = \frac{P_C \rho_C}{P_I}.$$

5.15 As long as there is some repair effort (that is, the fault reduction factor *B* is not 0), all faults will ultimately be eliminated from the program. The interval between failures will approach infinity. Thus it is possible to have a finite number of failures in infinite time.

5.16 We experience and can readily count *total* failures. The best measure of the degree to which the software is repaired, with the resultant change in failure intensity, is *net* (not total) faults corrected.

5.17 It is assumed that each person involved in failure identification can run and examine the results from any test that is made. Failure correction personnel are assumed to work only on failures that have been attributed to their respective design areas. If a person has enough background to work at either failure identification or failure correction, depending on where staff is required, that person should be included in *both* counts. This might sound like duplication, but remember that, except in rare circumstances (see solution to Problem 5.14), only one resource at a time can be limiting.

5.18 No, because they do not directly constitute a limiting resource. Of course, the amount of support available may affect the environment in which the project operates, so that the resource usage parameters may be a function of the support level. That is, a higher level of support may reduce the amount of work done by the failure identification and failure correction personnel for each failure or per unit execution time.

5.19 No. They must all be available if needed (or suitable replacements must be provided, where "suitable" implies that the overall average skill level of the group remains the same). However, they will usually be far from fully employed in the latter part of the system test phase. Hence for practical purposes we can transfer some to other projects, with infrequent demands made for correction of failures in their programs.

5.20 Establish the maximum number of hours the computer can be used by your project each week. Subtract items such as maintenance time and down time. The result is hours of availability, which should be expressed in terms of prescribed work periods.

5.21 No. The ρ_C and ρ_F factors that are supplied as inputs relate to utilization during the computer-limited and failure-correction-personnel-limited periods, respectively, and are *maximum* figures. Each will have lower values during the other two periods.

5.22 An overhead factor should be applied to the parameters μ_F, μ_I, and θ_I. The overhead factor provides an allowance for training, vacations, absences, and administrative activities. A typical value is 1.67 (equivalent to the assumption that 60 percent of a person year is effective work time). This results in lengthening of all calendar time estimates to account for overhead activities on an *average* basis. You cannot, of course, predict the time of correction of a particular failure with any decent accuracy. The time required is a random variable. Also, the particular person who must do the correction *can* be sick or on vacation.

5.23 Change them. You may notice a "jump change" in many of the quantities you are monitoring as a result, but your predictions should henceforth be more accurate.

5.24 Usually not. The field test period is often a computer-time-limited one. Then only computer resource parameters need be known.

5.25 Yes. This can be handled in two ways:

1. You can reduce the number of available failure identification personnel by an amount proportional to the size of these activities relative to total test activities.
2. If the activities require work proportional to the amount of testing (execution time) or the number of failures or both, the resource expenditure parameters μ_I (failure identification work per failure) and θ_I (failure identification work per unit execution time) can be adjusted to reflect them.

5.26 Yes, a somewhat longer queue would probably be permissible. A modular-by-function program would be tested in a modular fashion, and a failure in one function would have little impact on another. Thus there would be less effect on the work of another program or on other work of the same programmer as a failure queue lengthens.

5.27 Note that you are really estimating *observable* failure intensity and the observability has suddenly changed. You might view this in the same light as a program being tested in a new environment. This violates the general assumptions of software reliability models, to some extent, but the effects are usually not serious. A new crop of failures will occur. Behavior will be analogous to behavior occurring when a substantial number of design changes are made at one time.

5.28 Let r_1 and r_2 be the instruction execution rates of the "failure identification" and "failure correction" computers, respectively. View all quantities as being referred to the failure identification computer. Then the failure correction computer can simply be considered as an additional computer resource with prescribed work periods P_{C_2} which adds an effective

$$P_{C_2} \frac{r_2}{r_1}$$

prescribed work periods to the original resource P_{C_1}.

5.29 Remember you are estimating what the initial failure intensity *must have been*, not what the present failure intensity is now. You *will* usually see an increase in present failure intensity. However, the occurrence of a number of short time intervals between failures indicates the proportion of faults that has been removed is not as high as we thought. In other words, the present failure intensity does not represent as much progress from the initial failure intensity as we had believed. This means we must have been overestimating the initial failure intensity.

   Note that the situation described will happen when a number of design changes are made, introducing new faults. The present failure intensity will rise, but the estimate of initial failure intensity will drop.

5.30 After a fashion. Later predictions are approximations to reality. Hence we can use them as a standard against which quality is measured, but only to a degree. We can check the execution time component parameters in this way, since they should be constant if there are no perturbing circumstances. A convenient way to do this is to use plots of the quantities against execution time. Project horizontal lines from the confidence limit boundaries at the point whose predictions are to be checked. If these are, for example, 75 percent confidence limits, then 75 percent of the points spanned by the succeeding confidence intervals should lie within the horizontal lines. This may be checked by comparing the ratio of the area inside the confidence intervals *and* the horizontal lines to the area inside the confidence intervals.

5.31 Providing that the quality of the estimation is good, they (particularly the total execution time plot) can be considered as an indication of the stability of the software. The plots should be horizontal in a stable situation. A rising plot usually indicates that design changes are introducing additional faults into the system and thus prolonging the completion time.

5.32 This time is *not* execution time. It represents failure identification time for the person (or persons) examining the data. If the same computer is used as that used for failure identification and correction, it also represents computer time expended.

5.33 Yes. Add 4 days to the predictions.

5.34 Yes. Test cases required would be determined by execution time expended in test. Treat the test case generation capability as an additional limiting resource.

5.35 We may include regression tests with the rest of the tests we are running. We can merge all the failure data, as long as the frequencies of the test cases match the operational profile.

5.36 Yes. The machine speed affects the linear execution frequency f.

5.37 Perhaps in absolute but not in relative terms. The effect mentioned is counteracted by the fact that the accuracy with which failure intensity can be estimated is increasing with execution time. This results from a larger sample of failure data being available. Software reliability models have at least two parameters, with associated accuracies. Both affect the geometry of the interaction of the failure intensity curve with the failure intensity objective. Therefore, a simple geometric analysis of this situation is not feasible. Instead, let's look at an example from an actual project [see Musa, Iannino, and Okumoto (1987), Table 13.1, project T1]. Using the basic model, estimates of hours of execution time required to reach various failure intensity objectives were made, along with the 75 percent confidence intervals. Results are indicated in Table E.1. Note that the absolute size of the confidence interval increases as the failure intensity objective decreases, but the relative size *decreases*.

5.38 Since there will be 200,000 object instructions, the linear execution frequency f of the program will be $333,333/200,000 = 1.67$ sec^{-1} or 6,000 hr^{-1}. Note that inherent faults $\omega_0 = 300$. Hence initial failure intensity λ_0 is given by $\lambda_0 = fK\omega_0 = 6000(1.67 \times 10^{-7})(300) = 0.3$ failure/CPU hr, where K is the fault exposure ratio.

5.39 The computer utilization factor is set to reflect the *available*, not actual, level of utilization. If the users of the computer in question have their usage carefully scheduled, a reasonable value might be 1. If demands for service are essentially unscheduled and hence random, utilization must generally be held in the range of about 0.5 to 0.8 for reasonable turnaround.

If turnaround requirements are stringent, the utilization should be set near 0.5; average, 0.65; not stringent, 0.8. However, you may wish to set the value at the value that minimizes overall development costs.

5.40 Failure correction work required per failure. Almost all projects are in the failure-correction-personnel-limited period at the start of system testing. Most remain in this period for most of system test. Some (particularly those released with a moderate failure intensity remaining) stay in the period for *all* of system test. It is desirable to collect data on all limiting resources, since all limiting periods can occur. However, you can take a calculated risk that a particular resource other than failure correction personnel will never be limiting. You then do not collect resource expenditure data for it, if the collection is particularly difficult or burdensome.

TABLE E.1
Execution times of reaching various failure intensity objectives, basic model, project T1

Objective (failures/CPU hr)	Execution time to objective (CPU hr)	
	Estimate	75% confidence interval
0.05	23.0	18.0–29.5
0.01	36.1	29.5–44.6
0.005	41.7	34.4–51.1
0.001	54.8	45.9–66.3
0.0001	73.5	62.4–88.0
0.00001	92.2	78.8–109.7

5.41 Yes, and the obvious generalizations of the calendar time component of the execution time theory should be made, unless one of the four resources can be considered to be nonlimiting. This is often the case with computer time for failure correction.

5.42 Generally not. Its effect is to place a time delay into the test and debug process that may be added to predicted completion dates.

5.43 Determine how many groups of such people exist (where any member can correct the failure) and the average group size. To determine the utilization factor, use the number of people and increase the acceptable queue length by a factor equal to the average group size.

5.44 You don't have to and should not. By finding more faults through code reading, you will reduce the failure intensity more rapidly than would normally be the case. The failures will be farther apart and the estimation process will automatically take care of this.

5.45 The parameter can be greater than 1 because computer time is used for more than testing. For example, recorded data must be processed and printed, and this requires computer time proportional to the length of the period of execution.

5.46 Note that each of these machines represents a separate resource. Thus we should apply an obvious generalization of the calendar time component of the execution time model. There will be three computer resources rather than one. Computer resource expenditures will be accounted for in three separate categories.

There can be as many as five resource-limited periods (three computer and two personnel) in this situation. Transition points between these periods and the calendar time to execution time ratio in each period may be computed in the same way as for the case of three resources.

5.47 No. Only the time used for general system testing by the failure identification (test) team that is devoted to initial failure identification. Additional selective testing undertaken to verify the existence of the failure or collect data on it is not counted. We do not count time required to diagnose the fault causing the failure. Neither do we count time needed to show that the failure has been corrected. Although we don't count these times as cumulative execution time, we do count them in determining computer resources used.

CHAPTER 6

6.1 It could do either. It would tend to increase if the simulator didn't adequately represent the environment. It would tend to decrease if you have underestimated the testing compression factor. Note that the software simulator itself may have failures due to faults, but you shouldn't be including these with the system you are testing. If the simulator itself represents deliverable software (for example, for system exerciser purposes), an estimate of its independent failure intensity may be desirable.

6.2 Yes. When applying software reliability measurement to monitoring system test, you will probably have a shorter test period because there will be fewer faults to remove. However, it seems likely that there will always be a substantial system test period before the release of any software product. It will always be necessary to run the code through a number of functional tests.

6.3 Yes, use a double randomization procedure. First choose the length of the period by picking a random number (uniformly distributed) from the range of possible period lengths. Then pick another random number that represents the location of the failure within the period. The following example may be illustrative.

Tester A runs tests for 3 hr following the previous failure with no new failures. Tester B, who keeps poor records, follows with more tests and experiences a failure, but does not record the time of the failure occurrence or the length of test. It is known, however, that the test period ran somewhere between 1 and 9 hr.

First, select a random number in the range 1 to 9 to establish the length of the period; assume that 3.7179 is selected. We now have the failure occurring sometime between 3 and 6.7179 hr since the last failure. Select another random number to fix the failure location. Assume that it is 6.3036. We have a failure interval of 6.3036 hr and 0.4143 hr of failure-free testing that follows it. This information may ordinarily be used directly in a software reliability estimation program.

The foregoing procedure will yield more accurate results than ignoring the failures and test periods that are not accurately recorded. An estimate of the inaccuracy in any derived quantity can be obtained by computing the quantity using the extreme values of the possible ranges of the unknown failure intervals.

Note that the first step of the procedure will prove useful in establishing the length of a failure-free test period that is uncertain.

6.4 Only if we can characterize the changes as the addition of a new subsystem(s), so that it can be combined with the previous subsystem using combinatorial rules for reliability. If not, then it is best to work with both pre- and post-change data together. The larger sample size generally means that perturbations in estimated quantities resulting from changes are reduced, and recovery from the perturbation is faster.

6.5 No. Ignore the second and following occurrences of the same failure, just as you would for faults not yet fixed in single site testing.

6.6 As noted in the solution to Problem 6.5, eliminate from consideration failures that reoccur at the field site but have already been detected at the development site. The data can then be merged as you do for multiple sites with the same release. If design changes have been introduced in the later release, then the situation is similar to that of design changes being introduced at a single site. However, the effects are somewhat moderated for the period during which failure data are being merged from the different releases. For example, a sharp increase in estimated total failures due to new faults introduced with the design changes will be "softened" and occur more gradually due to the overlap. Since this problem assumes few new features, their effect will be neglected.

6.7 By "actual environment more severe than test environment" we really mean that a substantial part of the input space of the operational phase was not or could not be covered in test. It's best that the test environment realistically represent the operating environment of the program. You can't expect to obtain good reliability predictions without a well-planned testing effort. (You couldn't do this with hardware either.) However, suppose you can estimate the probability of selection of that part of the input space that was not covered and the failure intensity for that part. Then you can estimate overall failure intensity using Equation (6.17).

6.8 First determine whether the versions are substantially different. Two versions are different if the code of one contains appreciable additions and modifications with respect to the other. If they are not substantially different, we can merge the failure data from the two directly. If they *are* different, the techniques of failure time adjustment or breakdown into subsystems should be considered for combining the data.

Sometimes it may be possible to directly merge failure data from different subsystems, with acceptable error occurring in the estimations based on the data.

If one version has repaired faults that have not been repaired in other versions, the reoccurrence of failures due to these faults should not be counted.

6.9 The approach is best illustrated by an example. Assume two testers with the following test and failure patterns indicated for a particular day:

Tester 1	Tester 2
8:00 A.M. Start test	
8:36 A.M. Failure A	
	9:00 A.M. Start test
	9:15 A.M. Failure B
9:40 A.M. Failure C	
10:00 A.M. End test	
	10:24 A.M. Failure D
	11:00 A.M. End test

Total execution time accumulated is measured as follows:

Time	Execution time (min)
8:00 A.M.	0
9:00 A.M.	15
10:00 A.M.	45
11:00 A.M.	60

The utilization for each hour is readily found from the above table to be:

Time	Utilization
8–9 A.M.	0.25
9–10 A.M.	0.5
10–11 A.M.	0.25

Since both testers are running on the same system we compute:

$$\text{execution time to failure A} = 36(0.25) = 9 \text{ min}$$
$$\text{execution time between failures A and B} = 24(0.25) + 12(0.5) = 12 \text{ min}$$
$$\text{execution time between failures B and C} = 28(0.5) = 14 \text{ min}$$
$$\text{execution time between failures C and D} = 20(0.5) + 24(0.25) = 16 \text{ min}$$
$$\text{execution time from failure D to end of test} = 36(0.25) = 9 \text{ min}$$

Thus the execution time intervals between failures are given by:

Failure	Execution time interval from previous failure (min)
A	9
B	12
C	14
D	16
end of test	9

If the two testers were testing different subsystems and we wanted to keep the failure data separate (to get subsystem reliability estimates) we could proceed as follows. Note that execution time measured between 9 and 10 A.M. is for both subsystems. Thus it must be allocated. The utilizations for each subsystem for each hour are

	Utilization	
Time	Subsystem X	Subsystem Y
8–9 A.M.	0.25	
9–10 A.M.	0.25	0.25
10–11 A.M.		0.25

We would compute for subsystem X:

$$\text{execution time to failure A} = 36(0.25) = 9 \text{ min}$$
$$\text{execution time between failures A and C} = 64(0.25) = 16 \text{ min}$$
$$\text{execution time from failure C to end of test} = 20(0.25) = 5 \text{ min}$$

For subsystem Y we would calculate:

$$\text{execution time to failure B} = 12(0.25) = 3 \text{ min}$$
$$\text{execution time between failures B and D} = 72(0.25) = 18 \text{ min}$$
$$\text{execution time from failure D to end of test} = 36(0.25) = 9 \text{ min}$$

The execution time intervals for the two subsystems are:

Subsystem X		Subsystem Y	
Failure	Execution time interval from previous failure (min)	Failure	Execution time interval from previous failure (min)
A	9	B	3
C	16	D	18
end of test	5	end of test	9

6.10 Yes. Weight clock time by an estimate of utilization. A good approximation of the utilization in any time period is given by the ratio of current users to maximum feasible users, multiplied by the utilization that corresponds to this maximum.

6.11 You shouldn't assign a trend because you do not know what the trend is (form) or what its parameters are.

CHAPTER 7

7.1 Each system experiences, on the average, 0.1 failure/week. Total failures will average 60/week or 12/day, requiring 6 service persons. Each doctor will require an average of 5.2 calls/yr at $200 each. Applying the profit margin to the annual cost of $1040 yields a contract fee of $1248.

7.2 The basic execution time model will be applied here, since we want to relate failure intensity to number of faults.

Consider first the situation without design reviews. We compute a value of $\nu_0 = \omega_0 = 400$ failures, using the program size and average fault density. Since initial failure intensity $\lambda_0 = 10$ failures/CPU hr, we have

$$\Delta\mu = \frac{\nu_0}{\lambda_0} (\lambda_P - \lambda_F) = \frac{400}{10} (10 - 0.1) = 396 \text{ failures}$$

and

$$\Delta\tau = \frac{\nu_0}{\lambda_0} \ln \frac{\lambda_P}{\lambda_F} = \frac{400}{10} \ln \frac{10}{0.1} = 40 \ln 100 = 184 \text{ CPU hr}.$$

The resource expenditures will be identical to the requirements, since no resources are allowed to be idle. Now

$$\chi_C = \mu_C \Delta\mu + \theta_C \Delta\tau$$
$$= 0.5(396) + 2(184)$$
$$= 566 \text{ CPU hr},$$

$$\chi_F = \mu_F \Delta\mu$$
$$= 6(396)$$
$$= 2376 \text{ person hr},$$

and

$$\chi_I = \mu_I \Delta\mu + \theta_I \Delta\tau$$
$$= 3(396) + 5(184)$$
$$= 2108 \text{ person hr}.$$

The cost of system test will be

$$\$1000 \, \chi_C + \$50 \, (\chi_F + \chi_I) = \$1000 \, (566) + \$50 \, (4484)$$
$$= \$790,200 \, .$$

Now, consider the case *with* design reviews. Since the programs are of the same size and executed on machines of the same speed, they will have the same linear execution frequency f. Since they are similar in type also, K may be assumed to be the same. Thus, $fK = \lambda_0/\omega_0 = \lambda_0/\nu_0 = 0.025$ is the same also. We have $\nu_0 = \omega_0 = 300$ failures and

$$\lambda_0 = fK\omega_0 = 0.025(300) = 7.5 \text{ failures/CPU hr}.$$

Hence

$$\Delta\mu = \frac{\nu_0}{\lambda_0} (\lambda_P - \lambda_F) = \frac{300}{7.5} (7.5 - 0.1) = 296 \text{ failures}$$

and

$$\Delta\tau = \frac{\nu_0}{\lambda_0} \ln \frac{\lambda_P}{\lambda_F} = \frac{300}{7.5} \ln \frac{7.5}{0.1} = 173 \text{ CPU hr}.$$

We have

$$\chi_C = \mu_C \Delta\mu + \theta_C \Delta\tau$$

$$= 0.5(296) + 2(173)$$

$$= 494 \text{ CPU hr},$$

$$\chi_F = \mu_F \Delta\mu$$

$$= 6(296)$$

$$= 1776 \text{ person hr},$$

and

$$\chi_I = \mu_I \Delta\mu + \theta_I \Delta\tau$$

$$= 3(296) + 5(173)$$

$$= 1753 \text{ person hr}.$$

The cost of system test *with* reviews is

$$\$1000 \chi_C + \$50(\chi_F + \chi_I) = \$1000(494) + \$50(3329)$$

$$= \$670,450 .$$

Thus the saving in system test costs from design reviews is $119,750. The design reviews require a total of 380 person hours of time, which costs $19,000. Thus the design reviews are cost effective, producing a net saving of $100,750.

7.3 (*a*) For the logarithmic Poisson execution time model

$$\Delta\mu = \frac{1}{\theta} \ln \frac{\lambda_P}{\lambda_F}$$

$$= \frac{1}{0.05} \ln \frac{10}{0.1} = 20 \ln 100 = 20(4.61) = 92 \text{ failures}$$

and

$$\Delta\tau = \frac{1}{\theta} \left[\frac{1}{\lambda_F} - \frac{1}{\lambda_P} \right]$$

$$= \frac{1}{0.05} \left[\frac{1}{0.1} - \frac{1}{10} \right] = 20(9.9) = 198 \text{ CPU hr}.$$

Hence

$$\chi_I = 2(92) + 3(198)$$
$$= 778 \text{ person hr},$$

$$\chi_F = 6(92)$$
$$= 552 \text{ person hr},$$

and

$$\chi_C = 1(92) + 1.5(198)$$
$$= 389 \text{ CPU hr}.$$

(b) No, somewhat less. Note that $\Delta\tau$ is approximately doubled but increases logarithmically. Thus the resource increase will be between a logarithmic increase and a linear increase for changes in failure intensity objective.

7.4 We compute a value of $\nu_0 = \omega_0 = 500$ failures, using the program size and average fault density. The linear execution frequency, determined by dividing object instruction execution rate by number of object instructions, is 2.5 CPU sec^{-1} or 9000 CPU hr^{-1}. Hence, $\lambda_0 = fK\omega_0 = 9000(2.222 \times 10^{-7})(500) = 1$ failure/CPU hr. Now

$$\Delta\mu = \frac{\nu_0}{\lambda_0} (\lambda_P - \lambda_F) = \frac{500}{1} (1 - \lambda_F) = 500(1 = \lambda_F)$$

and

$$\Delta\tau = \frac{\nu_0}{\lambda_0} \ln \frac{\lambda_P}{\lambda_F} = \frac{500}{1} \ln \frac{1}{\lambda_F} = -500 \ln \lambda_F .$$

The resource expenditures will be identical to the requirements, since no resources are allowed to be idle:

$$\chi_C = \mu_C \Delta\mu + \theta_C \Delta\tau$$

$$= 0.5 \left[500 - 500\lambda_F \right] + 1 \left[-500 \ln \lambda_F \right]$$

$$= 250 - 250\lambda_F - 500 \ln \lambda_F,$$

$$\chi_F = \mu_F \Delta\mu = 5 \left[500 - 500\lambda_F \right]$$

$$= 2500 - 2500\lambda_F,$$

and

$$\chi_I = \mu_I \Delta\mu + \theta_I \Delta\tau$$

$$= 2 \left(500 - 500\lambda_F \right) + 4 \left(- 500 \ln \lambda_F \right)$$

$$= 1000 - 1000\lambda_F - 2000 \ln \lambda_F.$$

The cost of system test will be

$$\$1000 \; \chi_C + \$50(\chi_F + \chi_I) = \$250,000 - \$250,000\lambda_F - \$500,000 \ln \lambda_F$$

$$+ \$50 \left(3500 - 3500\lambda_F - 2000 \ln \lambda_F \right)$$

$$= \$425,000 - \$425,000\lambda_F - \$600,000 \ln \lambda_F \;.$$

The number of failures during operation will be the total operating lifetime multiplied by failure intensity, or $4000 \; \lambda_F$. Hence the cost of failures will be $\$40,000,000\lambda_F$. The expression for the sum of these costs,

$$\$425,000 + \$39,575,000\lambda_F - \$600,000 \ln \lambda_F,$$

is of the form

$$a + b\lambda_F - c \ln \lambda_F.$$

A simple minimization using calculus yields

$$\lambda_F = \frac{c}{b} \;.$$

Thus we obtain a value of 0.01516 failure/CPU hr for the failure intensity objective that minimizes system life cycle costs. The cost of system test and operational failures for this value is $3,538,000.

To determine the duration of system test, note that since there is only one limiting resource period, we have $\Delta\chi_{FF} = \Delta\chi_F$ and

$$t = \frac{\Delta\chi_F}{P_F \rho_F} \;.$$

Since no debugger can have more than 2 failures, with 90 percent probability, no debugger can have 3 *or* more with that probability. Thus the utilization factor is

$$\rho_F = \left[1 - P_{m_Q}{}^{1/P_F} \right]^{1/m_Q} = (1 - 0.9^{1/25})^{1/3} \approx 0.16 \;.$$

Hence

$$t = \frac{\Delta\chi_F}{P_F \rho_F} = \frac{2500 - 2500\lambda_F}{25(0.16)} = 625 - 625\lambda_F \;.$$

At the minimum cost point, the system test period will require 616 hr or 77 days, each 8 hr long.

The reliability of the software for one day (8 CPU hr) of operations, assuming the failure intensity objective of 0.01516 failure/CPU hr is attained, is given by

$$R = \exp\left[-\lambda\tau\right] = \exp\left[-8(0.01516)\right] = 0.886,$$

where τ is the period of operation and λ is the failure intensity. This figure can be combined with reliabilities of hardware components to give overall system reliability.

7.5 Note that each installation will have an operational life of 10,000 CPU hr. The total number of failures over all installations will be $50,000\lambda$, where λ is the failure intensity. The cost impact of operational failures is $\$5,000,000\lambda$.

Using the table that was furnished, the following table can be constructed:

Failure intensity objective (per 100 CPU hr)	Operational cost(K$)	System test cost(K$)	Total cost(K$)
1	50	1585	1635
2	100	1490	1590
3	150	1440	1590
4	200	1400	1600
5	250	1360	1610

Minimum cost occurs at about 2.5 failures/100 CPU hr.

At the high and low ends of system test cost we have:

Failure intensity objective (per 100 CPU hr)	Operational cost(K$)	High end		Low end	
		System test cost(K$)	Total cost(K$)	System test cost(K$)	Total cost(K$)
1	50	1840	1890	1230	1280
2	100	1710	1810	1160	1260
3	150	1650	1800	1100	1250
4	200	1600	1800	1070	1270
5	250	1560	1810	1040	1290

Note that the minimum cost occurs at 3.5 and 3 failures/100 CPU hr, respectively. Thus the range of values of failure intensity objective is 2.5 to 3.5 failures/100 CPU hr.

7.6 The normalized failure time is 5. With no failures experienced, Figure 7.9 shows that the objective has been met with high confidence.

7.7 The base program had 500 faults at the start of system test. Since $B = 1$, $\nu_0 = 500$ failures.

The number of failures experienced during test was

$$\Delta\mu = \frac{\nu_0}{\lambda_0}(\lambda_P - \lambda_F) = \nu_0\left[1 - \frac{\lambda_F}{\lambda_0}\right]$$

$$= 500 \left[1 - \frac{0.06}{2} \right]$$

$$= 500(0.97)$$

$$= 485 \text{ failures}.$$

Since $B = 1$, 485 faults have been corrected and 15 remain. The modification will add 10 faults, making a total of 25 remaining.

The failure intensity in the operational phase is proportional to the faults remaining, hence

$$\lambda = \frac{25}{15} (0.06) = 0.10 \text{ failure/CPU hr} .$$

Thus the impact of modifying the code is to increase the failure intensity from 6 to 10 failures per hundred hours.

7.8 Yes. It can provide information on the present reliability of each subsystem. To decide on priorities for testing, you will also need information on the relative criticalities of the functions implemented by the subsystems and knowledge of how system failure is related to failures of the individual subsystems.

7.9 The entire fraction, during the failure-identification-personnel-limited segment, since failure identification personnel (unlike failure correction personnel) utilization is 1. The overtime cannot be profitably used when other resources are limiting. During the failure-identification-personnel-limited segment, a fraction of overtime to regular time of α will reduce elapsed calendar time by the factor $1 + \alpha$. The cost will be increased by a factor that is the product of α and the fractional increase for premium pay (typically 0.5).

7.10 The inefficient program will give a failure intensity that is realistic for that program. The system engineer must interpret failure intensity in the light of all other system characteristics, particularly performance, in establishing the quality of a particular implementation. For example, consider an airline reservation system that handles 10,000 reservations/CPU hr and has a failure intensity of 1 failure/CPU hr. It may be superior in quality to a system that handles 1,000 reservations/CPU hr and has a failure intensity of 0.5 failure/CPU hr. In a case such as this it may be useful for comparison purposes to transform time units to functional units. In other words, the systems have 0.1 and 0.5 failure/1000 reservations, respectively.

7.11 Not necessarily. You must take account of different cost impacts, perhaps due to different repair costs for the components.

7.12 The effects of "better testing" on the variation of failure intensity with time are illustrated in Figures E.2 and E.3.

Good test planning will increase the rate at which failure intensity decreases with execution time. Such planning will ensure that the most frequently occurring input states during operation are tested first. If faults are associated with these input states, the related failures will occur early. Thus failure intensity reduction will be rapid. Good test planning will also minimize inefficient duplicate activation of input states.

Proper execution of tests, with appropriate recording of relevant information, will maximize the value of the fault reduction factor B that can be attained. This will ensure that the rate of decrease of failure intensity with execution time is the maximum possible.

FIGURE E.2
Effect of better test planning.

7.13 This is really an "evaluation of software engineering technology" problem *except* that the technology in general cannot be evaluated. You can only evaluate the effect of the particular audits for the particular program in question. This must be done by a comparative test of the program with and without audits. The test must be sufficiently extensive that the part of the operational profile covered totals up to a high probability.

7.14 Plot the logarithm of the failure intensity function, given by

FIGURE E.3
Effect of better test execution.

$$\ln \lambda = \ln \lambda_0 - \frac{\lambda_0}{\nu_0} \tau \,.$$

You will note that it is a straight line (Figure E.4). Hence it is easy to project the model and read off execution times corresponding to various failure intensity objectives.

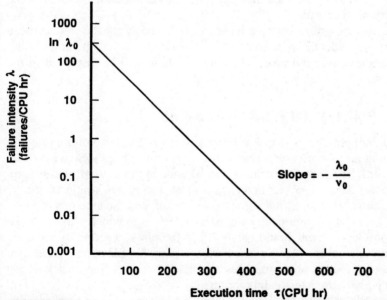

FIGURE E.4
Failure intensity for basic model, plotted on logarithmic scale.

RECOMMENDED SPECIFICATIONS FOR SUPPORTING COMPUTER PROGRAMS

Designing a software reliability estimation support program can be a time-consuming task. This appendix has been written in order to provide you with some guidance. The basic structures described here can handle most situations, though some customizing may be necessary.

Four computer programs that are most useful in the application of software reliability theory were identified in Section 5.3.1. These were the tabular, plotting, simulation, and log conversion programs. Each of these will be discussed in the following sections.

F.1 TABULAR AND PLOTTING PROGRAMS

The tabular program provides a snapshot of system status and the plotting program provides a running history of system status. It is generally a good idea to have two separate input files. The first file contains model and, in the case of plotting programs, plot control parameters. Examples of model parameters would be the resource usage parameters, the testing compression factor, and the amounts of available resources. Plot control parameters are used to determine which plots are to be drawn, what confidence level should be shown in the plots, whether or not there should be a grid, and so on. Many of the parameters in this file should have standard default values. Others are sometimes not needed. For example, if you just want a table, the plot parameters can be omitted.

The second file contains the actual failure data. Various formats are possible depending on whether the failure data are time data or grouped data. As an example, consider the case of failure interval data. One workable format consists of the following sequence per record:

1. execution time interval between the present and previous failure experienced in testing,
2. the number of days from the start of testing on which the present failure occurred (optional),
3. the number of instructions integrated (optional), and
4. the number of instructions of developed code integrated (optional).

We have generally found the following outputs useful:

1. a listing of parameters with their associated values,
2. an echo of the input failure data,
3. a listing of the adjusted data, days from start of test, and associated numbers of the failures in columnar format, in the situation where failure times are adjusted to account for a program that is changing in size,
4. program error and warning messages (if present),
5. a listing of plot messages and diagnostics (if present),
6. results in tabular format, and
7. results in graphical format.

The format of the third output should be compatible with the input failure data file. This allows the user to use the result as input to other software reliability programs. This is particularly useful when using software reliability programs that do not perform failure time adjustment.

A typical program structure is shown in Figure F.1. The first thing done is to read the data from the two input files. The data are checked and error flags are set so that appropriate messages can be printed in the output routine. The errors detected will abort all or part of the calculation, as appropriate.

The next step is to determine if a tabular or graphical output has been requested. Suppose tabular output is the case. Then a check is made to see if failure time adjustment is required. If so, then the failure adjustment routine is called. Once the failure data is adjusted a routine is called to calculate estimates of the unknown model parameters. Once these estimates are determined we move to a routine which computes all of the derived quantities. The final step is to output all the files described earlier.

Now suppose graphical output has been requested. A loop on the failure number is started. For each iteration of this loop the following calculations are performed. A check is made to see if the failure data should be adjusted. If so, the failure adjustment routine is called. As before, the parameter estimates are determined and used to calculate the quantities requested in the plot(s). The results are saved for final plotting and the loop is continued. When all of the failure data

FIGURE F.1
Basic program structure for tabular and plotting programs.

have been exhausted, the plots and any other appropriate information are outputted.

F.2 SIMULATION PROGRAM

The simulation program computes schedule and cost as a function of one of several parameters you choose to vary. Two modes of operation are useful: test-phase and pretest. In the test-phase mode the execution time component parameters are estimated from actual data, along with confidence levels to express bounds. In the pretest mode the parameters and bounds are both input.

As with the tabular and plotting programs, the use of two separate input files is recommended. The first file contains model and plot control parameters. Many of these parameters are the same as those in the previous programs. Additional parameters include the cost of computer time and personnel, predicted values of the model parameters, along with low and high bounds for these values, and the parameter which is to be varied.

The following outputs have been found useful:

1. a listing of parameters with their associated values,
2. echo of the input failure data (if test-phase mode is used),
3. program error messages, and
4. plots of schedule or cost against a selected parameter.

A typical program structure is shown in Figure F.2. The first thing done is to read data from the two input files. The input routine functions exactly the same as the one used for the previous programs.

After input processing has been completed a test is made to see if the test-phase or pre-test mode has been selected. If the former is the case a routine is called to calculate estimates of the unknown model parameters along with upper and lower bounds (confidence limits).

A print routine is called to handle any of the first three outputs mentioned above. Then a loop is begun on the parameter being varied. For each value of the parameter an estimate of project cost or completion date is made and saved. When the loop is finished the plot is generated and the program terminates. An additional loop can be included if more than one plot at a time is desired.

F.3 LOG CONVERSION PROGRAM

The final program is the log conversion program which calculates failure intervals for use in the other three programs. Three input files are recommended. The first consists of event entries. The second consists of control parameters which dictate

FIGURE F.2
Basic program structure for simulation program.

how the events are to be processed. The third is optional and contains a previously calculated set of intervals.

Separate event entries for the start of the test, the end of the test, a run duration, a stop duration, program growth specification, and a failure should exist. A provision to allow specification of window start and end times should be made in case an event is known only within a window.

The control parameters should give the user some selection capability over the data to be used for interval calculation. For example, one might have entries for several programs in the input file. The user may exclude event entries from a subset of the programs and may exclude all data before a certain start time and after a certain end time.

The program structure is relatively simple in this case. An input routine reads the data from the various input files and checks the data for validity. If no fatal errors are detected, a routine which performs the failure interval calculation is called. The program terminates with the output of the failure intervals to a specified file.

REFERENCES

Adams, E. N. 1980. "Minimizing Cost Impact of Software Defects," IBM Research Division, Report RC 8228 (35669).

Adams, E. N. 1984. "Optimizing Preventive Service of Software Products," *IBM Journal of Research and Development*, **28**(1), pp. 2–14.

Akiyama, F. 1971. "An Example of Software System Debugging," *Information Processing 71*, North-Holland, New York, pp. 353–359.

Albin, J. L., and R. Ferreol. 1982. "Collecte et Analyse de Mesures de Logiciel," (in French), *Technique et Science Informatique*, **1**(4), pp. 297–313.

Anderson, T., and P. A. Lee. 1981. *Fault Tolerance: Principles and Practice*, Prentice-Hall, Englewood Cliffs, NJ.

Angus, J. E., J. B. Bowen, and S. J. VanDenBerg. 1983. "Reliability Model Demonstration Study," Rome Air Development Center, Technical Report RADC-TR-83-207, Rome, NY.

Bardsley, I. 1984. Unpublished communication.

Basili, V. R., and D. H. Hutchens. 1983. "An Empirical Study of a Syntactic Complexity Family," *IEEE Transactions on Software Engineering*, **SE-9**(6), pp. 664–672.

Basili, V. R., and B. T. Perricone. 1984. "Software Errors and Complexity: An Empirical Investigation," *Communications ACM*, **27**(1), pp. 42–52.

Basin, S. L. 1973. "Estimation of Software Error Rates via Capture-Recapture Sampling: A Critical Review," Science Applications Report, Palo Alto, CA.

Belady, L. A., and M. M. Lehman. 1976. "A Model of Large Program Development," *IBM Systems Journal*, **15**(3), pp. 224–252.

Bendick, M. 1976. "Error Rate as a Management Tool," Computer Sciences Corporation, Report of June 8, 1976.

Boehm, B. W. 1981. *Software Engineering Economics*, Prentice Hall, Englewood Cliffs, NJ.

Brooks, F. P., Jr., 1975. *The Mythical Man Month*, Addison-Wesley, Reading, MA.

Budd, T. A., R. J. Lipton, R. A. De Millo, and F. G. Sayward. 1979. "Mutation Analysis," Department of Computer Science, Research Report 155, Yale University.

Burington, R. S., and D. C. May. 1970. *Handbook of Probability and Statistics with Tables*, 2d ed., McGraw-Hill, New York.

Card, D. N., V. E. Church, and W. W. Agresti. 1986. "An Empirical Study of Software Design Practices," *IEEE Transactions on Software Engineering*, **SE-12**(2), pp. 264–271.

Cox, D. R., and P. A. W. Lewis. 1966. *Statistical Analysis of Series of Events*, Methuen, London.

Cox, P. R. 1981. "Specification of a Regression Test for a Mini Computer Operating System," *Performance Evaluation Review*, **10**(1), p. 29.

Currit, P. A., M. Dyer, and H. D. Mills. 1986. "Certifying the Reliability of Software," *IEEE Transactions on Software Engineering*, **SE-12**(1), pp. 3–11.

Dale, C. J. 1982. "Software Reliability Evaluation Methods," British Aerospace, Report ST26750.

Davis, H. T. 1962. *The Summation of Series*, The Principia Press of Trinity University, San Antonio.

Dhillon, B. S. 1983. *Reliability Engineering in Systems Design and Operation*, Van Nostrand Reinhold, New York.

Downs, T. 1985. "An Approach to the Modeling of Software Testing with Some Applications," *IEEE Transactions on Software Engineering*, **SE-11**(4), pp. 375–386.

Duran, J. W., and S. C. Ntafos. 1984. "An Evaluation of Random Testing," *IEEE Transactions on Software Engineering*, **SE-10**(4), pp. 438–444.

Endres, A. 1975. "An Analysis of Errors and their Causes in System Programs," *Proceedings 1975 International Conference on Reliable Software*, Los Angeles, pp. 328–329. Also *IEEE Transactions on Software Engineering*, **SE-1**(2), pp. 140–149.

Feuer, A. R., and E. B. Fowlkes. 1979. "Some Results from an Empirical Study of Computer Software," *Proceedings Fourth International Conference on Software Engineering*, Munich, Germany, pp. 351–355.

Fries, M. J. 1977. "Software Error Data Acquisition," Rome Air Development Center, Technical Report RADC-TR-77-130, Rome, NY.

Gilb, T. 1977. *Software Metrics*, Winthrop, Cambridge, p. 28.

Goel, A. L., and K. Okumoto. 1979. "Time-Dependent Error-Detection Rate Model for Software Reliability and other Performance Measures," *IEEE Transactions on Reliability*, **R-28**(3), pp. 206–211.

Grant, E. L., and R. S. Leavenworth. 1980. *Statistical Quality Control*, McGraw-Hill, New York, p. 559.

Gremillion, L. L. 1984. "Determinants of Program Repair Maintenance Requirements," *Communications ACM*, **27**(8), pp. 826–832.

Halstead, M. H. 1977. *Elements of Software Science*, Elsevier, New York.

Hamilton, P. A., and J. D. Musa. 1978. "Measuring Reliability of Computation Center Software," *Proceedings Third International Conference on Software Engineering*, Atlanta, pp. 29–36.

Hecht, H. 1981. "Allocation of Resources for Software Reliability," *Proceedings COMPCON Fall 1981*, Washington, DC, pp. 74–82.

Herndon, M. A., and N. T. Keenan. 1978. "Analysis of Error Remediation Expenditures During Validation," *Proceedings Third International Conference on Software Engineering*, Atlanta, pp. 202–206.

Howden, W. E. 1980. "Functional Program Testing," *IEEE Transactions on Software Engineering*, **SE-6**(2), pp. 162–169.

Inglis, J., F. Gray, Jr., D. M. Kane, and M. K. Kaufmann. 1986. Unpublished work.

Institute of Electrical and Electronics Engineers. 1983. *IEEE Standard Glossary of Software Engineering Terminology* (Standard 729-1983), IEEE, New York.

Jelinski, Z., and P. B. Moranda. 1972. "Software Reliability Research," (W. Freiberger, Editor), *Statistical Computer Performance Evaluation*, Academic, New York, pp. 465–484.

Jones, C. 1986. *Programming Productivity*, McGraw-Hill, New York.

Kapur, K. C., and L. R. Lamberson. 1977. *Reliability in Engineering Design*, Wiley, New York.

Knight, J. C., and N. G. Leveson. 1986. "An Experimental Evaluation of the Assumption of Independence in Multi-Version Programming," *IEEE Transactions on Software Engineering*, **SE-12**(1), pp. 96–109.

Koch, H. S., and P. Kubat. 1983. "Optimal Release Time of Computer Software," *IEEE Transactions on Software Engineering*, **SE-9**(3), pp. 323–327.

Laner, D. 1985. Commentary on War, Public Television series.

Laprie, J. C. 1984. "Dependability Evaluation of Software Systems in Operation," *IEEE Transactions on Software Engineering*, **SE-10**(6), pp. 701–714.

Lawson, D. J. 1983. "Failure Mode, Effect, and Criticality Analysis," (J. K. Skwirzynski, Editor), *Electronic Systems Effectiveness and Life Cycle Costing*, NATO ASI Series, **F3**, Springer-Verlag, Heidelberg, pp. 55–74.

Leveson, N. G. 1986. "Software Hazard Analysis Techniques," (J. K. Skwirzynski, Editor), *Software System Design Methods*, NATO ASI Series, **F22**, Springer-Verlag, Heidelberg, pp. 681–699.

Littlewood, B. 1976. "A Semi-Markov Model for Software Reliability with Failure Costs," *Proceedings Symposium on Computer Software Engineering*, Polytechnic Press, New York, pp. 281–300.

Littlewood, B. 1979. "Software Reliability Model for Modular Program Structure," *IEEE Transactions on Reliability*, **R-28**(3), pp. 241–246.

Littlewood, B., and J. L. Verrall. 1973. "A Bayesian Reliability Growth Model for Computer Software," *Journal Royal Statistical Society-Series C*, **22**(3), pp. 332–346.

Lloyd, D. K., and M. Lipow. 1977. *Reliability: Management, Methods, and Mathematics*, 2d ed., published by the authors, Redondo Beach, CA.

McCabe, T. J. 1976. "A Complexity Measure," *IEEE Transactions on Software Engineering*, **SE-2**(4), pp. 308–320.

Mendis, K. S. 1981. "Quantifying Software Quality," *Proceedings American Institute of Aeronautics and Astronautics*, pp. 300–308.

Mills, H. D. 1972. "On the Statistical Validation of Computer Programs," IBM Federal Systems Division, Report FSC-72-6015, Gaithersburg, MD.

Misra, P. N. 1983. "Software Reliability Analysis," *IBM Systems Journal*, **22**(3), pp. 262–270.

Mittermeir, R. T. 1982. "Optimal Test Effort for Software Systems," (E. Lauger and J. Moltoft, Editors), *Reliability in Electrical and Electronic Components and Systems*, North-Holland, Amsterdam, pp. 650–654.

Miyamoto, I. 1975. "Software Reliability in Online Real Time Environment," *Proceedings 1975 International Conference on Reliable Software*, Los Angeles, pp. 194–203.

Motley, R. W., and W. D. Brooks. 1977. "Statistical Prediction of Programming Errors," Rome Air Development Center, Technical Report RADC-TR-77-175, Rome, NY.

Musa, J. D. 1975. "A Theory of Software Reliability and its Application," *IEEE Transactions on Software Engineering*, **SE-1**(3), pp. 312–327.

Musa, J. D. 1979. "Software Reliability Data," report available from Data and Analysis Center for Software, Rome Air Development Center, Rome, NY.

Musa, J. D. 1985. "Software Engineering: The Future of a Profession," *IEEE Software*, **2**(1), pp. 55–62.

Musa, J. D., P. A. Hamilton, and R. B. Hollander. 1983. "Program for Software Reliability and System Test Schedule Estimation—Revised for Staged Failure Interval Adjustment—Program Documentation," available through J. D. Musa.

Musa, J. D. and R. B. Hollander. 1983. "Program for Software Reliability and System Test Schedule Estimation—Revised for Staged Failure Interval Adjustment—User's Guide," available through J. D. Musa.

Musa, J. D., A. Iannino, and K. Okumoto. 1987. *Software Reliability: Measurement, Prediction, Application*, McGraw-Hill, New York.

Musa, J. D., and K. Okumoto. 1984a. "A Comparison of Time Domains for Software Reliability Models," *Journal of Systems and Software*, **4**(4), pp. 277–287.

Musa, J. D., and K. Okumoto. 1984b. "A Logarithmic Poisson Execution Time Model for Software Reliability Measurement," *Proceedings Seventh International Conference on Software Engineering*, Orlando, pp. 230–238.

Myers, G. J. 1976. *Software Reliability: Principles and Practices*, McGraw-Hill, New York.

Myers, G. J. 1979. *The Art of Software Testing*, Wiley, New York.

Okumoto, K. 1985. "A Statistical Method for Software Quality Control," *IEEE Transactions on Software Engineering*, **SE-11**(12), pp. 1424–1430.

Okumoto, K., and A. L. Goel. 1978. "Availability and Other Performance Measures of System Under Imperfect Maintenance," *Proceedings COMPSAC*, pp. 66–71.

Okumoto, K., and A. L. Goel. 1980. "Optimum Release Time for Software Systems Based on Reliability and Cost Criteria," *Journal of Systems and Software*, **1**(4), pp. 315–318.

Ostrand, T. J., and E. J. Weyuker. 1982. "Collecting and Categorizing Software Error Data in an Industrial Environment," New York University. Technical Report 47.

Pressman, R. S. 1982. *Software Engineering: A Practitioner's Approach*, McGraw-Hill, New York.

Presson, P. E. 1981. "A Study of Software Errors on Large Aerospace Projects," *Proceedings National Security Industrial Association Conference on Software Technology and Management*, Alexandria, VA.

Putnam, L. H. 1976. "A Macro-Estimating Methodology for Software Development," *Digest of Papers: Fall COMPCON 1976*, Washington, DC, pp. 138–143.

Ramamoorthy, C. V., and F. B. Bastani. 1982. "Software Reliability—Status and Perspectives," *IEEE Transactions on Software Engineering*, **SE-8**(4), pp. 354–370.

Rubey, R. J., J. A. Dana, and P. W. Biché. 1975. "Quantitative Aspects of Software Validation," *IEEE Transactions on Software Engineering*, **SE-1**(2), pp. 150–155.

Rudner, B. 1977. "Seeding/Tagging Estimation of Software Errors: Models and Estimates," Rome Air Development Center, Technical Report RADC-TR-77-15, Rome, NY.

Saunier, P. 1983. "Fiabilité du Logiciel: Quelques Remarques Tirées d'une Expérimentation de Trois Modéles à Taux de Panne," (in French), *L'Industrie Face a la Qualité du Logiciel*, Belvedere, Toulouse, France, Oct. 20–21, 1983, pp. 257–290.

Schafer, R. E., J. F. Alter, J. E. Angus, and S. E. Emoto. 1979. "Validation of Software Reliability Models," Rome Air Development Center, Technical Report RADC-TR-79-147, Rome, NY.

Shen, V. Y., T. J. Yu, S. M. Thebaut, and L. R. Paulsen. 1985. "Identifying Error-Prone Software—An Empirical Study," *IEEE Transactions on Software Engineering*, **SE-11**(4), pp. 317–324.

Shooman, M. L. 1972. "Probabilistic Models for Software Reliability Prediction," (W. Freidberger, Editor), *Statistical Computer Performance Evaluation*, Academic, New York, pp. 485–502.

Shooman, M. L. 1983. *Software Engineering*, McGraw-Hill, New York.

Shooman, M. L. 1986. *Probabilistic Reliability: An Engineering Approach*, McGraw-Hill, New York, 1968. Updated and reprinted, Krieger, Malabar, FL, 1986.

Shooman, M. L., and M. I. Bolsky. 1975. "Types, Distribution, and Test and Correction Times for Programming Errors," *Proceedings 1975 International Conference on Reliable Software*, Los Angeles, pp. 347–357.

Shooman, M. L., and A. K. Trivedi. 1976. "A Many-State Markov Model for Computer Software Performance Parameters," *IEEE Transactions on Reliability*, **R-25**(2), pp. 66–68.

Stover, R. E., Jr. 1977. "A Statistics Collection Package for the JOVIAL J3 Programming Language," Rome Air Development Center, Technical Report RADC-TR-77-293, Rome, NY.

Sunohara, T., A. Takano, K.Uehara, and T. Ohkawa. 1981. "Program Complexity Measure for Software Development Management," *Proceedings Fifth International Conference on Software Engineering*, San Diego, pp. 100–106.

Takahashi, N., and Y. Kamayachi. 1985. "An Empirical Study of a Model for Program Error Prediction," *Proceedings Eighth International Conference on Software Engineering*, London, pp. 330–336.

Thayer, T. A. 1976. "Software Reliability Study," Rome Air Development Center, Technical Report RADC-TR-76-238, Rome, NY.

Trachtenberg, M. 1985. "The Linear Software Reliability Model and Uniform Testing," *IEEE Transactions Reliability*, **R-34**(1), pp. 8–16.

Walston, C. E., and C. P. Felix. 1977. "A Method of Programming Measurement and Estimation," *IBM Systems Journal*, **16**(1), pp. 54–73.

Watson, I. A. 1981. "Review of Common Cause Failures," National Centre of Systems Reliability, Report NCSR R27.

Weiss, D. M. 1981. "Evaluating Software Development by Analysis of Change Data," University of Maryland Computer Science Technical Report TR-1120.

AUTHOR INDEX

SUBJECT INDEX

A

Accuracy:
  calendar time component:
    effect of parameter errors, 130
  of estimation, 126–127
  execution time component:
    effect of grouping failure data, 127–128
    effect of parameter errors, 47
Additional number of failures to objective, 43–45
Additional time of objective, 45–46
Adjustment of failure times (*see* Failure time
        adjustment)
Allocation, reliability, 197–198
Alternatives, investigation of, 65, 67, 193–194
AND configuration, 89
Applicability of model and size of project, 32
Application:
  overview, 75–76
  planning for, 69–73
  procedures, 182–213
  software reliability measurement to design,
    209–210
  software reliability measurement to hardware
    design, 209–210
Application procedure, overview of, 75–76
Applications, 61–73, 182–213
  evaluation, 62
  quality of results, 61–62
Approximation of data, 216
Approximation to execution time, 156–158
  clock time, 156
  natural units, 157–158
  weighted clock time, 156–157
Assignment of debuggers, random, 134–135

B

Attribution of failures to components, 87
Automated data collection, 218
Automated failure reporting system, 152
Automated testing, effect of, 79
Availability, 18
Availability, software, 18

B

Basic execution time model, 30–60
  application areas, 32, 35
  calendar time component, 50–58
  description, 32–43
  failure intensity, 33–34, 38–43
  failures experienced, 36–37
  mean value function, 36–37
  parameters:
    calendar time component, 52, 57–58
    execution time component, 40–43, 47–48
  reasons for selection, 30–32, 58–59
Batching of repairs, 17
Bebugging, 114
Boundaries of limiting resource periods, 55–56,
    184–186

C

Calendar time:
  definition of, 8
  relationship to execution time, 54–57
Calendar time component:
  description, 50–57
  parameter determination, 57–58

282